Children's Services Today

PRACTICAL GUIDES FOR LIBRARIANS

About the Series

This innovative series written and edited for librarians by librarians provides authoritative, practical information and guidance on a wide spectrum of library processes and operations.

Books in the series are focused, describing practical and innovative solutions to a problem facing today's librarian and delivering step-by-step guidance for planning, creating, implementing, managing, and evaluating a wide range of services and programs.

The books are aimed at beginning and intermediate librarians needing basic instruction/guidance in a specific subject and at experienced librarians who need to gain knowledge in a new area or guidance in implementing a new program/service.

About the Series Editor

The **Practical Guides for Librarians** series was conceived by and is edited by M. Sandra Wood, MLS, MBA, AHIP, FMLA, Librarian Emerita, Penn State University Libraries.

M. Sandra Wood was a librarian at the George T. Harrell Library, The Milton S. Hershey Medical Center, College of Medicine, Pennsylvania State University, Hershey, PA, for over 35 years, specializing in reference, educational, and database services. Ms. Wood worked for several years as a Development Editor for Neal-Schuman Publishers.

Ms. Wood received a MLS from Indiana University and a MBA from the University of Maryland. She is a Fellow of the Medical Library Association and served as a member of MLA's Board of Directors from 1991 to 1995. Ms. Wood is founding and current editor of *Medical Reference Services Quarterly*, now in its 35th volume. She also was founding editor of the *Journal of Consumer Health on the Internet* and the *Journal of Electronic Resources in Medical Libraries* and served as editor/co-editor of both journals through 2011.

Titles in the Series

1. *How to Teach: A Practical Guide for Librarians* by Beverley E. Crane.
2. *Implementing an Inclusive Staffing Model for Today's Reference Services* by Julia K. Nims, Paula Storm, and Robert Stevens.
3. *Managing Digital Audiovisual Resources: A Practical Guide for Librarians* by Matthew C. Mariner.
4. *Outsourcing Technology: A Practical Guide for Librarians* by Robin Hastings.
5. *Making the Library Accessible for All: A Practical Guide for Librarians* by Jane Vincent.
6. *Discovering and Using Historical Geographical Resources on the Web: A Practical Guide for Librarians* by Eva H. Dodsworth and L. W. Laliberté
7. *Digitization and Digital Archiving: A Practical Guide for Librarians* by Elizabeth R. Leggett
8. *Makerspaces: A Practical Guide for Librarians* by John J. Burke.
9. *Implementing Web-Scale Discovery Services: A Practical Guide for Librarians* by JoLinda Thompson
10. *Using iPhones and iPads: A Practical Guide for Librarians* by Matthew Connolly and Tony Cosgrave
11. *Usability Testing: A Practical Guide for Librarians* by Rebecca Blakiston
12. *Mobile Devices: A Practical Guide for Librarians* by Ben Rawlins
13. *Going Beyond Loaning Books to Loaning Technologies: A Practical Guide for Librarians* by Janelle Sander, Lori S. Mestre, and Eric Kurt
14. *Children's Services Today: A Practical Guide for Librarians* by Jeanette Larson

Children's Services Today
A Practical Guide for Librarians

Jeanette Larson

PRACTICAL GUIDES FOR LIBRARIANS, NO. 14

ROWMAN & LITTLEFIELD
Lanham • Boulder • New York • London

Published by Rowman & Littlefield
A wholly owned subsidiary of The Rowman & Littlefield Publishing Group, Inc.
4501 Forbes Boulevard, Suite 200, Lanham, Maryland 20706
www.rowman.com

Unit A, Whitacre Mews, 26-34 Stannary Street, London SE11 4AB

British Library Cataloguing in Publication Information Available

Library of Congress Cataloging-in-Publication Data

Larson, Jeanette.
   Children's services today : a practical guide for librarians / Jeanette Larson.
     pages cm. — (Practical guides for librarians ; 14)
     Includes bibliographical references and index.
     ISBN 978-0-8108-9324-5 (hardback : alk. paper) — ISBN 978-0-8108-9132-6 (pbk. : alk.
   paper) — ISBN 978-0-8108-9133-3 (ebook) 1. Children's libraries—United States. I. Title.
   Z718.2.U6L37 2015
   027.62'50973—dc23

                                        2014042217

Printed in the United States of America

To the many wonderful children's book authors and illustrators who have made it so much fun to be a children's librarian. Especially Jack Gantos. I point the finger at his Rotten Ralph books for luring me into this profession.

Contents

List of Illustrations

Preface

I was probably the last person my library school colleagues expected would become a children's librarian. I loved research so I had big plans to be a reference librarian. Working at Anaheim Public Library during a period when every librarian was a generalist, I discovered children's books, storytime, and summer reading programs. When I moved to Texas, the only job available during an economic downturn was as a children's librarian, so I took it, learning on the job from talented librarians like Ann Furche Sampson.

The library world has certainly changed a lot since 1975. Libraries are emerging as technology centers and community gathering places. Access to electronic materials means patrons may not need to ever step foot into the library. The Internet makes information readily available to anyone, even when that information is outdated, wrong, or satirical. E-publishing means anyone and everyone can get their book published.

While their interests may be different and they seem to be born with a cell phone in their hand already taking selfies, children today are essentially no different from the children of yesterday. They crave attention, soak up information, love hearing stories, and need guidance to grow into healthy, productive adults. Through my experience I have seen firsthand the difference a good children's librarian makes to a child's life. The work we do is important!

I have worked as a children's librarian, children's library consultant, administrator, and, most recently, library educator. *Children's Services Today: A Practical Guide for Librarians* comes out of my teaching the Youth Programs course at Texas Woman's University. While I was able to use many fine textbooks, I always found myself supplementing the textbook with practical information—the stuff I learned on the job, from other librarians, and through trial and error. And children's librarians never stop learning. We always need to know more, try new things, and keep a step ahead of our patrons.

Not every good children's librarian has a master's degree in library science. Some great librarians never took a youth services or children's literature course. I didn't. It was offered during a time when I could not attend classes in the pre-online learning era when I had to drive 60 miles each way to classes in downtown Los Angeles. *Children's Services Today: A Practical Guide for Librarians* is based on my teaching experience but also my experience working with children and children's librarians. The focus is on public libraries, although, of course, school librarians use many of the same skills and face similar issues. *Children's Services Today: A Practical Guide for Librarians* has been written for use by university classes but also for that person who walks into the library one day and is told she will be the children's librarian.

Children's librarians, in my opinion, have the most fabulous jobs. We get to play and sing and dance. We introduce children to books that will take them to new places and bring them new ideas. We help children experience the wonder of learning and reading and exploring. We are educators, mentors, and friends to the children we serve. We have wonderful opportunities to experiment, learn new skills, and meet amazing people. We get to meet the rock stars of literature—the authors and illustrators of books that I love to share with young patrons. And nothing beats knowing that you have helped a young person grow into the person he wants to be. Every children's librarian has stories of hugs, invitations to graduations, and the best compliment—new parents bringing their child to your storytime because they remember how wonderful the experience was for them.

Another great thing about being a children's librarian, as Elizabeth Bird notes: "I believe that even if all other forms of librarianship were to crumble to the ground and wash away with the tides, children's librarians would remain standing. New parents and children appear every day. They need your opinions, your thoughts, your recommendations, and your help in finding the best books, websites, apps, and materials out there" (Bird, 2012: 22). So even when jobs are hard to find or you are feeling overwhelmed and exhausted by the day's work, remember that the kids make a difference in our lives.

◎ Organization of the Book

The work of a children's librarian can seem overwhelming at times. We are expected to be teachers, storytellers, performers, researchers, tutors, administrators, managers, and more. Our coworkers often believe that we spend the day reading books to children and playing games. *Children's Services Today: A Practical Guide for Librarians* is designed to walk you through the range of skills children's librarians use and provide a foundation for carrying out your work. Some of the information overlaps and is dealt with within the broader topics.

Children's librarianship is a young profession, starting in the late 19th century and hitting its stride in the 20th. Chapter 1 explores this history and some of the pioneers of the profession. Chapter 2 examines our primary populations, delving into the development and capabilities of babies, toddlers, preschoolers, and elementary-age children. We also consider the other groups with which you will work, including child care providers, families, and children with special needs.

The collection, in whatever formats that includes, forms the heart of the children's department and provides the basis for reference and homework help as well as programming and reader's advisory. So in chapter 3 we take an in-depth look at the collection and its development and maintenance. Chapter 4 discusses the various services provided in the children's department, focusing on reference services, reader's advisory, and educational support. While we look at partnerships and outreach in chapter 4, programs such as preschool storytime, book discussion groups, and summer reading are covered in chapters 5, 6, and 7. The concluding chapter looks at the administrative and managerial aspects of running a children's department, including policies that affect children's services, budgets, and marketing.

In *Children's Services Today: A Practical Guide for Librarians*, established librarians, trustees, and library directors will find information to help them understand what children's librarians do on a daily basis. If you are using this book as part of your library course work or because you are the newly appointed children's librarian, I hope you will find it to be practical and useful in preparing you for your work.

As you begin to delve into the wonderful world of children's librarianship, I say to you what Dr. Seuss (1990) says in *Oh, the Places You'll Go!*:

Congratulations!
Today is your day.
You're off to Great Places!
You're off and away!

References

Bird, Elizabeth. 2012. "Want to Work with Kids in a Public Library? Here's the Inside Scoop." *School Library Journal* 58, no. 9 (July): 18–22.
Seuss, Dr. 1990. *Oh, the Places You'll Go!* New York: Random House.

Acknowledgments

It has been my privilege to work with many outstanding children's librarians during my career and to teach and mentor many students who have excelled in the field. Many of their contributions to this book are uncredited. I want to thank the librarians who provided photographs of their activities and programs; some of those people don't know me personally. I especially want to thank Sally Meyers, children's librarian at Tom Green County Library System in San Angelo, Texas. Over the many years that I have known her, Sally has been a strong advocate for children and a creative children's librarian, and she tirelessly took photographs and created activities for me. Sally is the heart of Texas libraries! I also want to thank the many friends I've made in the children's book publishing world who cheerfully responded to my requests for images and permissions and never considered me to be a pest. You know who you are.

This book would not have been possible without the trust placed in me, and the patience of Charles Harmon, who first suggested that this would be "an easy" book for me to write. When I was ready to give up, my editor, Sandy Wood, gently nudged me back on task and she has worked tirelessly to ensure that the book is as complete as possible. Of course, I also must acknowledge the support of my husband, James W. Larson, who over the years has done enough to support my work that he is surely due the honorary title of children's librarian. There are many colleagues—especially my first supervisor, Ann Furche Sampson; my mentor, Julie Beth Todaro; and Texas Library Association executive director, Pat Smith—who have encouraged me, supported me in my work, and urged me to do even more. With librarians and colleagues like these, and others too numerous to mention for fear of leaving someone out, our children and the profession are in good hands.

Children's Services in Public Libraries

THE CONCEPT OF A PUBLIC LIBRARY, a place that provides access to books for the public's use, goes back to the early days of the Romans, when scrolls were provided for use in common areas, but were not circulated. Generally, even when the public was permitted access to early libraries, use of the materials was strictly on-site and any lending regulations were extremely prohibitive. The push for true public libraries, supported by taxpayers and open to the citizenry, took hold during the 19th century when Progressive leaders in Great Britain recognized the importance of education to common people and the need to add cultural and intellectual energy to their lives. As public libraries expanded throughout the United States, thanks in great part to Andrew Carnegie, library service to children was usually not included.

The ages for childhood are not consistent across disciplines, or even across libraries, but the Association for Library Services to Children (ALSC), a division of the American Library Association, defines their charge as serving young people from birth through age 12. This part of librarianship, serving children, is a relatively new concept, developed primarily in the 20th century. To set the stage for all that children's librarians do, it is useful to review a bit of this history and to understand how these services contribute to the whole of the public library's mission.

Although most people take it for granted that their public library will have a children's department with services and programs geared specifically for young patrons, in the early days of libraries children were not included in the target audience for services. While public libraries as an institution developed beginning in the 1800s, philanthropists and city leaders intended them to be for adults. The materials in those public libraries were there to help educate the populace, provide means for new immigrants to assimilate into American life, and offer access to high-quality literature for those who could not afford to buy books. Rarely were there materials intended for children. In fact, until after the Civil War, children were actually barred from most public libraries. William Fletcher, writing about public libraries and young people, noted that "one of the first questions to be met in arranging a code of rules for . . . the public library relates to the age at which young persons shall be admitted to its privileges" (Fletcher, 1876: 412). He noted that, in his opinion, most libraries chose the wrong solution to this question, fixing the age at 12 or 14 instead of having no age restrictions whatsoever.

William Fletcher was a staunch advocate for the removal of age restrictions on public library use, arguing that if the mission of public libraries was to help people develop good reading habits, they should begin that process early in life. He noted that one of the "special requirements of the young" is that "the library shall interest and be attractive to them" (Fletcher, 1876: 416). He was a proponent of moving libraries away from being "clubs" that offered "an economical supply of reading" (Fletcher, 1876: 416) to the idea of educational service, a kind of "people's university." Logically, then, education should begin at an early age. Of course, Fletcher also felt that if public libraries did not provide children with access to good books that "have something positively good about them" and that were "instructive and stimulating to their better nature," then children would instead develop a taste for less lofty reading, such as pulp novels and serialized books (Fletcher, 1876: 416). Interestingly, many tenets that are held by today's youth librarians, while not necessarily stated specifically the way we would do so today, find their roots in Fletcher's writing.

Librarians, along with educators, psychologists, and social workers, began to understand that the needs of children differed from the needs of adults. Support was required to help them develop into intelligent, responsible adults. The crusading spirit of reforms in child welfare and education helped open the library doors to children. In 1885, Melvil Dewey created the Children's Library Association and Miss Emily Hanaway, a grammar school principal, opened a reading room for children, which, a few years later, became a branch of the New York Free Circulating Library. As of 1894, 70% of public libraries did not serve children (Marco, 2011), but within a few years, Pratt Institute in Brooklyn and

FLETCHER'S TENETS OF CHILDREN'S LIBRARY SERVICE

- Books change lives.
- Cooperation with schools is important.
- Librarians help children select reading materials.
- Parents, not the librarians, are responsible for deciding what their child reads.
- Appropriate library behavior is expected of all, not just children.

Figure 1.1. Children's Room, Dayton Public Library, 1897. *Courtesy of the Dayton Metro Library, Ohio*

the Providence (Rhode Island) Public Library had dedicated children's rooms designed specifically to serve young patrons. Children's areas were often small but could be larger, such as the children's room that opened in the basement of Dayton Public Library in 1897 (figure 1.1). The library was open two days a week for children, and only "boys and girls, who had accepted an invitation, issued through the schools, to become members of the Library League, were permitted to borrow one book per week from the collection" (Horlacher, 2014). At the time there were few books published specifically for children, so most of the books were books for adults, and for many libraries, the primary mission of the children's room was to prepare children to use the adult collection. The first children's room, as marked by a separate collection, is credited to England.

While early libraries were expected to help poor people and immigrants improve themselves, even when children were admitted to the library, people of color were not generally allowed or they would only be admitted to segregated facilities. As of 1886, Enoch Pratt Free Library in Baltimore provided service to users of all races. More commonly, separate facilities were provided, such as the one-room annex in Henderson, Kentucky, which opened in 1904 and is recorded as the first library structure for African Americans in the United States. It housed 100 books (Jones, 2001)! Galveston, Texas, opened a branch of the Rosenberg Library in an addition to the high school in 1905 to serve as a public library for African Americans, and the same year Charlotte, North Carolina, opened the first independent public library to serve the black community.

It's not entirely clear where the first separate collection of materials for young people was established in the United States. Some of the earliest collections were gifts from a benefactor and, consequently, rather limited. For example, a donor in Salisbury, Connecticut, gave 150 books "suitable for children" to the town in 1803, apparently to be housed in the regular collection and without any funds to add to the collection (Wiegand and Davis, 1994: 127). In 1893, Minneapolis Public Library moved all the children's books to a separate room with open shelving. In her entry in Wiegand and Davis's *Encyclopedia of Library History*, Christine Jenkins noted that when the circulation of children's books reached 15% at the Cleveland Public Library in 1876, the "problem" was handled by curtailing all purchases of additional children's books until 1884 (Wiegand and Davis, 1994: 128).

Effie Louise Power is recorded as the first children's librarian, appointed in 1895 by Cleveland Public Library specifically for this job (Marco, 2011). A year later, in 1896, Anne Carroll Moore began story hours at Pratt Institute, and at the 1897 American Library Association conference, children's library work was discussed for the first time. By the turn of the century, most of the larger urban libraries had a children's department.

One of the early leaders in children's librarianship was Augusta Baker, notable not only as an African American librarian but as a premier children's librarian. Baker is described as "a catalyst for social change brought about through books that give a positive portrayal of people regardless of race, culture, or religion and made an impact on literature and libraries as a promoter of accurate portrayals of ethnic, cultural, and religious groups in children's literature" (Dawson, 2000: 56). In 1921, Pura Belpré became the first Puerto Rican to be hired by the New York Public Library and quickly became an advocate for services to the Spanish-speaking community, buying Spanish-language books and holding bilingual storytimes.

Just as the profession was beginning, there were questions about the viability of the "genus children's librarian." In an article in *Public Libraries*, Alice I. Hazeltine, supervisor of children's work for St. Louis Public Library, questioned whether, after only 30 years, children's librarians were extinct. The feeling was that because children's librarians were so young—generally under 30 years old—and prone to marrying, they were leaving the profession. Noting that children's librarianship was an "undercrowded profession," Hazeltine clearly identified a children's librarian as "a librarian whose vision of library work with children as an integral part of library work as a whole . . . is clear and compelling" (Hazeltine, 1921: 518, 513), while she also established the roles of the children's librarian and the value of her work.

Early training for children's librarians was mostly handled on the job, through training classes at larger libraries, and through courses at the New York State Library School and Pratt Institute. By 1900, larger cities had a children's department, headed by a female staff member. These early librarians set the norm for the pattern of service still seen today: age-appropriate collections, a special room or area for children's services, programs designed for young people, cooperation with schools, and specially trained staff (Marco, 2011).

The first decade of the 20th century saw many firsts for children's services, including the establishment of the American Library Association's Children's Service Section; the American Library Association's publication of *Booklist*, which included reviews of children's books; and the first edition of *Children's Catalog*, H. W. Wilson's list of a basic collection for public libraries.

It only took until the end of the 1920s for most public libraries to stock children's books, but by then many were providing storytimes and summer reading programs. By the end of the 1930s, "service for youth was found nationwide in separate alcoves, rooms, and buildings" (Marco, 2011: 430).

A place within the national professional association, the American Library Association (ALA), was important to legitimizing children's services and professional children's librarians. The full history of the place for youth librarians in ALA includes a number of name changes and restructuring as children's services became more prevalent in libraries and as children's literature hit its golden age. In 1941, the Division for Children and Young People merged three groups within ALA: the Children's Services Section, the School Libraries Section, and Young People's Reading Round Table. In the 1950s, the group was renamed the Children's Services Division of the American Library Associa-

A picture book biography (figure 1.2) of Anne Carroll Moore, *Miss Moore Thought Otherwise*, by Jan Pinborough is a good way to explain the history of children's services to young people.

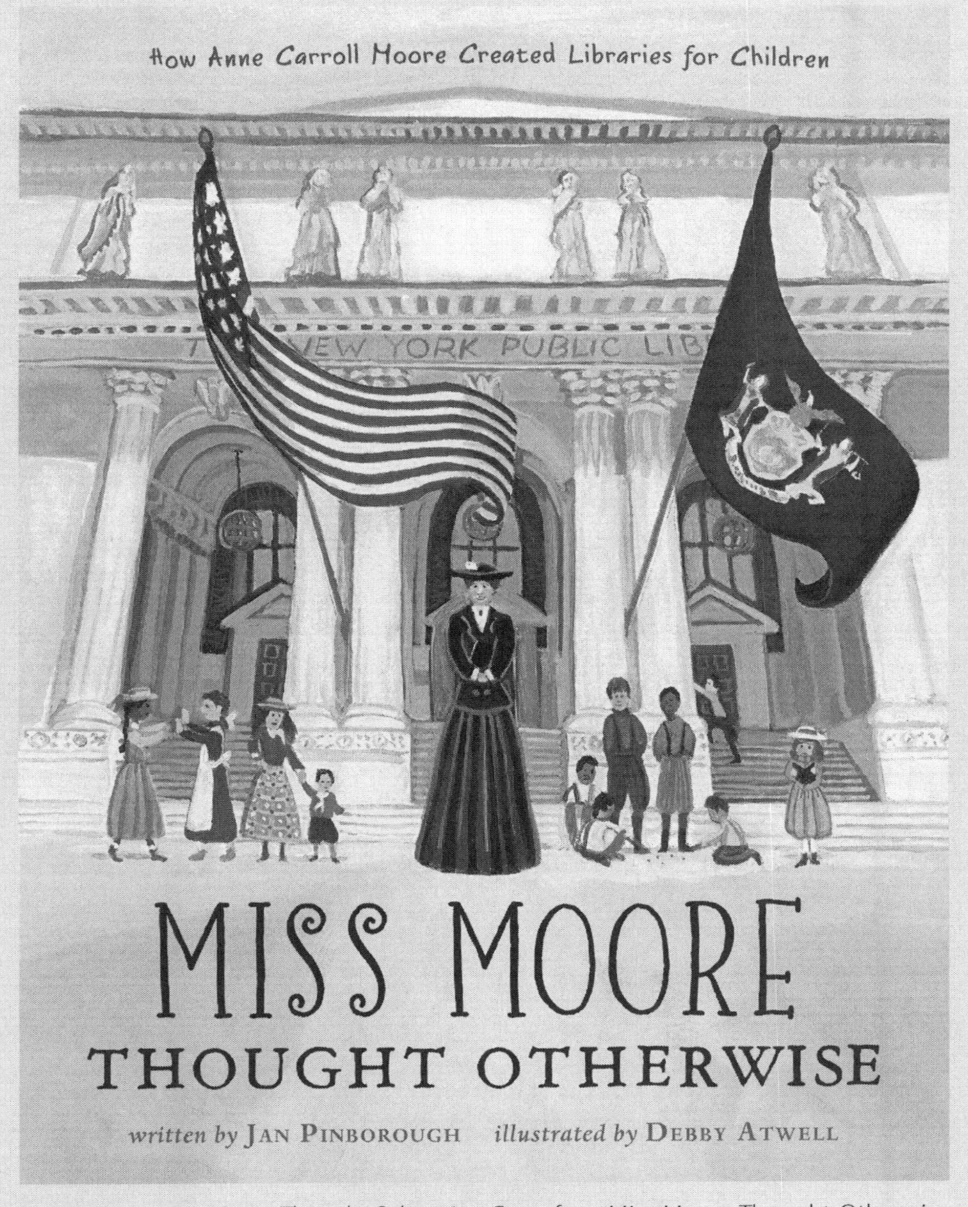

How Anne Carroll Moore Created Libraries for Children

THE NEW YORK PUBLIC LIBRARY

MISS MOORE
THOUGHT OTHERWISE

written by JAN PINBOROUGH   *illustrated by* DEBBY ATWELL

Figure 1.2. *Miss Moore Thought Otherwise.* Cover from Miss Moore Thought Otherwise *by Jan Pinborough. Cover illustrations copyright ©2013 by Debby Atwell. Reprinted by permission of Houghton Mifflin Harcourt Publishing Company. All rights reserved.*

tion, but beginning in 1976, children's librarians found their home in the Association for Library Services to Children (ALSC, 2014). Although after 1941 children's librarians and young adult librarians had separate associations within ALA, the official journal for both groups of librarians serving youth was combined, first *Top of the News* and then *Journal of Youth Services in Libraries*, until 2003. The associations each established their own journal, with ALSC establishing *Children and Libraries* as a vehicle for continuing education and reporting on research for those working specifically with children, defined as those 12 and under.

In many ways youth services faltered in the 1960s and 1970s, with some libraries abandoning targeted efforts to attract youth patrons and eliminating specialized librarian positions in favor of generalists who worked with all ages without specialization. By the end of the 20th century, circulation of youth materials increased from 29% of total circulation in 1993, as reported by the National Center for Educational Statistics, to 35% in 2005. Library usage by people of all ages has been increasing, and most libraries today identify at least one person responsible for children's services.

While the basic services such as storytimes, special collections, and summer reading programs remain as touchstones of children's public library services, new programs are also being introduced. These range from early literacy classes to homework centers to Makerspace programs that encourage self-production of technology and innovative projects. Today children's services and programs are often the most visible in the community and the most valued by the public.

⊚ The Role of Children's Services within the Public Library

Although the provision of services for young people—those under the age of 12 usually—did not become an expected part of public library services until the 20th century, it quickly developed into an essential part of public library services. Few people today can imagine a public library without children's services and a substantial children's collection. These services play a number of roles within the public library that foster and further the library's organizational mission.

One of the core beliefs of children's services is that they drive libraries. Adults often have access to library services from more than one source, including college and business libraries. They also are more likely to be able to purchase books and information and to travel to other libraries. The services offered for children—storytime, picture books, afterschool programs, tutoring—are a great draw for a wide range of people. These services and programs bring adults to the library who then discover the other services and resources available. An interesting phenomenon happens to former non-library users when they become parents: they discover the public library as if it were a new invention! Of course, children's librarians play an important role in service to more than just young people. Among others, these services reach parents, grandparents, teachers, and child care providers.

Children's library services also support the library's mission as part of the education infrastructure in the community. Not only does the collection support the public school curricula, but it also serves a growing homeschool community. Teachers rely on the public library to provide additional resources for classroom learning, and many public libraries serve as homework centers or provide space for afterschool tutoring. Early literacy starts with preschool and infant storytime and pre-reading programs. Programs and services for school-age children set the stage for lifelong learning, a legacy role established with the first public libraries.

Many libraries are viewed as community gathering places—the community's living room—and children's services play an important part in the role. In addition to providing space for programs and for caregivers to interact with their child's early learning, children's programs provide opportunities for children to socialize and learn to behave as part of a group or audience. Libraries are seen as safe havens for children, and while not intended to replace appropriate supervision of young people, library programs provide a means for them to be involved in productive and enriching activities.

Foundations of Children's Services

Beginning in 1876 William L. Fletcher argued that public libraries should be working to influence children's reading habits as early as possible. Although his concern was mainly focused on helping children find high-quality educational reading, his passionate message has remained a major part of the foundation of children's services.

The foundations of librarianship are based on Ranganathan's laws of library science, set forth in 1931. These laws have been updated to reflect modern formats for information (Crawford and Gorman, 1995) but remain relevant to and are reflected in children's services.

The mandate to promote reading in general grew out of the work of some of the pioneers of children's library service who recognized that books were not only a means to education and knowledge, but also a way to shape lives, entertain, and bring unknown worlds to the reader's front door. Books are for use, and children's librarians work to put books into the hands of readers. Children's librarians are true believers in the power of reading both as a necessary skill for success in life but also for the ability of reading to enrich lives.

Anne Carroll Moore, one of the first librarians to work in a designated children's room, set the tone for attractive, inviting spaces tailored to the comfort of children. Most libraries today not only have child-sized furniture and comfortable reading chairs designed for little bodies, but some also have elaborate and built-in reading cubbies like the ones in Tom Green County Public Library shown in figure 1.3, unique spaces, such as treehouses and castles, that allow children to imagine different worlds and special features that encourage play and learning. Shelves are of heights appropriate to allow children to browse, and books for babies and very young children may even be placed in bins on the floor for easy reaching.

RANGANATHAN'S FIVE LAWS OF LIBRARY SCIENCE

1. Books are for use
2. Every reader his or her book
3. Every book its reader
4. Save the time of the reader
5. The library is a growing organism

Figure 1.3. Reading Cubby. *Courtesy Tom Green County Library System, San Angelo, Texas; Sally Meyers, children's librarian*

The library is a growing organism, and the spaces change to reflect changes in the users' needs. The library also grows through the changes in programs and the places where services are provided. Outreach efforts take library services to children who can't easily get to the physical location. Often these children are in child care centers, low-income housing developments, health clinics, and even juvenile detention centers. New types of programs are implemented to reach audiences that are underserved or not being served at all.

Collections are selected from the array of materials available from a wide variety of publishers and are tailored to the needs and interests of children. In the past, librarians often saw themselves as gatekeepers of good literature, restricting materials in the collection only to "worthy" reading and quality materials. In part this was a consequence of the low volume of materials published specifically for children. Librarians established selection criteria that emphasized accuracy, originality, relevance of illustrations, and quality writing in part "to position children's books as real literature" (Walter, 2001: 20) at a time when children's books were often considered to be second-rate or trivial. Since the 1970s or thereabouts, collections have focused more on providing popular reading materials along with materials for leisure reading and that support the formal education curricula. Children's librarians are fierce proponents of the idea that there is a book for every reader and a reader for every book!

At the same time, children's librarians understand the importance of a collection that is up-to-date, includes accurate and timely information, and helps the reader. Each book is selected or deselected based on the idea that every book should have someone interested in reading it or it is not an asset to the collection. Currency of information in the collection's materials is especially critical for young people who don't have the education and maturity to discern that information may be outdated or superseded by new knowledge. While conducting research for schoolwork, they are also learning to look at copyright dates and the authority of the author or creator of the information being used but may not yet be experienced enough to know what is current. Therefore, part of what children's librarians do is to help children become information literate.

Equal and open access to materials and services is part of the children's librarian's belief that young people deserve respect and dedication. Policies should ensure that children are offered equitable access to everything the library has to offer. By adhering to the Library Bill of Rights, children's librarians support the rights of children to read and view library resources without restriction. Children are entitled to privacy and confidentiality about their selections and their use of the library, and only their parents can restrict their child from checking out materials. Intellectual freedom is a cornerstone of librarianship, and nowhere is this concept more challenging than in children's and teen collections when adults want to restrict access or censor reading.

Equal access also plays an important role in collection development and programming that serves to bring minority and underserved children into the library. Many of the early leaders in children's libraries were African American, notes Virginia Walter (2001). Although we still struggle to build collections and provide services that reflect the full diversity of the community, Walter believes that people like Augusta Baker, Charlemae Rollins, Effie Lee Morris, and Pura Belpré raised awareness of the need for less stereotyped books than were being published during their careers. They also helped children's librarians focus on the diversity of the American culture, diversity found even within the majority population, and the need to be sensitive to the cultures, ethnicities, and races of the children served. Outreach service and inclusion of service for underserved populations and children with special needs remains a basic principle of children's librarianship.

Children's librarians save the time of the reader by helping young people find appropriate information through reference and homework assistance and through reader's advisory and booktalks. Creating booklists and special displays helps children and parents quickly find materials for annual activities like the science fair or holiday reading.

The Legacy of Children's Librarianship

Virginia A. Walter lists three enduring legacies of children's librarianship: the concept of the child as reader, a tradition of outreach to the unserved or the underserved, and a renewed commitment to accountability and managerial excellence (Walter, 2001). Throughout the chapters in this book, readers will discover how to make these things happen and how to implement the principles of librarianship to service to young people and their families. From this foundation, children's librarians of the future will create new services and continue to grow the wonderful organism that is the public library.

Key Points

Children's services is a fairly young profession, so remember:

- Children's services really began in the 20th century.
- Ranganathan's Laws of Library Science continue to be applicable to children's services.
- Children's librarians continue to build on the legacies of service that began in the early days of the profession.

Today's children's librarian continues to promulgate the philosophies of service developed by leaders like Anne Carroll Moore, who believed that children's librarians could put "the right book into the hands of the right child at the right time." These ideas, along with information to help those studying to be children's librarians or those wanting some background for on-the-job training, will be explored in subsequent chapters. Best practices will provide the material needed to gain the competencies to excel in children's services. Before we hone our skills, we will look at the various groups children's librarians serve in public libraries.

References

ALSC (Association for Library Services to Children). 2014. "A Brief History of ALSC." Accessed May 16, 2014. http://www.ala.org/alsc/aboutalsc/historyofalsc.

Crawford, Walter, and Michael Gorman. 1995. *Future Libraries: Dreams, Madness & Reality*. Chicago: American Library Association.

Dawson, Alma. 2000. "Black Women, Civil Rights, and Libraries." *Library Trends* 49, no. 1 (Summer): 49–87.

Fletcher, William I. 1876. "Public Libraries and the Young." In *Public Libraries in the United States: Their History, Condition and Management*, 412–418. Washington, DC: Bureau of Education.

Hazeltine, Alice L. 1921. "What Is a Children's Librarian?" *Public Libraries* 26, no. 10 (November): 513–519.

Horlacher, Nancy. 2014. E-mail to the author. August 20.

Jones, Reinette F. 2001. *Library Service to African Americans in Kentucky, from the Reconstruction Era to the 1960s*. Jefferson, NC: McFarland.

Marco, Guy A. 2011. *American Public Library Handbook*. Oxford, England: ABC-Clio.

Pinborough, Jan. 2013. *Miss Moore Thought Otherwise*. Boston: Houghton Mifflin.

Walter, Virginia A. 2001. *Children and Libraries: Getting It Right*. Chicago: American Library Association.

Wiegand, Wayne A., and Donald G. Davis Jr., eds. 1994. *Encyclopedia of Library History*. New York: Garland.

Resources Mentioned in This Chapter

ALSC (Association for Library Services to Children). http://www.ala.org/alsc/.

ALSC (Association for Library Services to Children) and ALA (American Library Association). 2003. *Children & Libraries*. Chicago: American Library Association.

Booklist. http://booklistonline.co/.

H. W. Wilson Co. 1916. *Children's Catalog*. New York: H.W. Wilson Co. (new title *Children's Core Collection*).

Makerspace. http://makerspace.com/

National Center for Educational Statistics. http://nces.ed.gov/.

Additional Readings and Resources

ALA (American Library Association). 2014. "Access to Library Resources and Services for Minors: An Interpretation of the Library Bill of Rights." Adopted June 30, 1972. Last amended July 1, 2014. http://www.ala.org/advocacy/intfreedom/librarybill/interpretations/access-library-resources-for-minors.

ALSC (Association for Library Services to Children). 2009. "Competencies for Librarians Serving Children in Public Libraries." American Library Association. http://www.ala.org/alsc/edcareeers/alsccorecomps.

McDowell, Katherine. 2007. *The Cultural Origins of Youth Services Librarianship, 1876–1900*. PhD dissertation. University of Illinois at Urbana-Champaign.

Who We Serve

WHILE CHILDREN ARE, OF COURSE, the main focus for the work of children's librarians, children's services bring in many other groups of people connected to children. These people include parents and grandparents, homeschooling families, children from new immigrant families, children with special needs, educators, students in college courses, child care providers and caregivers, and others. There will also, of course, be overlap between these groups so that today's patron in the children's department may be a new immigrant mother who just had her first baby and wants to know how to help that child develop good literacy skills while maintaining his home language. After we understand whom we are serving, we can also look at ways to serve each group based on our understanding of their needs and can consider best practices for serving our patrons.

Children as Patrons

While everyone should be welcome to utilize the services of the public library and the children's department, and many of the services offered for children will be similar to those offered to adults, children are not simply smaller human beings. Defining children as individuals from birth through age 12, there are several developmental stages children's librarians need to recognize and understand in order to provide quality service. Few children's librarians take child development courses as part of their training, yet they still need to understand and be comfortable with the abilities of, limitations of, and expectations for children at each stage if only because of their implications for library services. An overview of this information provides some of the knowledge needed to plan appropriate activities, select materials that will best serve each group, and connect children and their caregivers with the best services possible. This information also helps children's librarians advocate for age-appropriate programs and services when these are discussed with administration, funders, and other groups that want to know why services and programs are important and should be funded.

While it is not possible to provide a full course in child development within the scope of this book, an overview provides some foundation in the generalities of child development, particularly those areas dealing with language development and speech acquisition, cognitive development, and social development. It is also useful to have an understanding of the stages of physical development so that appropriate activities can be incorporated into storytimes for specific groups of children. Understanding the stages of physical development and the relationship of these abilities to learning provides context for including fingerplay, dance, song, and craft activities as part of early literacy activities.

Brain development has been a much discussed topic among librarians in recent years, in part because of the role libraries and literacy programs play in helping children reach their full potential as their brains grow over the first decade of life. Many of the optimal learning windows for skills like math and language occur in the early years, as do the best times for developing vocabulary, motor skills, and social skills. While people continue to learn throughout their lives, the "optimum 'windows of opportunity for learning' last until about the age of 10 or 12" (Begley, 1996: 59), exactly the age span children's librarians serve. Be sure to think about both developmental age, which will vary with individual children, and chronological age; each child may vary in abilities at a particular age. Also, boys learn and develop differently than girls do. Studies show that boys read less than girls, use the library less frequently, and require different opportunities for learning. Some of these differences may be nature, while others are based on how boys are nurtured. Regardless, children's librarians actively work to find ways to reach boys and engage boys in library programs.

Parents may look at the children's librarian as an expert not only in children's literature but also in child development and parenting. They will frequently request help in selecting books and other materials for their child and seek suggestions for helping a struggling reader succeed. To aid with these endeavors, some libraries provide a parenting collection within the children's department. A parenting collection offers parents guidance on child development, issues their child may face, and ways to encourage their child's literacy and brain development through books and reading. If these materials are not housed in the children's department, the children's librarian will still want to know what is available and should make selection recommendations.

Babies

Some of the best library customers are the parents of newborns, and this is a great time to be in the library surrounded by books, media, and activities because baby brains are super sponges. Very young children, through about 18 months old, change rapidly, moving from helplessness through the beginnings of discovering their world. Much research has been done about baby brain development, and it would behoove any children's librarian to be familiar with these new ideas and theories. Infants respond to various stimuli and react to sound, colors, tactile objects, and smells. Research shows that there is a dramatic link between the number of words that a baby hears and verbal intelligence as a baby learns to speak. Babies who are read to during the first years of life are better prepared for school and have a head start on learning, and public libraries play an important role in helping parents achieve these outcomes.

Babies are all different, but within a few months they are beginning to distinguish between parent/mother and self. They react to voices and sounds and begin to ask for things verbally and nonverbally. By 12 months a baby understands "no" and "stop," and by 18 months she can follow simple instructions and say simple sentences.

Library services for babies are directed by necessity to the parents. Special lapsit programs, where the baby is in a caregiver's lap, or Mother Goose storytimes encourage parents to do the things that will help develop their baby's brain. Librarians model rhymes, songs, and fingerplays that parents can emulate and reinforce at home. Programs like the Association for Library Services to Children's Every Child Ready to Read program or Mother Goose on the Loose provide structure and instruction for field-tested programs, but many public libraries offer nonbranded lapsit storytimes and other playtime programs that encourage babies and caregivers to participate in brain development and early literacy activities. More detail on these programs is provided in chapter 5.

Librarians are also introducing parents and caregivers to the collection of books and materials to use with their baby and encourage them to develop library and reading habits. Most popular will be board books that tiny fingers can clutch and chew on. Pile these durable books in tubs on the floor of the library, and they circulate like crazy. The collection should include an assortment of nursery rhymes and songbooks, as well as musical recordings for young children. Books should show babies of many different races and ethnicities, and generally books with simple, clear illustrations and few words work best. Babies don't begin to see colors until they are a few months old, but they begin to distinguish patterns early on so have books that are in black and white available. Tactile books like *Pat the Bunny* by Dorothy Kunhardt or *Peekaboo Kisses* by Barney Saltzberg allow babies to explore books with all of their senses. These books will wear out within a few months so budget to replace them frequently.

Toddlers

As the name implies, toddlers enjoy a lot of activity! The term *toddler* refers to a stage of development—beginning to walk and function independently of a parent—but generally occurs around age two. Toddlers are in the early stages of acquiring literacy skills and are learning to control their own environment. This results in some amazing accomplishments and some interesting challenges. A toddler experiences rapid growth, often with mood swings, and a healthy dose of free will. They may say "no" quite often to test their boundaries, and they can become frustrated because their lack of language skills can hinder their desire to express themselves. Toddlers try to distinguish themselves from parents and peers but are also still very possessive of their parents and personal objects such as toys. Safety is a major concern as toddlers very actively explore their environment.

Between the ages of about two and three years old, a child can begin to play simple pretend games and form simple sentences. Their hands can hold a pencil or crayon, and they can follow simple directions. While toddlers have a limited attention span, they can memorize short songs and rhymes. Although they want to make choices between things, they have trouble doing so; we can help them be successful by limiting the options from

Figure 2.1. Toddler Busy Box. *Courtesy Tom Green County Library System, San Angelo, Texas; Sally Meyers, children's librarian*

which they will choose. Many libraries provide developmental toys and games, such as the busy box shown in figure 2.1, so that toddlers and parents can work out puzzles and play together while in the library. It's also a good idea to put out tubs of board books that toddlers can grab.

Library services for toddlers are still aimed primarily at parents and caregivers, but these popular programs also begin to involve the child more in the presentation and in doing things during the program. These are shorter, fast-paced sessions, generally about 20 minutes with a lot of activity and movement. Wordless picture books and concept books encourage toddlers to label items and participate in telling the story. Stories that encourage action help release toddler energy in a constructive manner, and they can learn repetitive participatory stories like *Clap Your Hands* by Lorinda Bryan Cauley. Children's librarians will be encouraging parents and caregivers to read to their child throughout the day and to use dialogic reading methods to allow discussion between the child and the reader about the story. Programs can include activities like flannel board stories that are tactile and involve the child in telling the story while they begin to learn how to follow a sequence of events.

Parents may express concerns to the children's librarian about their child's development, and this is a great opportunity to share parenting books and brochures with them to help as they cope with common, albeit challenging, issues. Programs and services are

Figure 2.2. *Read to Your Bunny. © Rosemary Wells 1999, published by Scholastic Books*

frequently directed to helping parents succeed as their child's first teacher by providing information and modeling ways parents can work with their child.

Because toddlers may be in child care facilities during the business day, programs might be provided off-site at these centers, or programs can be scheduled at times when parents are able to bring toddlers to the library. The library may also implement branded programs, such as Every Child Ready to Read, a project of the Association for Library Services to Children, or author/illustrator Rosemary Wells's Read to Your Bunny program (figure 2.2), that foster early literacy development and help children get ready to learn to read when they enter school.

Preschoolers

Preschoolers, generally between the ages of three and five, are independent individuals who have developed personalities and know their likes and dislikes. While they still cling to the familiar, they want to separate themselves from their parents and caregivers. Librarians are often the first nonfamilial adult with whom preschoolers will build a relationship, giving the storytime presenter hugs and small gifts, such as drawings.

These are the years when children are getting ready for school and preschoolers are eager to learn. Libraries play an important role in getting them ready for formal education, making this an especially glorious age for library use! While any age is the right age for a child to get his own library card, frequently this is a preschool rite of passage. Preschoolers are eager to read, even if it is only play reading, and they consume a lot of books. With a greater command of language, preschoolers know what they want and are not reluctant to speak up. "Why?" may be the favorite word for a preschooler and their curiosity can test the patience of many adults.

Fears may begin to manifest themselves at this age, and books like *Where the Wild Things Are* by Maurice Sendak can help children learn to cope and overcome problems.

They are developing social skills, including teamwork, learning that there are consequences for actions, and beginning to understand the concept of fairness, as well as learning manners and how to behave as a member of an audience at storytimes. Children are also learning to solve problems and are honing their reasoning and classification skills. Preschoolers are able to distinguish between reality and fantasy. They have active imaginations and enjoy pretending. Because their language skills are developing, preschoolers can be quite talkative and will help tell stories at programs.

Library programs for preschoolers can include a lot of variety. Storytimes can be longer and more intricate, combining a lot of different activities and longer, more involved books. Because children learn languages easily at this stage, libraries may offer bilingual programs, including programs with sign language, or programs presented entirely in another language that is spoken in the community. Special programs may feature pajama or bedtime storytimes, as well as family programs, puppet shows, and crafts.

Children will have definite subject preferences for the books they check out, often with vocabulary that will amaze their parents. A four-year-old boy who loves dinosaurs has no problem with the big words, quickly learns to name the different species, and is

CHECK IT OUT!

Lola discovers the joy of books in *Lola at the Library*, a storybook by Anna McQuinn. Lola gets her own library card, has a backpack full of books to read, and enjoys storytime (figure 2.3).

Figure 2.3. *Lola at the Library. Used with permission. Charlesbridge Publishing.*

eager to share his knowledge with anyone who will listen. Folk and fairy tales provide a sense of familiarity but preschoolers also enjoy variants of these familiar tales, such as *Little Red Hot*, Eric Kimmel's Southwestern retelling of Little Red Riding Hood, and easily recognize the similarities and differences between the versions.

Elementary

School-age children have pretty fully developed egos, and they are the most important person in the world. While they usually do well in groups, they can be possessive and selfish, needing some time alone. Their communication skills are developing rapidly and they can write, tell stories, and create art. They do not deal well with failure or criticism, so adults often try to set them up for success and should address mistakes and problems gently. They want adult attention, sometimes even when that attention is negative, and want to figure out the rules, expect fairness and consistency, and are watching important adults to determine their own moral code. As they reach the upper end of this age group, children may be deliberately disobedient to express their independence and test the rules.

As children enter school they learn to read, although some may have already started as preschoolers. They practice reading to become fluent and are also developing an interest in reading for pleasure. From about age 6 through age 10, children may read books that are longer and more complex. By age 10 and older, most children will be reading longer and more varied books, as well as listening to audiobooks or reading e-books. School-age children can use computers for research and to write but also rely heavily on help from librarians to find what they need and for reader's advisory. Elementary children often have a well-developed sense of humor and generally enjoy word play and silliness, but they also develop intense interests in fiction and nonfiction topics.

The collection should offer a wide range of materials, including beginning readers with short sentences and simple vocabulary for developing reading skills. Short chapter books serve as a transition to full-length novels and complex nonfiction books, but fluent readers may also enjoy longer picture books that ease the transition from short, controlled vocabulary books to longer, more grown-up books. Series books offer a level of comfort from familiar characters and settings, while allowing children to practice reading and to read for entertainment with a sense of accomplishment. It is especially important to maintain an up-to-date nonfiction collection as elementary children lack the skills necessary to understand when information is outdated or erroneous.

Library services will include homework help, afterschool programming, special guests that introduce children to careers, the arts, and other subjects. Many school-age children enjoy activities around celebrations such as Children's Book Week and setting reading goals for programs like summer reading that encourage retention of skills during the school vacation. Because they have a great deal of independence, elementary-age children may hang out at the library, with both the positive result of building relationships with the librarians and staff and discipline issues that may ensue when they are bored and restless.

As this group ages and enters the tweens, they may look to the librarian for friendship and want to share their reading interests with you. Be sure to understand the library's policies on patron behavior expectations and intellectual freedom. Elementary children who can read above their grade level may begin to venture into the teen and even adult collections for reading material.

Special Needs Children

Children with disabilities may need special assistance to fully participate in programs or use the library's materials and services. Their ability to access the library may be hindered by physical barriers to the building, especially older buildings that lack ramps or elevators. Access can also be hindered by furniture that blocks paths or is not appropriate for use by people in wheelchairs or with visual disabilities. Behavioral, cognitive, or developmental disabilities may make it more difficult for children to participate in programs or serve themselves adequately, requiring additional intervention and assistance from library staff.

The Americans with Disabilities Act, federal legislation passed in 1990, requires that public facilities make reasonable accommodation to provide equal service to people with disabilities. Accommodation may include providing personal help on request, providing assistive technology, or providing an alternate method for communication. It may mean that a sign language interpreter is provided during public programs. Staff must take more time and patience to ensure that the patron is getting what is needed. Children with autism spectrum disorders may not follow social norms or understand appropriate group behavior. It is important that library staff be as flexible and understanding as possible. Speaking too loudly or having to repeat instructions several times may be annoying, but usually the child can't control that behavior and is not intentionally being disruptive. Try to disregard the behavior and help the patron unless it is truly interfering with the ability of others to use the library. The American Library Association's Association of Specialized and Cooperative Library Agencies (ASCLA, 2014) provides fact sheets (online at http://www.ala.org/ascla/asclaprotools/accessibilitytipsheets) to help librarians understand special needs and how libraries can accommodate the needs of these patrons.

Although few public libraries maintain large collections of Braille books, most have large print collections with larger type that can be used by those with low vision. The book collection should include materials that feature characters that use a wheelchair, are blind, or have other disabilities. This can take a conscious effort on the part of the selector; checklist research by Williams and Deyoe found that "one-third of public libraries spending over $100,000 annually on materials did not achieve the minimal level for representations of diversity in their youth collections" (Williams and Deyoe, 2014: 97). Additionally, adults with low literacy levels may find materials in the children's collection more appropriate for their reading abilities.

Audiovisual materials can be especially useful for children with learning disabilities and dyslexia. Consider allowing the use of audiobooks for summer reading programs, for example. Be familiar with how to refer patrons to the National Library Service for the Blind and Physically Handicapped. Regional and subregional locations make it easy to receive free material by mail and any U.S. resident "who is unable to read or use regular print materials as a result of temporary or permanent visual or physical limitations may receive service" (National Library Service, 2014).

The trend today is toward inclusiveness, encouraging children with disabilities or special needs to participate in the programs that are routinely scheduled. Programs like summer reading clubs can be advertised as being for children of all abilities. Rules may need to be relaxed or modified; for example, some libraries recognize that older children with mental disabilities may benefit from attending preschool storytimes even though they are technically too old for the program. In some communities, programs tailored to specific needs are held. For example, if the community has a large deaf population, schedule monthly signed storytimes (figure 2.4). The local school for the deaf or another

Figure 2.4. Signed Storytime. *Courtesy of Austin Public Library, Texas*

organization that works with the deaf community may be willing to partner with the library to provide this service. In most cases the needs will vary from child to child, and asking them or their caregivers how to provide assistance will ensure that they get what they need.

Non-English-Speaking Families

The United States is a nation of immigrants and many new arrivals do not speak or read English as their first language. While many new arrivals come from Spanish-speaking countries, many also come speaking Vietnamese, Russian, Chinese, and other languages. Often children will learn to communicate in English and then serve as translators for their parents. While most librarians will not be fluent in languages other than English, often someone on staff is available to assist with languages spoken within the community.

Keep in mind that some other countries do not have the tradition of free, tax-supported publicly accessible libraries, and parents may not know about all the services and programs offered. In some countries, libraries are more archives of older books or are for use by the wealthy intelligentsia. It is frequently pointed out that the English word *library* resembles the Spanish word *librería*, which means "bookstore," so people may not immediately recognize they are not expected to pay for services. Children's librarians will need to work with community organizations to reach these children and parents.

Schools, Head Start programs, churches, and cultural centers in the community offer great partnership opportunities to bring library services to non-English speakers and new immigrants and to attract members of these communities to the library.

The library may have a collection of materials for young readers in languages other than English. Public library collection policies often address what languages will be purchased and what types of materials will be included in the world languages collection. Some books published in other countries are not bound as well as those typically added to library collections, so flexibility in purchasing may be necessary. Librarians who don't speak the language can usually find help in selecting materials by asking for suggestions and advice from educators or community members who do speak the desired language. This subject is covered in more depth in chapter 3, but book publishers like Lee & Low, Arte Público Press, Lorito Books, Milet Books, and Star Bright Books can provide books in many languages. Look also for respected bookstores, many with their catalogs online, for recommendations. Birchbark Books, for example, has an assortment of books by Native Americans from a variety of publishers, many of which are bilingual in Native American languages. It may take a little extra effort to find books from these and others publishers, but the quality materials with multicultural themes by writers from other cultures make it worth the time.

Many programs strive to be inclusive, and non-English-speaking parents will want their children to be immersed in English language storytimes. Try to provide some of the publicity and information in the preferred languages of the community. Incorporating multicultural books and activities into the programs also helps nonnative English speakers feel comfortable. Also look at holding bilingual programs and cultural celebrations such as those included in chapter 7. Bilingual celebrations like El día de los niños/El día de los libros offer opportunities for multicultural and multilingual activities and programs. Although this "children's day/book day" celebration is titled in Spanish, it is really aimed at recognizing and celebrating all languages. Many branded programs, such as Every Child Ready to Read, also provide materials in Spanish. While it may be extra work to develop programs for speakers of other languages, these offerings will attract the families to the library and will also serve the many English-speaking families who want their children to learn other languages.

Working with Other Educational Organizations

School Libraries

Although the public library serves a broader population than do school libraries, children's librarians share the same clientele with school librarians. Students rely on the public library for materials not found in their school library and during times when the school library is not accessible. Children's librarians may frequently partner with the school librarians to provide appropriate materials and programs, and a popular field trip may be a trip to the public library. Schools also may invite the children's librarian to present storytimes, booktalk programs, or other programs in the school.

Many of the reference-type questions that public librarians get from children are related to school assignments. These assignments, and standards for teaching set by state education departments, also may drive the types of materials selected for the children's collection. While no public library would be expected to have classroom sets of a book—enough for every student to have a copy to use—the collection provides support for major assignments and district-wide projects like the science fair and term papers. The public library collection might highlight materials that are regularly used for school reading assignments or for school-based reading incentive programs like Accelerated Reader. Children's librarians also often offer to pull books for classroom use, setting them aside for the teacher to pick up.

Cooperation may be formal or informal. Some libraries establish formal assignment alert programs to help public librarians know what students will be asking for. Schools may staff homework help centers or tutoring programs in the public library. A relationship with the school librarians in the area also makes it easier for children's librarians to share information about summer reading programs, obtain an invitation to speak to the PTA (Parent Teacher Association), and coordinate special events and programs so that they don't overlap or interfere with major school events.

Homeschool Families

Homeschooling continues to grow in the United States. According to the National Home Education Research Institute (2014), "home-based education has grown from nearly extinct in the United States in the 1970s to now about 2 million school-age students." Another growing initiative is cyberschooling, which allows for online learning and dual enrollment.

Reasons for homeschooling or cyberschooling vary widely but may include factors like geographical isolation, low performing local schools, ideological or religious values, and behavioral problems or special needs. Homeschool philosophies range from unschooling, based on the idea that children will pursue their own areas of interest, to school-at-home that looks much like a typical classroom, just not housed in a public school building. Each philosophy and eclectic variation has its own curriculum interests and needs that the children's librarian will need to clarify before helping the students.

Public libraries can play an important role in the education system of homeschooling families as well as distance education or cyberschooling. While public library collections usually can't and shouldn't include all of the various homeschooling textbooks or specialized materials homeschoolers need, the general collection serves as a great resource for homeschooling families. Parents may request assistance from the children's librarian to teach students how to use specific reference tools or to pull specific materials for use with projects. Homeschool families may also use interlibrary loan frequently in order to get older material that meets their philosophical requirements.

Students may come to the library during the school day to use computers and other technology and to access online databases and reference materials. Some libraries where there are large populations of homeschoolers establish homeschool centers in the library or homeschool resource links on the library's website. These centers may include specialized equipment, such as microscopes and science kits, as well as educational software and board games. Meeting rooms or study areas may be used for group teaching. Homeschooling families who are looking for educational opportunities may also be interested in guest programs and educational events that the library offers so that they can add enrichment opportunities to their children's learning.

Child Care Center

Child care centers may call on the children's librarian to provide early literacy programs, either in the library or off-site at the child care facility. These are children who may not regularly visit the library with their parents, so the contact with the library is important.

Many libraries provide preselected sets of books and other age-appropriate items for child care staff to use with the children in their care. Often, such as with Pierce County, Washington (figure 2.5), the program has a specific name to identify it and its purpose. These books and accompanying materials may be checked out for extended periods to

Figure 2.5. Child Care Center Box. *Ready for Books bin for licensed child care centers; Courtesy of Pierce County Library, Tacoma, Washington*

allow for use by several different classes. These may be theme based to make it easy for child care providers to teach about specific areas, such as the seasons, animals, or numbers, or may be broad based to be used for regular reading times at the center. The kits generally include some way to account for circulation numbers and get feedback on how the materials were used.

Child care centers range from large corporately managed centers that have accreditation from organizations like the National Association for the Education of Young Children to small home-based businesses with caregivers who have little or no training or education for working with very young children. The children's librarian may offer short training sessions to help the child care providers use books to develop early literacy skills. Children's librarians may also model appropriate group reading practices and methods that support developmentally appropriate behavior. Child care providers who lack training in children's literature may not know how to select books that are appropriate for toddlers as opposed to preschool children. They may read too fast or not hold the book properly so that every child can see the illustrations. In some communities, the library is recognized as a provider of continuing education for child care providers and the training counts toward professional development credit for child care providers.

Smaller home-based child care providers may bring small groups of children to the library for regularly scheduled storytimes. Small groups that are scheduled ensure that the program has attendance, but larger groups will overwhelm the program. In that case, the library may provide outreach storytimes. This is a great way to bring early literacy programming to children who may not get to visit the library. Usually these programs are scheduled on a rotating basis to ensure that all of the organizations in the community have an opportunity to host library storytimes. Specially trained volunteers are sometimes used for these outreach programs when staff cannot meet the demand.

Working with child care centers increases use of the collection and allows for opportunities to market library services to parents, encouraging them to bring their children to the library.

◎ Key Points

Children's librarian's work with a range of patrons and groups, and the extent of services will vary depending on the library's location, the community's demographics, and other factors.

- Children have different abilities and needs at various ages.
- Programs will be tailored to meet the developmental needs of various ages of children.
- Many patrons will be from non-English-speaking families.
- Children's librarians must learn to serve the needs of children with disabilities.
- It's important for children's librarians to work with other organizations that also serve children.

The children's librarian and the public library make a difference in the lives of these children and families and the rewards of working with them are great. In the next chapter, you will learn about the children's collection and the literature that forms the basis for the collection. Additionally, some of the standard selection tools will be introduced.

References

ASCLA (Association of Specialized and Cooperative Agencies). 2014. "Library Accessibility: What You Need to Know." Accessed June 16, 2014. http://www.ala.org/ascla/asclaprotools/accessibilitytipsheets.

Begley, Sharon. 1996. "Your Child's Brain." *Newsweek*, February 19: 55–61.

National Home Education Research Institute. 2014. Home page. Accessed June 18, 2014. http://nheri.org/.

National Library Service for the Blind and Physically Handicapped. 2014. "That All May Read." Accessed June 16, 2014. http://www.loc.gov/nls/reference/factsheets/annual.html.

Williams, Virginia Kay, and Nancy Deyoe. 2014. "Diverse Population, Diverse Collection? Youth Collections in the United States." *Technical Services Quarterly* 31, no. 2: 97–121.

Resources Mentioned in This Chapter

Arte Público Press. https://artepublicopress.com/.

Association for Library Services to Children. 2014. "Every Child Ready to Read @ Your Library." Accessed November 21, 2014. http://www.everychildreadytoread.org/

Birchbark Books. http://birchbarkbooks.com/.

Cauley, Lorinda Bryan. 1992. *Clap Your Hands*. New York: Putnam.

Children's Book Week. http://www.bookweekonline.com/.

Every Child Ready to Read. http://www.everychildreadytoread.org/.

Kimmel, Eric. 2013. *Little Red Hot*. Las Vegas, NV: Amazon Children's Publishing.

Kunhardt, Dorothy. 1968. *Pat the Bunny*. New York: Golden Books.

Lee & Low Books. http://www.leeandlow.com/.

Lorito Books. http://loritobooks.com/.

McQuinn, Anna. 2006. *Lola at the Library*. Watertown, MA: Charlesbridge.

Milet Books. http://www.milet.com/.

Mother Goose on the Loose. http://www.mgol.net/.

Rosemary Wells's Read to Your Bunny program. http://rosemarywells.com/index.php/parents/read-to-your-bunny/.

Saltzberg, Barney. 2002. *Peekaboo Kisses*. San Diego: Harcourt.

Sendak, Maurice. 1963. *Where the Wild Things Are*. New York: Harper.

Star Bright Books. http://www.starbrightbooks.org/.

Additional Readings and Resources

Banks, Carrie Scott. 2014. *Including Families of Children with Special Needs: A How-To-Do-It Manual for Librarians*. Chicago: Neal-Schumann.

Crawford, Walter, and Michael Gorman. 1995. *Future Libraries: Dreams, Madness & Reality*. Chicago: American Library Association.

Family Place Libraries. http://familyplacelibraries.org/index.html.

Farmer, Lesley S. J. 2013. *Library Services for Youth with Autism Spectrum Disorder*. Chicago: American Library Association.

Furness, Adrienne. 2008. *Helping Homeschoolers in the Library*. Chicago: American Library Association.

Johnsburg Public Library District. 2014. "Homeschool Resource Center." http://www.johnsburglibrary.org/content/homeschool-resource-center.

Larson, Jeanette. 2011. *El día de los niños/El día de los libros: Building a Culture of Literacy in Your Community through Día.* Chicago: American Library Association.

Okyle, Carly. 2014. "Program Diversity: Do Libraries Serve Kids with Disabilities?" *School Library Journal,* May 1. http://www.slj.com/2014/05/diversity/program-diversity-do-libraries-serve-kids-with-disabilities/#_

Squires, Tasha. 2009. *Library Partnerships: Making Connections between School and Public Libraries.* Medford, NJ: Information Today.

Sullivan, Michael. 2003. *Connecting Boys with Books: What Libraries Can Do.* Chicago: ALA Editions.

CHAPTER 3

The Children's Collection

IN THIS CHAPTER

▷ Understanding the children's collection

▷ Selecting materials for the children's collection

▷ Building a diverse collection

▷ Supporting intellectual freedom and the freedom to read

▷ Promoting library materials and reading

AFTER THE LIBRARY'S STAFF, THE COLLECTION is the most important component of the services librarians provide for children, families, and others who work with children. The collection provides the basis and support for programming, reference assistance, homework help, and essentially every other offering. One of the great things about working with a children's collection is that many of the materials remain useful long after the audience we originally acquired the materials for has aged out of the children's department. For example, books like *Charlotte's Web* by E. B. White or *Goodnight Moon* by Margaret Wise Brown will always be important titles in most collections. At the same time many recent titles will also remain useful and circulate for many years, with a new audience discovering them every year.

Children's needs, reading abilities, and interests change rapidly as they age, so it is important to know the collection and understand what children of various ages might need. While adults may want to read the latest *New York Times* best seller this year and can, in fact, read that book at any age, a child requires material that satisfies both her or his reading abilities, which may be developing, and maturity level, for the actual topic and for the depth of content. Children are also less experienced in determining for themselves whether information is up-to-date, accurate, and still valid, making it especially critical that the nonfiction and reference collections be kept current.

Collection management is a process that includes assessing the collection to determine its strengths and weaknesses, selecting new materials to add to the collection, acquiring the selected materials, preparing them for circulation, and maintaining the collection. Maintenance includes repairing or refurbishing items when practical, pulling items for withdrawal from the collection when they are no longer useful, and replacing lost or withdrawn items with new copies, updated editions, or different titles. The children's librarian will play an important role in most of these steps at least to some degree. Even when the children's librarian has no direct role in the actual acquisition, cataloging, or repair of the materials, it is helpful to be familiar with the business side of the processes in order to understand how the collection budget is spent and what is supposed to happen, as well as what can go wrong on the path from publisher to patron.

ⓖ Building the Collection

In most libraries the children's librarian will be responsible for selecting appropriate materials for the collection. Selection tools can help identify what is available, and reviews help the librarian determine the potential usefulness of the item in the collection. Selections are made based on criteria mentioned in the collection development policy, reviews, and the selector's professional assessment of the books' value or usefulness to the community. Your choices will be limited by the budget but also may be influenced by ordering cycles and the availability, or lack of availability, of an item at the time it is needed. Books go out of print or out of stock quickly. Orders must often be placed early enough to allow materials to be received or canceled for nonfulfillment before the end of the fiscal year. You may be asked to order a percentage above the amount actually available for spending in order to ensure that all funds are spent. Excess items are cancelled once the spending threshold has been met. On rare occasions you may be asked to quickly spend a windfall amount of money; for this reason many librarians maintain wish lists of items they would order if funds allowed.

Some larger libraries centralize the selection of materials, making one person or a small committee responsible for selecting materials for all library locations in a system. A 2004 survey found that more than 40% of library systems used centralized selection, with that figure even higher when smaller libraries with only one or two locations or branches were excluded (Hoffert, 2004). The selection process may also be streamlined a bit by using vendor-generated lists to narrow the available materials. In some cases the entire selection process is outsourced to a vendor who makes selections based on profiles developed by the library staff.

Book selection is viewed by many librarians as a critical part of their professional responsibilities. Although it is a time-consuming process, it is also important that the selector know the collection—what is already there—and the community and their needs and interests. It doesn't take a lot of skill to figure out that the collection probably needs the latest best sellers, but the librarian who is working directly with the children will know whether it is likely that the newest title in a specific series is still being voraciously read by young readers in the community. If profiles are used, funds should be available to fill gaps that have been missed. Profiles should be changed and tweaked to refine choices that are made. Money should also be set aside to fill unanticipated needs or to purchase items that have been missed by the in-house or outsourced selectors.

The Print Collection

Figures vary but it is safe to estimate that more than 20,000 books are published in print format each year in the United States for readers through the sixth grade. That figure doesn't count the increasing number of self-published books and books from very small publishers, which may raise the number as high as 100,000. It is impossible for any librarian to know every title that is released each year, much less to be familiar with the many titles that are already in print. To find the best items that are most suited for the collection librarians use checklists, reviews, patron suggestions, vendor websites, award lists, and other tools. While the amount of material may seem overwhelming, simply being able to peruse catalogs, scan websites, and look at lists that provide a good overview of all that is available results in a surprisingly high level of retention and understanding of the many titles, plots, and concepts available.

The print collection will include a mix of hardcover and paperback books. Become familiar with the terminology like *library edition*, *board book*, and *prebind*. For some audiences, or in situations where the book will receive intense use, the type of binding and production quality will make a difference in its longevity. Paperback copies will rarely provide the service needed for a popular picture book like *The Very Hungry Caterpillar* by Eric Carle, but a board book version for toddlers might be a good supplement to a well-bound library edition of the title. Many librarians have stopped selecting the library-bound editions with reinforced bindings for nonfiction because the bindings outlast the useful life of the content, and many libraries are reluctant to weed books that are in good condition even though they are outdated. Library bindings generally receive a smaller discount so are best used for books that will have a long, useful life span in the collection. We will explore the various formats and genres of books later in this chapter.

TYPES OF BINDINGS

Board book: a book printed on thick paper; usually eight pages and small enough for tiny hands to hold

Library edition: a book with a hardcover binding that has been reinforced for rigorous library use

Paperback: a book with a soft cover and glued binding; often smaller in size than a hardcover book

Prebind: a book that has been rebound prior to delivery to the library; intended to strengthen the binding and reinforce the covers for durability

Trade book: a hardcover book that usually has a glued binding and is intended for general consumer use

---

Audiovisual Materials

Public library collections may include a range of nonprint or nonbook materials such as film, sound recordings, and visual items or realia. Formats change with the technology so that few libraries now provide film in VHS format, and 16 mm has almost disappeared entirely. Sound recordings are almost entirely on compact disc or in downloadable digital formats. Newly emerging are devices with preloaded content. Playaway and Playaway View offer one or more books or films on a self-contained media player. This eliminates the need for the patron to own the equipment to access the material and eliminates potential for damaging or losing one disc in a set.

Audio and film, including DVDs, Blu-ray, and streaming video, are standard items in library collections and may include audiobooks, music, popular movies, educational films, and documentaries. Some items will be reviewed in the same journals that are reviewing books, but there are also specialized journals and review sources for audiobooks, music, and film.

Visual and other nonbook items may also include art prints, video games, computer programs, and educational toys. The list of nonbook items is limitless, with some libraries lending educational toys, cake pans, car seats, and other materials that meet the recreational needs of the community. The collection development policy should address the types of nonbook materials that will be collected, linking them to the idea that information is communicated through a variety of methods and different learning styles will be accommodated when possible.

Each format comes with its own set of issues: Are reviews available to help with selection? Are reviews necessary for selection? How will items be cataloged and labeled for circulation? How often are they checked for damage or use? These items also must be maintained and weeded on a regular basis. Additionally, some library policies restrict children from checking out DVDs and audiobooks on the assumption that they are more expensive than books if they are damaged or lost. Of course, that is not always the case and care should be taken not to restrict children's access to the materials they want and need.

E-books and Digital Collections

E-books and digital downloads of audiobooks and films are essentially variations of the physical formats already discussed. Instead of the item being utilized in a physical format—printed book, compact disc, or DVD or Blu-ray—the content is downloaded onto a device for listening or viewing. The device may be a computer, an MP3 player, a smartphone or tablet, or whatever new technology comes along next. Although some content is produced exclusively for digital download, currently much of the content is also available in a physical format. Use is growing, and will continue to grow, but as of 2012 only 46% of children reported having read an e-book according to Scholastic's *Kids & Family Reading Report*. The Scholastic study also found that e-books are of more interest to boys and may stimulate them to read more (2013: 8), something that is a challenge for many educators and parents.

Currently, selection and maintenance of digital materials are in great flux. Many publishers are not selling e-books and digital audiobooks directly to libraries. Selection of individual titles may not be possible, or will be very limited, because the digital content is often part of a package that is licensed by the library. Often the library gets what is available in the package and may not be able to add additional copies to meet greater demand for a specific title. Current business models favor licensing, rather than owning, digital content, meaning that when the library no longer pays for the service, the items will no longer be available. As with every technology, this may change as use and demand grows.

Some books, especially reference books, are now only available in electronic format. This works well as the content is outdated within a short time of publication. The electronic format is easier and less expensive to update more frequently. Although there are some books that are published directly as digital books, particularly in the self-publishing world, most audiobooks start as a print book and are available in downloadable format as well as on compact disc. Audiobooks may include computer files that offer enhanced materials like photographs, images, and replicas of historical documents that were in the print book and links to websites with more, or corrected, information.

Some books may never translate well to digital format. For example, a board book in digital format would simply be a picture book because board books are printed on thick glossy paper that can withstand rough handling, and chewing, by infants. There is also some research indicating that comprehension may not be as good when reading material on an e-reader. "Compared with paper, screens may also drain more of our mental resources while we are reading and make it a little harder to remember what we read when we are done" (Jabr, 2013). This is particularly important for students who are reading to understand a subject.

When selecting nonprint material that was based on print items, keep in mind that reviews may be based on the original content published in the traditional formats without evaluation of the digital format or enhancements that may be achieved with technology. Reviews are also not as easily available for content that is available solely in digital format. Many of the standard library review journals do not review self-published works or reformatted material like e-books and audiobooks, or if they do so, it is not comprehensive so a lot of material is never reviewed.

While the children's librarian's role in selection and weeding may be limited, he or she still needs to know what is available in digital formats. There are many different e-book platforms and readers available, with more to come. Some downloads will only work on specific readers. Some content will be current materials, but a lot of the content for e-books may come from freely available classics and public domain works. It's important for users to be aware of the copyright date because many older books in the public domain are in digital format and may show up in a catalog search. Children may never even consider that the e-book on astronomy was released in 1856!

The Collection Development Policy

Much of the collection management process will be addressed in the library's collection development policy that the children's librarian should refer to regularly. This policy provides guidance when materials are being selected for the collection, when you are responding to complaints or concerns expressed about materials, and as you weed the collection or decide what to discard without replacement.

Many libraries, especially small and medium-sized public libraries, have a comprehensive collection development policy that addresses all areas of the collection, including the children's collection. Larger or specialized libraries may have separate policies for various sections of the collection, or subsections. The children's librarian may or may not be involved in the development of all policies but should have input into the development and revision of policies that involve the children's department.

The collection development policy sets priorities for the types of materials, formats, and subjects that will be included—or excluded—from the collection. While it is best not to get overly detailed or specific, the collection development policy will provide guidance in shaping the collection so that it will fulfill the goals established for the library's children's services. Although some parts of the policy may apply to all areas of the collection, the needs of children will often vary from the needs of adults and the policy should address these differences. For example, textbooks may not be an important component of the adult collection but would be essential in a public library collection that is supporting the local schools by offering homework assistance or that serves many homeschooled children.

The collection development policy will usually include a statement about its purpose, including the ages of the patrons covered by the collection (often birth through age 12) and assign responsibility for carrying out aspects of the policy (for example, "A professional children's librarian is responsible for selecting appropriate materials based on the selection criteria established in this policy."). The policy should also provide selection criteria or factors that will influence choices, set priorities for formats (for example, "Books, e-books, and audio or video materials may be given priority over other formats such as games, toys, or art."), and include information about intellectual freedom and collection maintenance. The policy will also usually refer to the procedures for requesting that materials be considered for removal from the collection because a patron objects to the content. Sample policies can be found on the library websites provided on this page, as well as in *Public Library Policy Writer: A Guidebook with Model Policies on CD-ROM* by Jeanette Larson and Herman L. Totten (2008), which includes topics for consideration while developing specific policies.

Needs Assessment

One of the main goals of the library is to provide for the information and recreational reading, listening, and viewing needs of the community it serves. In order to do that effectively, the library staff needs to understand the community and the interests of its members. Data is received on this daily via feedback from patrons as they find, or don't find, what they are looking for in the collection. However, it is good practice to occasionally take a more structured look at the community to ensure that the collection, and other services, of course, are meeting user needs. Community analysis also helps to identify the needs of *nonusers* who may not be coming to the library because the collection doesn't have anything for them. Of course, the collection will be broad based and include some materials that are only used by a small percentage of the population, but as your community grows, or shrinks, and as the demographics change over time, a community analysis can help reestablish collection priorities and ensure that needs are being met.

Although it is not likely that the children's librarian will embark on a full-scale community analysis independently of the rest of the library, it is good practice to regularly update and review demographic information to ascertain whether the number of children in the community is increasing or decreasing, the education level of children and parents, what languages are spoken at home, the percent of young children who are in child care during the day or who live with grandparents, and economic factors such as household income. Changes in these demographics and lifestyle factors can impact the collection and the programs and services provided. If, for example, a large percentage of preschool children are in child care facilities, the library might want to set up mini-collections to lend to those facilities as part of an outreach program. Demographic data is helpful in planning, marketing, and executing many library programs and services.

⌾ Children's Literature

Since physical books continue to be the mainstay of most children's collections, even with the increasing popularity of e-books, the collection is generally divided and described by a variety of labels. Sometimes distinctions are made with regard to the format of the material (for example, paperbacks) or by the intended group of users (for example, beginning readers), but most public library children's collections will include some or all of the various types of children's materials. We'll explore a few of the types of material here, but anyone who has never taken a course on children's literature will be well served by reading a good textbook that can provide much more information than is provided in this chapter. For example, in addition to a good, quick overview of the history and foundations of the discipline, *Children's Literature, Briefly* by Michael O. Tunnell, James Jacobs, Terrell A. Young, and Gregory Bryan (2012) outlines the various aspects of each genre and format within the field of children's literature.

There are two major divisionary elements for books: format and genre. Although these terms are often used interchangeably, *format* refers to the design and layout out of the book. Picture books, paperbacks, and graphic novels have specific design features, but the content can be about any subject and in any genre. Some elements of format may go out the window when a book is transferred into e-book format as pagination is usually

Format	Genre
Board book	Historical fiction
Graphic Novel	Humor
Hardcover	Mystery
Paperback	Nonfiction
Picture book	Poetry

lost or can be manipulated by the reader. *Genre* refers to the type of literature and the shared literary elements that define the content. Genres include mystery, folklore, poetry, historical fiction, and other styles of literature. New genres, such as urban fiction, appear occasionally.

A specific book may overlap genres or incorporate elements of several genres, sometimes making it a little difficult to offer a concise label for a book that is being described. A picture book may be any of a multitude of genres, just as mysteries and biographies can be presented in graphic novel format. Each format and genre has elements to consider as selections are made for the children's collection.

Picture Books

Picture books, or picture storybooks, are what people often think of when they hear the term *children's books*. The format is usually 32 pages long and the pages are larger than standard books for adults. The trim size may be 8" x 10" or 10" x 11" or 11" x 9" or something else. The orientation of text and art may be horizontal or vertical, and the book might even be squared rather than rectangular. There are usually illustrations on every page with some illustrations spanning two facing pages to create a double-page spread. The illustrations are integral to the telling of the story. These books are usually read *to* a child; therefore, the vocabulary can range from fairly simple to extremely complex. In fact, research by Hayes and Ahrens, as well as others, shows that children's books usually have richer and less commonly used vocabulary than other books, providing children with opportunities to learn more words and enrich their own vocabulary (Hayes and Ahrens, 1988).

Keep in mind that while all picture books are illustrated, not all illustrated books are picture books. Some illustrated books may be 32 pages long but will have extensive text, tell a complex story, and be divided into chapters. The pictures are more illustrative or decorative rather than being integral to telling the story.

Picture books are read to children from babies and toddlers through kindergarten and primary grades. These are the mainstay of storytime and bedtime reading, and the majority offer fictional stories. Picture books can, however, be any genre, including nonfiction. A great thing about picture books is that many stay in print and remain popular for decades. Although it may seem that the vocabulary is dated or the illustrations muted by today's standards, books like *Caps for Sale* by Esphyr Slobodkina, first published in 1938, and *Millions of Cats* by Wanda Gág (1928) are still in print and remain staples of storytime.

In addition to introducing children to a wide range of stories and folktales, picture books introduce children to vocabulary and reinforce the connection between the symbols on a page and the words they stand for. The illustrations in picture books help children develop visual literacy, a term coined by John Debes in the late 1960s to describe the competencies a human being needs to have in order to discriminate and interpret the objects and symbols, whether natural or man-made, that we encounter in our environment. Art styles are diverse, ranging from realistic illustrations that faithfully reproduce people, objects, and places as they really appear, to impressionistic illustrations that appear mixed up and distorted. Other styles include naive, cartoon, and surrealistic. The artist can select from many different mediums, including fabric, paint, woodblock print, collage or paper pulp, pen and ink, and photography. Today illustrations are being created using computer software, and artists may use a combination of materials or enhance computer-created art with other media.

A growing number of picture books are written for older children and include more sophisticated content that is targeted for a more mature reader. These books might be disturbing or frightening to many in a younger audience. While books like *Patrol: An American Soldier in Vietnam* by Walter Dean Myers or *Baseball Saved Us* by Ken Mochizuki meet the general definition of a picture book, the subjects, a soldier's fear in the jungles of Vietnam and a Japanese American child in an American internment camp, are not appropriate for preschoolers. These picture books may be read aloud to a group of older children or they may read them on their own.

Although there is no consensus about a specific canon of books that *every* children's librarian should know, a good children's librarian should be familiar with a large number of books. Not only will knowing these books help with selection as new items are compared with what is already in the collection, but it also helps with reader's advisory. To most parents, whether accurate or not, the children's librarian is viewed as an expert in children's literature. For new children's librarians, the books on the list "100 Books Every Child Should Hear Before Kindergarten" compiled by Pierce County Public Library (2014), offer a good start in reading the best picture books. The annual notable lists (http://www.ala.org/alsc/awardsgrants/notalists) compiled by the Association for Library Services to Children (ACLS, 2014a) also provide good benchmarks for current titles to familiarize yourself with.

Many of the picture books in the collection will provide a story with characters, plot, and a progression of activities. The format also includes concept books that provide basic information without much of a storyline, although there may be connecting factors. Concept books are created to help children learn the alphabet, numbers, colors, and more. Picture books may present factual information and biographies in a narrative form that is highly illustrated and simplified. Pop-up books or books with parts that can be manipulated by the reader are also considered to be picture books. A wordless picture book, such as *Pancakes for Breakfast* by Tomie dePaola, tells the entire story through the pictures without words, or with only one or two words. Wordless picture books allow the child to "tell" the story and are an excellent way to encourage children to look closely at the illustrations and discuss the story. Since there is no right way to read the story, wordless picture books are also great for parents who are not themselves proficient readers to share a book with their child.

Be sure that the collection includes a good mix of diversity of art styles and story content, including characters from diverse communities. Subjects should include contemporary stories, but also traditional folk and fairy tales retold with a variety of illustration styles. Look at how David Wiesner treats the familiar story of the Three Little Pigs in his Caldecott Medal–winning book, using visual codes to break the boundaries of the traditional tale. Compare this with Paul Galdone's more traditional version of the same story. Older preschoolers and kindergarten children will delight in variants of the familiar story like Jon Scieszka's quirky *The True Story of the Three Little Pigs* or spin-offs like *The Three Little Gators* by Helen Ketteman. Multicultural or bilingual retellings like *Los tres cerdos/The Three Pigs: Nacho, Tito y Miguel* by Bobbi Salinas may also be used to introduce words in Spanish along with cultural distinctions.

In addition to variety in art styles and media, the collection should include original and traditional stories that reflect different cultures, which are written and illustrated by people from various ethnic and racial groups. As a multicultural nation, people come from many areas of the world, belong to different religious groups, and hold differing cultural beliefs. Literature should reflect this variety so that children see people like themselves

EVALUATING PICTURE STORY BOOKS

When evaluating picture books, you are looking for a perfect marriage of text and illustration. The illustrations should reinforce the story, which is told through strong text. Although the text often could stand alone, it is enriched by illustrations that supplement and expand on the story. As you gain experience reading and using picture books, some of the evaluation process becomes automatic and innate.

Whether you are examining the book to write a review of it or selecting something for use in storytime, these considerations should be kept in mind:

- Is the content appropriate for the *intended* age level?
- Is this a book that will appeal to children?
- Are the illustrations accurate? Do they correspond to the story?
- Do the illustrations complement the story? That is, do they help create meaning?
- Do the text and pictures avoid stereotypes?
- Is the theme worthwhile? What is the purpose for sharing the book?
- Are style and language appropriate?
- Are the text, illustrations, format, and typography in harmony?
- Is the medium chosen by the illustrator appropriate for the mood of the story?

in the stories and retain their cultural rights and cultural equality. Additionally, books help us see commonalities among people as well as differences and introduce readers to different cultures and ways of living.

Board Books

A special type of picture book worth noting is the board book, a specific type of binding and format. The book is chunky and printed on pressed cardboard that usually has a glossy coating. The books are generally 8 to 12 pages with very simple and minimal text and large illustrations on uncluttered pages. Sometimes the board book is original but it may be an abridgement or condensation of another picture book. The books are durable so that very young children, 18 months and younger, can hold them, chew on them, and play with them. Some board books incorporate nursery rhymes or songs, but some tell a very short story or are adapted from longer books, such as *The Carrot Seed* by Ruth Krauss. They can be used in baby storytimes and circulate a lot in communities with young families. Often multiple copies are provided so that the book can be used in lapsit storytimes and other parent/child programs.

Board books are meant to get parents into the habit of sharing a book with a child while stimulating the baby's senses and introducing them to the sounds that will be the building blocks for language. Babies also begin to learn how to handle a book by turning the pages of a board book, so board books should be sized for tiny hands. Some are small but chunky, but most are more squared. Some board books may include mirrored paper, tactile components, or flaps that allow the infant to engage with the book.

When evaluating board books, look for high contrast so that the baby's eyes can focus. Pictures should be simple with clear edges that define what is being shown. Cartoonlike illustrations or photographs work best, especially when they depict baby faces and familiar objects.

Easy Readers

Easy or beginning readers serve as a transition between picture books and chapter books. They have a controlled vocabulary so that they can be read by children who are learning to read. They help new readers be successful in their attempts at reading a book. Early beginning readers were often basal readers, repeating the same set of a few words in varying sentences without telling a story. The Dick and Jane books are a prime example of this. *The Cat in the Hat*, by Dr. Seuss, was published in 1954 in response to criticism of these basal primers that had uninspiring and uninteresting stories.

In the mid-1950s, Harper & Brothers, at the request of librarians, began publishing I Can Read books written and illustrated by some of the best people in the business. The first title released was *Little Bear*, written by Else Holmelund Minarik and illustrated by Maurice Sendak. The quality of the writing and illustration can be seen in beginning readers like *Frog and Toad Together* by Arnold Lobel and *Little Bear's Visit* by Else Holmelund Minarik and Maurice Sendak that have won many awards including Newbery and Caldecott honors. The Geisel Award was established by the Association for Library Services to Children in 2006 to specifically recognize the highest literary and artistic achievements in books that are intended for children who are beginning to read. Beginning readers are available in many genres, including mystery, western, and nonfiction. Many of the books first published over 50 years ago are still in print and widely used, remaining fresh reading for children in kindergarten, first, and second grades who are practicing their reading skills.

The best early readers tell a great story but use a controlled vocabulary that is appropriate for a specific level of reading skill. They have illustrations that provide clues to help readers understand new vocabulary, but the illustrations don't move the story along the way they do in a picture book. Pages have larger print (12 to 18 point), fewer words, shorter sentences, and a lot of white space to facilitate the physical development of children's eye muscles. The books are generally sized more like a typical book for older children, are divided into chapters or short stories and run 32 to 64 pages in length. Often these books will have an indication of the difficulty level or a code that indicates whether it is a very basic, middle, or advanced beginning reader.

Fiction Books

As children become proficient readers by second or third grade, they move from beginning readers into the broad category of longer books commonly referred to as fiction or chapter books. These can be as short as 64 pages or as long as 400 or more pages. Fiction books come in many genres, from science fiction and fantasy to mystery and historical fiction. These books tell a story and are primarily intended for recreational and leisure reading, although some may be assigned for class reading. They may be in a series, where the same characters appear over and over again. A key factor for these books is that children are often picking them out for themselves, or will select them to read based on recommendations from peers, teachers, and librarians. Many are classics that have been in collections for years, but every year a new crop of great stories can be added to the shelves.

Evaluating fiction can seem very subjective. In addition to general criteria, each genre and subgenre will have elements that are considered standards for excellence. Historical fiction, for example, is expected to be accurate for the history portion of the story, while anything goes in fantasy since the author is creating a world. In general, fiction is evaluated by considering these elements:

- Believability of the plot
- Satisfactory plot development and conclusion
- Style and language
- Natural-sounding dialogue (suited to the audience, characters, and story)
- Pacing appropriate to the tone of the story
- Character development (including cultural considerations)
- Setting
- Theme, avoiding overt didacticism
- Mood and tone

Series Books

Not every fiction book that is included in the collection will be of the highest literary caliber. Series books, such as the Nancy Drew and the Hardy Boys, are written by a stable of writers who follow a formula. Even more contemporary series, such as The 39 Clues, while written by some highly regarded authors, are designed to be fast, engaging reading, with strong characters and plots that compel the reader to pick up the next title. Entertaining reading, series books often encourage kids to read and to read a lot.

Having a successful experience reading one book and then being able to find another book "just like it" is a good way to build reading confidence, and series books accomplish this because of their familiarity. Some of the best books from a literary standpoint won't be the most popular reading with children, but studies have shown that to be proficient readers, as well as to enjoy reading, children need to be able to choose from a wide variety of books, including books that would be considered marginal from a literary standpoint. The important thing is for children to be surrounded by a lot of reading material and to be able to choose what they want to read.

There are also series of nonfiction titles that are useful for filling curriculum needs. Many of these books are well written but still follow a pattern to provide consistent information across topics within a predetermined number of pages. Nonfiction series like the Scientists in the Field from Houghton Mifflin or Seymour Simon's fabulous SeeMore Readers published by Chronicle Books provide an excellent introduction to a topic and are written by outstanding authors. More information on nonfiction books is provided later in the chapter.

Tip: Midcontinent Library System provides an online resource, Juvenile Series and Sequels (http://www.mymcpl.org/books-movies-music/juvenile-series) to organize over 28,000 books in 3,700 series by subject, series, and author. This is a great help in determining the order of series books and to find gaps in the collection.

We can slice and dice fiction into a myriad of genres; often there are subgenres or a book will overlap more than one genre. These are labels for categorizing fiction so new genres sometimes may be coined to enhance marketing a book. Remember that any format, including picture books, beginning readers, and graphic novels, can be categorized into genres, but patrons tend to regularly request fiction by genre more than other formats. Each genre has some specific elements that reviewers and evaluators consider. For every genre, you will want to familiarize yourself with examples for each of the major types so that you have touchstones for comparison as you read reviews and make selections, and for reader's advisory.

Fantasy and science fiction are sometimes dealt with as separate genres. Fantasy takes place in an imaginary world created by the author, but that world can be in the past, present, or future. Fantasy is further divided into high fantasy and low fantasy with high fantasy taking place in a totally imaginary world. Low fantasy may occur in our world but include magical elements, or it may set up a parallel world that coexists with ours. *The Sinister Sweetness of Splendid Academy* by Nikki Loftin, a version of Hansel and Gretel that takes place today in a community much like yours, is an example of low fantasy. *The Lion, the Witch, and the Wardrobe* by C. S. Lewis and many of the books by Lloyd Alexander are high fantasy. Fantasy can also be arranged by the elements of the story: magical powers, talking toys, tiny people, time warps, dystopia, and more.

The success of modern fantasy rests on the authors' ability to suspend the reader's disbelief in characterization, setting, theme, and point of view. The reader *knows* this is all made up and very different from our real world, yet within the context of the story the reader can believe that everything is possible.

Science fiction usually takes place in the future (measured from when the book was written), and the imaginary world must operate within the laws of science rather than magic. Even if robots can't currently do certain things, their actions and characterization and the technology available must be explainable within science.

Realistic fiction occurs in the real world, either in the present or in the past. The genre can be further divided into subcategories like school stories, sports stories, mystery, and survival. Books that are primarily categorized as realistic fiction can include elements of more than one subgenre.

Contemporary realistic fiction is the most popular genre for children's fiction books and deals with issues, themes, and topics that are familiar to young people. Some of the themes may explore problems like drug use, divorce, abuse, and war—all of which may be controversial or disturbing for some readers. Books for older readers may use mild profanity when it is appropriate for the character to speak that way or when the character is reacting to a situation.

Historical fiction is a specific type of realistic fiction that is set in the real world, but in the past. Generally for a book to be called historical fiction, a contemporary author writes about events that occurred in a previous time. The story may include historical figures as minor characters or make reference to real people who lived at the time, although the main character is usually created by the author. Vocabulary should be appropriate to the time period, using words that were common to the time. The setting, events, and items mentioned in the story should be historically accurate. Often the author will include an author's note to let the reader know what is true and what was made up, as well as to share a little more historical information. *The Loud Silence of Francine Green* by Karen

Cushman is set in McCarthy-era Los Angeles and makes reference to cultural life of that time, mentioning Jerry Lewis and Dean Martin, radio shows like *Dragnet*, and the Sears catalog. While today's readers may not immediately recognize these references, they are integral to setting the story in its historical context. Historical fiction can be a great way to help history come alive and provides scaffolding between factual material and a good story.

Some children's literature scholars feel that with the passage of time, a book written as contemporary realistic fiction moves into the realm of historical fiction. Others believe that for a book to be considered historical fiction, it must have been written some period of time after the events in the story. Still others feel that books written several decades ago about children who were modern at the time, might more properly be called "period fiction" because they don't deal with historical facts or figures but are "historical" to today's reader. Children rarely consider these distinctions, however. As with other books of realistic fiction, some historical fiction will deal with unsavory historical events or include controversial figures and events. For example, *The Boy in the Striped Pajamas* by John Boyne is a historical allegory that looks at the Holocaust through the eyes of a young boy whose father runs a concentration camp.

Most of the genres have at least one type-specific award and some of these are included in appendix B.

Nonfiction

Nonfiction can be a real challenge for the collection. The possible subjects are broad and you are collecting materials for leisure reading, for lifelong education, and to support local school curriculum requirements. When most library users think of nonfiction, if they think of that term at all, they are thinking about the books and other materials that are classified with Dewey Decimal numbers. In fact, of course, fiction has a Dewey number but most libraries classify them as JF (juvenile or junior fiction), E (easy), or some other category that pulls them out of the Dewey system to facilitate patron browsing. Many libraries also prefer to use B (biography) instead of the 920 numbers. Because children are learning the Dewey Decimal system, many libraries provide decorative reminders, such as the stuffed animal shown in figure 3.1, to help children remember Dewey numbers and find popular sections.

Nonfiction is usually subdivided into biography and information books. Both should present current and accurate knowledge about the subject. The information is verifiable and is a report on real happenings in the real world. On the other hand, fiction, or prose, which certainly contains elements of fact, is made up by the author.

It is traditionally thought that most children read nonfiction primarily for homework assignments and not for pleasure. In the past many nonfiction books were written and published to be utilitarian. A number of books, particularly those in series from publishers that specialize in books for school libraries, are still arranged to be useful for research and reports and are written for specific reading levels. For example, books on the states in the United States will follow a very similar format with uniform information about the differences in each state. This facilitates children using the book for research but rarely would the book be read from cover to cover for enjoyment.

An increasing body of nonfiction literature being published today is compelling both in the subjects covered and in the writing. The author uses all of the tools and techniques of a great storyteller, but the story being told is true. Common Core State Standards for

Figure 3.1. Elephant Shelf Reminder. *Courtesy Tom Green County Library System, San Angelo, Texas; Sally Meyers, children's librarian*

schools across the country are also beginning to require that students read more literary nonfiction, including complex nonfiction books, across disciplines. Books like *Ain't Nothing but a Man* by Scott Reynolds Nelson or *We've Got a Job: The 1963 Birmingham Children's March* by Cynthia Levinson tell as compelling a story as any novel, but the facts are verified and the story is real.

Nonfiction is written for every age and reading level, including picture book formats like *Surfer of the Century: The Life of Duke Kahanamoku* by Ellie Crowe (figure 3.2) or *The Mangrove Tree: Planting Trees to Feed Families* by Susan L. Roth and Cindy Trumbore. Even beginning reader and graphic novel collections can include nonfiction titles like *What Happens to Our Trash?* by D. J. Ward, a second level reader, or *Houdini: The Handcuff King* by Jason Lutes, a graphic novel biography. Informational books can include activity books, such as science experiments and hobby books, as well as concept books, including basic board books that may introduce colors and seasons to a baby. Biographical books may include memoirs and autobiography or interviews and journals.

When selecting nonfiction, look for these elements, which are usually mentioned in reviews:

- Accuracy—Are the facts current and complete? Is there a balance of fact and theory, and are theories clearly identified as such? Is the author qualified to write about the subject or have experts vetted the work? Does the book include additional resources and sources for information? Are source notes provided for dialogue or is the dialogue made up?
- Organization—Is the level of information appropriate for the intended audience? Is the development of the information laid out in a logical, clear sequence? Does

Figure 3.2. *Surfer of the Century: The Life of Duke Kahanamoku. © Illustration by Richard Waldrep, reprinted with permission from Lee & Low Books.*

it move from general to specific or simple to complex or another appropriate pattern?

- Design—Is the book attractive, inviting, and readable? Do illustrations or photographs complement the text, and are they well placed to enhance understanding?
- Style—Is the writing interesting and stimulating? Does the author's enthusiasm for the subject come across through rich language and appropriate terminology?

Graphic Novels

Although comic books and comic book–like formats have existed since the 19th century, graphic novels are a relatively recent phenomenon in public library collections. Simply put, graphic novels are book-length comics with a narrative story told through a series of illustrated panels. Sometimes dismissed by parents and educators who don't understand their popularity, the stories in graphic novels can be quite complex and the vocabulary quite rich. The format reaches multiple literacies and learning styles, so has proven to be useful in helping struggling or reluctant readers become proficient readers and enjoy reading. They have become an essential component of many public library collections, and research is showing that they have great potential in education.

The Orbis Pictus Award is presented by the National Council of Teachers of English to the best nonfiction and information books published in the previous year. It is named to commemorate the work of Johannes Amos Comenius, *Orbis Pictus: The World in Pictures* published in 1657 and considered to be the first book actually planned for children. This is a good resource for identifying some of the best books for the library's collection (http://www.ncte.org/awards/orbispictus).

The term *graphic novel* refers to the format of the book but is not necessarily a novel. Graphic novels may cover any subject found in traditional text-dominant books, so you can have graphic novel histories and biographies, as well as graphic novels in mystery, science fiction, historical fiction, and other genres. Mythology and classics like *Hamlet* translate well into the graphic format, and some children's classics, such as *A Wrinkle in Time* adapted by Hope Larson, are being recast in graphic novel format. Even younger elementary children can enjoy *Nursery Rhyme Comics: 50 Timeless Rhymes from 50 Celebrated Cartoonists* edited by Chris Duffy, or Jennifer L. Holm's Babymouse series.

A challenge for collection development is the sheer number of graphic novels being published each year and the fact that many are in series, almost mandating that the library provide every title. Additionally some graphic novels meant for adult readers or mature teens may include controversial material or very serious topics, and the art may be a bit racy. Care should be taken in selecting to ensure that you don't automatically equate the comic format with young children.

Awards and core lists for graphic novels are beginning to come forth. One notable core list is created by the Association for Library Services to Children's (ALSC, 2014b) Quicklists Consulting Committee (http://www.ala.org/alsc/compubs/booklists/grphcnvls). Graphic novels are not specifically excluded from inclusion on award lists so they may show up on the annual Notable Children's Books list. So far most of the awards specifically for graphic novels focus on books for teens and adults, rather than those for younger children, but the Eisner Awards (http://www.comic-con.org/awards/eisners-current-info) include a category for Best Publication for Kids, as do the Cybil Awards (http://www.cybils.com).

Books in Languages Other Than English

Most public library collections now include some books and materials in languages other than English that are spoken in the community. Selecting books in a language you don't speak has its own unique challenges, and you may rely more on reviews and patron suggestions and requests than you do with other areas of the collection. While collections can include books in French, Vietnamese, Hmong, or any language, materials in Spanish are commonly included in most collections.

Be sure you understand what languages are spoken in your community and even what dialect or country of origin is preferred. While selectors rarely have the option to choose the same title from among a range that includes Cuban Spanish, Mexican Spanish, or the Spanish spoken is Spain, you don't want, if possible, to select a book that won't be useful to your patrons.

Many libraries put more emphasis on books in other languages for young children, such as picture books, because parents who may not be proficient in reading English will be reading those books to their child. Older children who are reading alone may read in English. When children seek out books in another language, their choices are often translations of popular books like the Harry Potter series. While not every person of Hispanic heritage reads or speaks Spanish, a growing number of non-Spanish readers are learning Spanish and want simpler, shorter books.

For Spanish-speaking patrons who want to read in Spanish, libraries can select books published in the United States. Many of these are translations of books that were first published in English or are published in dual-language format, having both English and Spanish on the same page. Some publishers focus most of their attention on books that deal with multicultural topics and themes and that are available in Spanish and other languages. Arte Público Press (https://artepublicopress.com/), through its Piñata Books imprint, publishes books for children that offer the realistic and authentic portrayal of the themes, languages, characters, and customs of Hispanic culture in the United States. Lectorum (http://www.lectorum.com) is both a publisher and distributor of Spanish language books.

Shen's Books (http://www.shens.com/) publishes titles that focus on introducing children to the cultures of Asia. Star Bright Books (http://www.starbrightbooks.com) publishes authors from around the globe and has popular titles translated into multiple languages.

Most of these books will be available through the jobber or wholesaler that is used for the rest of the library's materials and may be reviewed by the standard review sources. There is currently no one-stop source for reviews of books in Spanish, although most of the standard sources, such as *School Library Journal*, include some reviews on a regular basis. Be careful about selecting a book in another language based solely on a review of its English content because while that will help you determine if a book was well written and is on a subject you want, it won't address the quality of the translation.

Books are also available from publishers in Spanish-speaking countries, and those books will rarely have been reviewed in standard library review sources available in the United States. They are also often harder to obtain and may require that the acquisitions department order directly from publishers or through specialty jobbers. The publishing industry also differs in other countries and bindings may be weaker than we expect and the paper may be flimsy and of lower quality. You have to decide whether having books that meet your patrons' needs are worth the cost, even if they have to be rebound or replaced more frequently.

Diversity in Children's Books

Throughout the children's collection you want to ensure that you not only have the best material available for children but also that the books in the collection represent the totality of our diverse nation. Children gain a good sense of self-worth and enhancement of self-concept by seeing themselves and their cultural heritage in the books they read. This diversity should cut across all genres.

The collection will include some books, particularly books written in earlier times when our nation was less sensitive to cultural differences, which reflect stereotypes or images and ideas and attitudes that are now considered to be inaccurate or that represent people from another culture as being inferior to members of the predominant culture. Some titles may remain in the collection despite stereotyping or inaccurate information because of their popularity or literary value, but you should still be aware of the issues related to them. Some books, such as *Little Black Sambo* by Helen Bannerman, have been updated and revised to eliminate the derogatory elements while retaining the essence of the original story. *Sam and the Tigers*, written by Julius Lester and illustrated by Jerry Pinkney, shows Sam as a savvy young man who comically and cleverly outwits the tigers. Other classics, such as *The Story of Doctor Doolittle* by Hugh Lofting, have been updated by the publisher to remove negative and derogatory references to skin color in the text or, as with *Charlie and the Chocolate Factory* by Roald Dahl, to provide new illustrations for the 1973 version that are not offensive. You will want to know which editions of these books are in the collection and may decide to weed older dated versions in favor of new ones. Modern sensitivity to and heightened awareness of offensive stereotypes and cultural inaccuracies does not, of course, prevent them from continuing to be included in children's literature. *Of Thee I Sing: A Letter to My Daughters* by President Barack Obama has been criticized for both the stereotypical text used to describe Lakota Chief Sitting Bull and the illustrations by Loren Long that seem to dehumanize the only Native American in the book. Sitting Bull is represented as landscape while the other people are realistically portrayed. Critic Debbie Reese, in her blog *American Indians in Children's Literature*, regularly points to negative or romanticized aspects of books that include Native American characters while also offering suggestions for books that provide a better reflection of indigenous peoples. Reviews and your professional judgment will help you decide whether the positive elements of the book outweigh the negative.

Books like *Multicultural Children's Literature: Through the Eyes of Many Children* by Donna E. Norton provide extensive information on how to evaluate, select, and share multicultural literature. Generally, look for

- Characters with authentic and realistic behaviors that allow the reader to look, read, recognize, and positively respond to the text and illustrations
- Text and illustrations that avoid stereotyping the cultural, ethnic, or racial group
- Balance of gender and culture, as appropriate to the subject or theme
- Strong plots and well-developed descriptions of the setting and characters that reflect the cultural values of the group
- Historical accuracy that is presented appropriately for the point of view of the main character
- Books that avoid showing a group only in historical context as if the cultural group no longer exists

Some librarians express concern that they can't find enough books that represent the diversity of their communities. While it is certainly true that only a small percentage of the books published each year are by or about persons of color, librarians often overlook what is available. The Cooperative Center for Children's Books at the University of Wisconsin, Madison tracks publishing statistics based on the books they receive for review. Of books featuring human beings (as opposed to animal characters), less than 10% featured a person of color in 2013 (Horning, 2014). Author and educator René Saldaña Jr. points out that even when the books are available and displayed, such as at conventions and conferences, librarians walk by without seeing them (2014). It is imperative that we make the effort to seek out books that are diverse. As Saldaña points out, often the books are published by smaller companies that can't afford massive publicity campaigns.

Publishers like Lee & Low and Cinco Puntos Press specialize in providing culturally authentic literature representing the diversity of our culture in very positive ways. Also make a point to check out the books that win awards for high-quality literature that are also culturally authentic and present a positive view of members of the group. These include the Schneider Family Book Award for books that embody the disability experience, the Pura Belpré Award for works that affirm and celebrate the Latino cultural experience, the Coretta Scott King Awards for outstanding books by African American authors and illustrators that reflect the African American experience, the American Indian Youth Literature Award to identify and honor the very best writing and illustrations by and about American Indians, and the Asian/Pacific American Award for Literature for works about Asian/Pacific Americans and their heritage. Criteria for these awards are generally included on the organization's website and can serve as an excellent tool for reviewing and selecting multicultural titles.

◎ Selection Tools

It is not possible for any librarian to read every book, view every film, or listen to every piece of music before making a purchasing decision. Very rarely will you have the opportunity to handle and examine most of the items before you select them for the collection. You will rely on other people to identify upcoming materials and to give you information about the items. Reviews, often written by librarians and children's literature specialists, are one of the best tools available to help you determine which items are most suited for the collection. While there are other review sources available, be sure that you understand the primary purpose of those reviews. Reviews posted to book selling sites like Amazon.com are usually written by readers. Some are even written by the author and friends of the author. While these may be useful in learning what the book is about and its potential popularity, they may not be critical or consider elements that are important in selecting for your collection. Other sources, such as Common Sense Media (https://www.commonsensemedia.org/), clearly define how they rate and review materials but look at the materials from a child development point of view, evaluating factors like age appropriateness, language, sexual content, violence or scariness, and such.

Review Sources

Many review sources are available to help in the selection of materials for the children's collection. These reviews also provide support for the selection decision if a book or other item is challenged. Each review source has its own focus and scope of coverage and some are more suited to public library collections. Select a few that best match the needs of the community and the public library collection. Some, such as *Booklist* and *School Library Journal*, review media in addition to print materials. *AudioFile* reviews only audiobooks and includes a good supply of children's materials.

Most print review sources now also have an online component, included with the subscription, that offers additional content, such as lists of best books and awards, columns on specific areas of librarianship, and features or "roundups" that focus on materials for targeted areas of the collection. Often there is also a feature in the online version of the journal that allows users to generate book lists, a handy tool for preparing orders.

Reviews that are written by and for librarians focus more on the suitability of the item for a library's collection. These reviews are generally short (200 words or less) and

> Professional development opportunity: Several library review journals recruit frontline librarians to write reviews of new materials. Being a reviewer is a great way to learn more about critically evaluating children's books. *From Cover to Cover* by Kathleen T. Horning is an excellent guide for learning to critically evaluate children's literature and for learning how to write reviews.

contain only a brief description of the plot or content of the book. The main part of the review will focus on identifying the intended audience, the usefulness of the book to a library's collection, the quality of the content, the timeliness of the topic, and how the book compares to or would supplement similar items that are available. Most of these journals strive to publish reviews of new materials just prior to their release, using advanced copies sent out specifically so the item can be reviewed, allowing librarians to order materials so that they arrive and can be on the shelf as close to the publication date as possible.

You may also have access to a database like Children's Literature Comprehensive Database (http://www.clcd.com/) that pulls together reviews from multiple sources and also provides themed lists of books with their accompanying reviews. These one-stop shops can be especially helpful when you are searching for reviews to support retaining materials during a censorship challenge or when you are looking for books to fill gaps.

AudioFile Magazine

The only magazine currently devoted to audiobooks, *AudioFile* (http://www.audiofile magazine.com/) is published bimonthly. Approximately 400 audiobooks are reviewed in each issue and the online supplement with a focus on the audio presentation, not the written material. Articles also feature narrator profiles and information targeted to librarians and teachers.

Booklist

Published by the American Library Association, *Booklist* (http://booklistonline.com/) provides about 8,000 reviews annually of recommended books, audiobooks, reference sources, video, and DVD titles. Materials included are for adults, teens, and children. It is published every two weeks and includes *Book Links* (http://www.booklistonline.com/booklinks), specifically focused on children's books and curriculum use, as a supplement four times a year. Reviewers are librarians and subject specialists.

School Library Journal

School Library Journal is published monthly and, in spite of its name, includes news and articles relevant to both school and public libraries. Each issue includes positive and negative reviews of books, audiobooks, films, and other materials for children and teens. Reviewers are volunteer librarians.

Kirkus Reviews

Kirkus is published twice monthly and reviews about 7,000 books annually, with about half of that number being children's books. *Kirkus* is one of a few review sources that will review self-published books, but only a very small percentage (3% as of 2012) are for children's books. Some web-only reviews are published for books received too late for the print journal.

The Horn Book

The Horn Book is published bimonthly and features book reviews of a very select group of new titles, as well as commentary, articles, and other information related to children's and young adult literature. A companion publication, *The Horn Book Guide*, is published twice a year and includes brief reviews of almost every hardcover children's book published by traditional publishers during the previous six months. Reviewers include librarians, teachers, booksellers, and children's literature specialists.

The *Bulletin of the Center for Children's Books*

Published by the Center for Children's Books at the University of Illinois, *BCCB* is devoted entirely to the review of current books for children. Reviews provide a concise summary of the book, pointing out its strengths and weaknesses. Codes are used to quickly indicate whether a book is recommended, an additional purchase, marginal, or not recommended. Articles and editorials look at a few titles in more detail or explore trends in children's literature.

Other Sources

There are, of course, many other sources for reviews. Some, such as *Publisher's Weekly*, are geared more toward bookstores and include a limited number of reviews in each issue. The *New York Times Book Review* is an often cited source, but reviews are essays written for a general reading audience. Fewer than 30 reviews are published each week and only a few are of children's books. The archived reviews are available online for free, as are the weekly lists of bestselling children's books. *Library Media Connection* focuses on the appropriateness and value of reviewed items for a school library collection. A public library may find the reviews especially useful for selecting nonfiction series books that are published for curriculum support. The journal also reviews Internet resources, databases, and film resources that have educational use.

The aforementioned Children's Literature Comprehensive Database (http://www.clcd.com) provides a one-stop shop for reviews from many sources. There are also examination centers, such as the Cooperative Children's Book Center at the University of Wisconsin, Madison, that allow for hands-on examination of new materials. Of course, this is limited to regional selectors who can conveniently stop in to peruse new books. Some publishers or representatives who sell for those companies will also provide librarians with boxes of books "on approval." The books are shipped to the library, and after a period of time for review the books not wanted are shipped back. This provides an opportunity for hands-on evaluation but can become cumbersome, and the library may be billed if books are not returned in a timely manner.

Checklists

Some journals, associations, reference resources, and major libraries create lists of books on specific topics or lists of best books for the year. In addition to helping you determine whether you have missed some important selections, these lists are useful when building a brand-new collection or filling in gaps.

The Cooperative Children's Book Center, for example, publishes an annual list, *CCBC Choices*, of their best books. *Booklist* and *School Library Journal* also publish annual editor's choice lists. These checklists are popular collection development tools because the number of choices has been narrowed down to meet some specific criteria. It is easy to check a specialized list to be sure that important titles have not been missed. Award winners or items that have been identified as the best of the materials released during the previous year can streamline the process for adding high-quality books to the collection. It is not good practice, however, to simply use the checklist as a blanket ordering tool. Professional judgment is still used to determine if the item is appropriate for the community and needed in the library collection.

Some standard lists or catalogs are published that allow librarians to compare their library's collection against a list of titles to determine what percentage of those items your library owns. Theoretically the higher the percentage of holdings in comparison to the standard list, the better your collection but this is a somewhat tenuous assumption because there are no standards for what that percentage should be. Some core titles may not be appropriate or needed for your collection even though they have been well reviewed. Lists become outdated quickly and include titles that are already being weeded from collections because the information is no longer accurate or timely. However, these lists can be very useful for filling in gaps in the collection or beefing up an area when collection priorities have shifted. They are especially helpful for building a broad-based collection for a new library or branch. Look for the newest titles, such as *Building a Core Print Collection for Preschoolers* by Alan R. Bailey (2014) and *The Mother of All Booklists: The 500 Most Recommended Nonfiction Reads for Ages 3 to 103* by William Patrick Martin (2015), but remember that with the children's collection older titles may still have value, especially when selecting picture books and fiction.

A number of standard checklists or catalogs are now available online, instead of or in addition to print format. These may be used to evaluate your collection, benchmarking your collection against what a specific group of librarians and experts consider to be a standard or core set of materials. They are also useful when you need to replace a book that is no longer available with a newer title on the topic. Examples for children's collections include H.W. Wilson's *Children's Core Collection* for preschool through grade 5; *A to Zoo* by Carolyn Lima, which provides subject access to children's picture books; and *Best Books for Children Preschool through Grade 8* by Catherine Barr and John Thomas Gillespie.

Catalogs

Spring and fall used to herald the arrival of dozens of catalogs. Massive amounts of paper from publishers showing forthcoming items were distributed twice a year to coincide with publishing cycles. Some publishers, especially those that cater to children's collections in schools and public libraries, still provide print catalogs, but many have moved to electronic catalogs both to reduce costs and to be greener.

Catalogs are useful for quickly perusing the range of new items. Catalogs are especially handy for locating books in sets that are useful for homework assignments and for finding backlist or older items. Catalogs often include excerpts from reviews, special pricing for sets, links for bonus material like lesson plans or activities that go with the books, and information about the authors and illustrators. Many librarians appreciate being able to make notes on the catalog page, tear out pages, and forward marked-up catalogs to the acquisitions department. Catalogs can also be reviewed without access to a computer in between other duties, and it may be faster to skim through a catalog. On the other hand, it is expensive and often wasteful to produce paper catalogs, especially when librarians often receive multiple copies that pile up.

While many publishers have discontinued mailing paper catalogs, many are providing the same information on their websites, often in a format that mimics the paper catalog. Edelweiss (http://www.abovethetreeline.com/edelweiss) is an online, interactive, cross-publisher catalog service that supplements or replaces traditional hard-copy publisher catalogs. Many major publishers are now using this service to provide catalogs and as a way for librarians to request digital review copies of books to examine or read before making purchasing decisions.

Websites

Publisher websites can provide a lot of information on forthcoming, current, and backlist titles. Some allow you to save a "cart" or create, save, and retrieve ordering lists. Although some publisher websites include a digital replica of a paper catalog, it can be a bit of a challenge to quickly identify only new items on some sites. Websites also include a lot of extras, such as information on the authors and illustrators, excerpts from reviews, information about awards and honors for the item, and even sample pages of books or excerpts from audiobooks. Because websites can be updated frequently, the listing may also show when an item becomes available in alternate formats.

Vendors

Most libraries find that it is easier and more cost-effective to purchase library materials through vendors, sometimes called wholesalers, distributors, or jobbers. These wholesale companies aggregate materials from the multitude of publishers and sell them to libraries. Children's librarians are not usually actually placing orders, so the exact details of how libraries work with vendors may not be that important to you. However, these vendors usually also offer services that you may use. Vendors like Baker & Taylor, Ingram, and Brodart offer online ordering and the ability to create lists or shopping carts. You may be able to see real-time inventory so that you know immediately whether an item is available or will be backordered. This can be important when you are spending year-end funds and can't wait for an item that is not immediately available for shipping.

Vendors also often offer specialized catalogs that point out new titles or lists of books in Spanish that make it easier for you to quickly see what is currently available. They may offer to create customized lists based on parameters you provide, again narrowing your search to strengthen an area of the collection or help you prepare the collection for big events like summer reading programs. The library can also place standing orders with the vendor so that you automatically receive best sellers, titles in specific series or by specific authors, or titles on award lists that the library has not previously ordered.

Companies like Bound to Stay Bound provide books that are prebound to withstand heavy circulation. Unbound pages are obtained from the publisher and a sturdier library binding is used to bind the book. In other cases books are purchased from the publisher and the bindings are reinforced. The dust jacket is usually removed and replaced by a sturdy cover imprinted with the original art. The prebound books should last up to five times longer than standard bindings. Keep in mind that while that can be a great savings for a book that will be useful for many years, it may be unnecessary for books that have a limited useful life. Additionally, the condition of the pages, particularly with picture books that can get dirty and marked up or torn more quickly, may necessitate weeding long before the binding fails. On the other hand, for many books available in paperback only, prebinding may be a good choice.

While the library will have a contract with one or two vendors, many of the catalogs and specialized lists are available to any librarian, and you may find that you prefer the services provided by one vendor over another. A few vendors, such as Follett, focus on K–12 school libraries only and therefore won't be of great interest to public libraries unless the library serves as the school library also.

⑥ Awards

Literary awards are given for books and other media by a wide assortment of organizations and associations. Usually awards cover materials published during a very specific period of time, often the previous year, and they can provide a quick look at the cream of the crop. In addition to looking at national, state, and local award winners and honor titles or the nominees to locate quality materials for the collection that might have been missed, award lists serve as resources for patrons seeking good reading options and are often used by teachers as reading selection lists for students. Most libraries, even those with very limited budgets, will want to seriously consider having the major children's book award winners in the collection, but each librarian must still consider whether the item meets the selection criteria established by the library and the needs of the community.

There are a wide variety of awards for literature and media. Some are essential for public libraries to know about, while others will have local or subject-specific interest. Most that are of importance to American librarians are limited to books published and readily available in the United States, but other countries have their own awards. A few awards consider authors, illustrators, and literature outside the United States. For example, the Hans Christian Andersen Award is the highest international recognition given to an author and an illustrator of children's books. The Batchelder Award is given to the most outstanding children's book originally published outside of the United States in a language other than English that was later translated into English for publication in the United States. Awards may also be given for material in media formats, such as audiobooks and film. A few of the major awards are mentioned here and in appendix B, but you can find others from the library's vendors, local and state library associations, and on the Internet.

The American Library Association (ALA) awards a number of annual honors to literature and media. In addition to those mentioned here, be sure to check out the ALA website (http://www.ala.org) for others. In most cases, honor titles may be named in addition to the winning title.

The Newbery Medal is awarded to the author of the most distinguished contribution to American literature for children. The Caldecott Medal is awarded annually by the ALA to the illustrator of the most distinguished American picture book for children. The Coretta Scott King Book Awards are presented each year to the best books by African American authors and illustrators. The Pura Belpré Award is co-sponsored by ALA and REFORMA, an ALA-affiliate that promotes library services to Latinos and Spanish speakers. The award is presented to the best books by Latino or Latina authors and illustrators for works that reflect the Latino experience. The (Theodor Seuss) Geisel Award is given to the author(s) and illustrator(s) of the most distinguished American book for beginning readers, while the Robert F. Sibert Informational Book Medal is awarded to the author(s) and illustrator(s) of the most distinguished informational, or nonfiction, book published in the United States. Other national awards to watch are the Boston Globe-Horn Book Awards, the National Book Awards, and the Orbis Pictus Award.

More than 45 state and regional children's choice awards are sponsored by state library or reading associations. These programs allow children to select their favorite book or the book they consider to be the best from a list compiled by a committee of librarians or educators. These award programs encourage reading by involving children in the critiquing and voting. Programs like the Texas Bluebonnet Award or Missouri's Mark Twain Readers Award allow children to vote after reading a specified number of books from a list that usually includes current and prior year titles. While you will probably need most of the titles on your state's award list to meet local demand, the lists are also good for identifying books that are not only high-quality but also popular choices.

Awards are also given for audiobooks and film. ALA awards the Odyssey to the producer of the best audiobook produced for children and/or young adults and the Andrew Carnegie Medal for the most outstanding video production for children released during the previous year. *AudioFile* magazine awards Earphone Awards to their best selections, and the Audio Publishers Association honors the best productions in two children's categories.

⊚ Intellectual Freedom and the Collection

Intellectual freedom means that every individual has the right to seek and receive information from all points of view without restriction by government, groups, or individuals. The ability to have open access to information without restriction is a hallmark of our democracy and is supported by the First Amendment to the United States Constitution. Both the democratic principle of self-government and the concept of the public library as the "people's university" require that individuals have access to a wide range of materials. The material may be offensive to some, run counter to another individual's beliefs, or discuss topics that may make the reader feel uncomfortable. U.S. citizens have a constitutional guarantee to read material without interference from others who may object to the content.

The concept of intellectual freedom is important to collection development because the public library serves a broad and diverse society. As the children's librarian you will have a good sense of what the community wants to read or view, and what interests and topics are needed in the collection. You will select materials based on those interests and the selection criteria set forth in the collection development policy. While it is not possible to have a completely balanced collection, the collection will include diverse points of view and reflect the thoughts of a diverse population. Some of the ideas in these materials may be considered by some people as inappropriate for children to read. However, no individual can presume to know what others may or may not find to be offensive or inappropriate. What is offensive to one person may be appropriate for another to read.

Every collection will, and should, have materials that someone in the community may find objectionable. They may wish to keep that material away from children. It is important for you to know how to handle complaints about materials and requests to remove or relocate library materials from the children's collection, but before any librarian faces a challenge to intellectual freedom, the item must have been selected and acquired by the library.

It may be tempting to try to avoid conflict about items in the collection by self-censoring or through internal censorship. It can be easy to think that no one in the community wants to read a book that includes a topic that others might find objectionable or that could be controversial. Do not avoid selecting something out of fear of community pressure. Self-censorship occurs when the selector decides not to purchase an item primarily because the description or a review indicates that the book deals with mature or controversial subject matter or has explicit language. A good librarian is aware of her own prejudices, biases, and preferences and works to ensure that they don't influence the selection or rejection of materials. It is censoring when the library doesn't order materials that express a conservative viewpoint just as much as when an item is not purchased because the author takes a liberal stand on the subject. Selections should be made to serve the diverse needs and interests of the entire community, not to reflect the values and interests of a few people.

Another form of self-censorship may occur when the librarian decides not to select something for the collection because it lacks literary value. An ongoing topic of discussion in the library world revolves around quality versus demand. Do we give patrons what they want or what we think they need or should have? This is an especially tempting concept to consider when we are selecting for children, who often lack the critical thinking skills and experience to differentiate between literature and books that are popular or trendy. While you may not be able financially to purchase the latest fad book or every title in a

CHECK IT OUT!

The Boy and the Book by David Michael Slater (figure 3.3). In this wordless picture book, a young boy is unintentionally rough on a book while visiting the library.

Figure 3.3. *The Boy and the Book. Used with permission by Charlesbridge Publishing, Inc.*

series that lacks much literary value, don't avoid selecting titles that your patrons want to read simply because you and reviewers think that the writing is less than stellar or the topic is insignificant. Some materials are included in the collection simply because they will be in high demand.

The library's collection development policy should include references to the Library Bill of Rights (http://www.ala.org/advocacy/intfreedom/librarybill) and the various interpretations that pertain to collection development. These documents, endorsed by the ALA (1996), affirm the role of libraries as forums for information and ideas and the library's responsibility to provide material that presents all points of view on current and historical issues. Materials in libraries should not be proscribed or removed because of partisan or doctrinal disapproval. Of particular importance for children's librarians is the interpretation "Access for Children and Young Adults to Nonprint Materials" (http://www.ala.org/advocacy/intfreedom/librarybill/interpretations/accesschildren). This interpretation of the Library Bill of Rights reinforces the statement, "A person's right to use a library should not be denied or abridged because of origin, age, background, or views." The principle protects the rights of minors to access library material in all formats. Only the child's parent can restrict access for their child. Library policies should never restrict access based on age limitations.

Collection Maintenance and Weeding

Collections are living entities that are never finished products. They are not static and the items in the collection must be maintained on a regular basis. Depending on the size of the library and the staffing available, the children's librarian may have more or less responsibility for specific maintenance activities. Once a book or other item has been placed on the shelf, it hopefully begins to circulate but every book and piece of media in the collection has a useful life span. As important as it is to be adding new materials to the collection, maintenance keeps the collection healthy, vital, and reliable.

The material may become damaged, be shelved in the wrong place, or become lost. Some materials that haven't circulated well can be displayed and promoted to encourage use. Items that become worn and shabby need to be replaced. When the information becomes outdated, inaccurate, or no longer suited to meet patrons' needs, it is withdrawn. Tastes and fads change and an item may simply no longer be of interest to the community. Items that have outlived their usefulness should be weeded, or withdrawn, from the collection.

Librarians are often resistant to weeding because it seems anathema to them to throw away a book. We cherish the printed word, but it is really the content that is important so we need to weed out items that are not being used.

Weeding can feel like an overwhelming task that will take valuable time. You may be afraid that someone will need the item right after you discard it or that you will inadvertently discard something valuable and irreplaceable. Actually the collection is made healthier by culling out materials that are no longer useful. Like most people, children don't want to handle books that are dirty and worn. We do a disservice to our patrons when we retain material that is outdated and has inaccurate information; not only are we wasting their time but inaccurate information may be dangerous or cause a student to get a lower grade on school work. Articles on weeding are filled with overused gardening metaphors and imagery, but the fact remains that like a well-tended garden, a well-maintained collection is a beautiful thing.

PARETO'S LAW

Pareto's Law (or Pareto's Principle) is also sometimes called the 80/20 Rule. Based on observations, Pareto, a mathematician, determined that in almost any situation 20% of something is responsible for 80% of the results. For library collections, 20% of the materials will result in 80% of circulation. Removing trivial items or items that are no longer useful almost always results in higher borrowing, so don't be afraid to weed.

There are few hard and fast rules about weeding, and in many ways weeding requires more knowledge, thought, and experience than is required for selecting library materials. You will make mistakes and you will agonize over decisions. Ideally, the person who selects the materials for the children's collection should also be the person culling items, but you will almost always be making decisions based on what someone before you selected.

Before you begin weeding, be sure to review your current collection development policy. You will be determining what to keep and what to pull based on the current priorities for the collection and the current needs of your community. You will also make decisions about whether a specific title is replaced with a new copy or can be mended for further use. Few librarians have the time to dedicate several days or weeks to a large-scale weeding project once a year, so you will need to schedule time and develop a plan for weeding. You may decide to work your way through the Dewey classifications, but you probably won't work sequentially from the 000s to the 900s. It makes more sense to weed the science fair books either right after your local science fair is over or long enough before to acquire replacement titles. Ideally, you would weed about 5% of the collection each year although collections without room to grow may weed at least as much as is added. Some areas of the collection need to be weeded more frequently than others. For example, the 398 (folk literature) section probably is not going out of date, whereas some areas of the science collection need attention every year or two. A great deal of weeding may be almost automatic in areas like picture books, where much of what is pulled will be materials that have become soiled or worn.

Although there are no rules on what to weed and when, and your collection is not likely to be monitored for currency by any organization or association (although some state standards do include looking at the currency of the collection as one evaluation tool), there are some guidelines available. *CREW: A Weeding Manual for Modern Libraries* (https://www.tsl.texas.gov/ld/pubs/crew/index.html), updated in 2008 and 2012 by Jeanette Larson, has become a standard for public librarians and can be downloaded free of charge. First developed in the 1970s by staff at the Texas State Library, CREW offers a comprehensive look at weeding library collections. A key component of CREW is the MUSTIE formula, an acronym for misleading, ugly, superseded, trivial, irrelevant, and elsewhere available. These factors cover a range of reasons for pulling an item from the collection. For each item, consider if it is outdated and misleading or in disrepair. If an edition has been replaced by a more current one, remove the older from the collection. You can also safely discard material that was purchased to support a now-gone fad or books on topics that were once popular but are no longer of relevance to the community. The final element in the MUSTIE formula, elsewhere available, encourages the person weeding to be ruthless, especially in culling out material that is rarely used as well as items that are available elsewhere in the community, through online resources, or through interlibrary loan. Public libraries, especially children's collections, are not warehouses or archives for books!

CREW also provides guidance to help you consider copyright age and last use or circulation. These factors help you to determine if information is likely to be outdated, particularly in the nonfiction collection, or is no longer relevant to your community's needs and interests. Some information changes rapidly, and to keep the collection current you may have to weed a book after just a few years. Books on computer technology and some areas of science may need to be replaced frequently to remain current. Also be aware of changes in country names and political structure. How many collections still have books that talk about South Vietnam or list Pluto as one of the planets? Young people may not be attuned to current events and the news and pay less attention to copyright than adults will. Allowing young patrons to use outdated and inaccurate information because an old book was not weeded will harm the library's reputation and credibility!

While the general guidelines for weeding provided by CREW apply to all areas of the collection, it is noted that MUSTIE factors will be the primary consideration for picture books, beginning readers, and juvenile fiction. Books that receive heavy use become worn and dirty more quickly, and while the content remains relevant and circulation may be high, you will want to replace ugly and damaged books. Additionally, because they are so heavily used in public libraries, any picture book that hasn't circulated in the past year probably is no longer of interest to the community.

If an item has not circulated or been used in-house within a reasonable period of time, it is most likely no longer useful in the collection and may be weeded. CREW offers guidelines to help you determine how long is reasonable for a book to be unused before you consider it for withdrawal. Sometimes if the item has some useful life left and is in reasonably good condition but has not circulated, you can take steps to draw attention to give it one last chance. You also need to be sure to consider whether an item that doesn't get checked out is used in-house.

Books that are on the highest or lowest shelves typically get less use, so displaying these "shelf sitters" may draw attention to them. Children, like adults, do judge a book by its cover. A book may not have circulated because it is starting to look tacky and grimy. A book that has a dirty Mylar cover over the dust jacket can gain fresh life with a new cover. Similarly, a children's book that has the jacket art embedded in the hard buckram cover can be cleaned to remove grease, grime, and sticky residue, allowing for many more circulations. Keep in mind, however, that if a lot of time will be spent on repairing and mending to save the book, it will probably be cheaper to replace it. While a few torn pages can be taped and minor pencil or crayon markings removed, it's probably not cost-effective to spend more than about 15 minutes on repairs and cleaning.

Depending on the library's size and staffing, you may do some of these repairs or they may be handled in technical services. If staff or volunteers are doing the repairs, suppliers like Brodart (http://www.shopbrodart.com/book-care-repair/) offer free instructional guides and training videos.

Books that have clean pages but a broken spine can also be rebound by binding companies. The cost is usually about 25%–30% of the cost for a new book. Only rebind children's books that have clean pages and that have an anticipated life span that makes it worth the expense. You lose part of the illustrations if the book has double-page spreads, as is common with picture books, since the binder will trim part of the margins and gutters during the rebinding process. Few books in the children's collection will warrant archival-level preservation.

Similarly, copyright won't usually be a big concern for children's fiction and picture books, with titles like *Curious George* by H. A. Rey and Maud Hart Lovelace's *Betsy-Tacy* continuing to be read decades after publication. However, old-fashioned-looking cover art may mean the book is overlooked unless it is required reading for school. Books in series like the Boxcar Children Mysteries are still popular and being read more than seventy years after the first title was released in 1942, but updated art keeps the series fresh and circulating. Compare the 1977 cover (figure 3.4) with an updated cover from the 1980s (figure 3.5). Covers do make a difference with children!

Figure 3.4. 1977 cover art for *The Boxcar Children. Cover illustration by Charles Tang, published by Albert Whitman & Co.*

Figure 3.5. Later edition cover art for *The Boxcar Children. Cover illustration by Tim Jessell, published by Albert Whitman & Co.*

Collection Promotion

You may be asking yourself why libraries need to promote our services. After all, the materials, programs, and services are available for free! However, we can't count on our patrons knowing exactly what they want, and like bookstores, we often want to entice readers to borrow something they didn't know existed. While the children's librarian may join other staff in promoting the library in general to the community, you play a key role in promoting the collection inside the building. Marketing and promotion, especially of services and programs, is covered more thoroughly in chapter 8.

Promotion of the collection can include things like bulletin boards and posters that advertise titles and authors. It also includes the creation of booklist, displays, and special collections that make it easy for patrons to find something of interest when they are browsing. Parents and children are not necessarily aware of what is available and, except for books that are highly publicized in the media like the Harry Potter books, won't usually be aware of what is new. You will use a variety of methods to promote your collection and encourage use of materials.

Displays

Displays offer a simple and inexpensive way to highlight part of the collection. They can be used to pull out materials that you know from experience will be in high demand, making it easier for patrons to remember that they want to pick up a few books for the holiday or an audiobook for vacation travel listening. They can also shine a spotlight on less well-known materials and topics or on materials that would be scattered around the collection, such as a display of books by local authors. Many people want to pick from a smaller grouping of materials or want to read something they feel has been recommended or read by others.

Simple displays, such as an assortment of books, can be arranged on a table. More elaborate displays may take up floor space, such as the *Wizard of Oz* display in figure 3.6,

Figure 3.6. *Wizard of Oz Display. Display by Kristina Lareau and Jen Gardner of the Fairfield Public Library, Fairfield, Connecticut*

or include ornate table covers and eye-catching objects. Simple or elaborate, keep displays filled with appropriate material and inviting so that patrons know they are welcome to take the items to the checkout desk. The unifying theme should be obvious to the patron either because of decorative items, such as holiday greenery and ornaments for a display of Christmas and Hanukah books, or through signage. Change displays regularly; nothing is sadder than seeing books about bunnies and eggs three weeks after Easter. Even displays that don't have an expiration date should be changed and refreshed regularly so that they remain special.

Displays work best when they are in places where patrons will easily spot them, but they can also work well in less obvious locations. Displays can be set up on window ledges, countertops, small tables, or even on boxes used as risers on the floor. Drape a cloth over an old typewriter stand, a milk crate, or a cardboard box for small displays. Look for inspiration from bookstores and other retail outlets and set up a point-of-purchase display right by the checkout counter so that it's easy for parents to pick up a few paperback books while they are waiting in line.

Bulletin Boards

Children's departments often have either tackable wall coverings that allow posters and other materials to be mounted on the wall or bulletin boards to share information about books and programs. These vertical displays can be attractive attention-getters that showcase books and other resources in the collection or that promote services and programs that are coming up.

Bulletin boards that are eye-catching and spark interest in what is being advertised take time to plan and prepare. Traditional bulletin boards are usually rectangular but may also come in shapes. Tackable wall coverings, of course, cover all or part of a wall but allow

Figure 3.7. Mmmmm . . . More Books, Please! *Misti Tidman, Licking County Library, Newark, Ohio*

for the creation of smaller mini-boards. Displays may be thematic, such as a display that entices children to read mysteries, seasonal or tied to a holiday, or motivational, encouraging reading in general, such as the bulletin board "Mmmmm . . . More Books, Please!" that shows a soup bowl of books (figure 3.7).

Books like *Bulletin Board Power: Bridges to Lifelong Learning* by Katherine Hawthorne offer ideas and patterns. Social media sites like Pinterest also have photographs of interesting bulletin boards. Prepared pieces, such as letters to spell out titles or shapes to create decorations, can be purchased at local teacher supply stores, dollar stores, or from companies like Demco (http://www.demco.com) or Lakeshore Learning (http://www. lakeshorelearning.com/). Some libraries own die-cut machines like the ones from Ellison (www.ellison.com) that allow staff and volunteers to cut their own materials from various types of paper and other materials as needed.

Although bulletin boards don't have to be elaborate, they should be current and bright. Nothing is less attractive than faded paper and outdated information! Take time to plan out the year, with some flexibility for last-minute ideas or special events that need promoting. A summer reading bulletin board may be left up for 8 to 10 weeks, but even then minor changes will keep the board fresh and interesting.

Special Collections and Promotional Lists

"Save the time of the reader" is the fourth of Ranganathan's Five Laws of Library Science. Promoting the library's materials by providing specially developed collections makes it easier for patrons to find what they want. These specialty collections may be short term, such as pulling out the science fair project books when students are doing these projects or gathering an assortment of Halloween titles for use in October. They may also be long-term, possibly even designated as a special collection in the library's catalog. For example, the library might keep all of the books that won the Newbery Medal together so that they are easy to locate and browse.

Parents and teachers, who may need to pick up a variety of materials from lists, are especially appreciative of these collections that highlight specific books and other materials. Pulling books to display can also push usage of lesser used items. For example, if the fictional beginning readers, those limited vocabulary books for children who are learning to read, are heavily used during the summer, pull similar books that have been classified as nonfiction and temporarily shelve them with the other beginning readers.

Often special collections and displays are accompanied by booklists that make it easy for patrons to locate more of the same type of books. These are usually created by the librarian and include the call numbers for the items in the particular library. If bibliographies from other sources are used, the call numbers may be written in next to the listing.

There are many other ways that librarians promote the collection. These may include booktalking, reader's advisory, book discussion clubs, and author programs. These, and others that are more interactive with specific patrons, will be covered in subsequent chapters.

⊚ Key Points

The children's collection offers a wide and varied array of materials. It is worth putting effort into learning about specific titles, authors, and genres because a good percentage of the collection remains relevant to new generations of readers. Children also require more guidance in locating materials to help them learn to read proficiently, for pleasure reading, and for school assignments.

- Children's librarians must develop a varied and diverse collection that includes books and materials in other formats.
- It is imperative that the children's collection be kept up-to-date and in good condition through regular weeding of materials.
- There are many resources in print and digital formats, including reviews and standard selection tools, to help the children's librarian select materials and use the collection.
- The children's librarian must be prepared to handle challenges to items in the collection, which should include materials that are controversial or offer points of view that differ from the beliefs of some members of the community.
- Promoting materials in the collection is important. Children do not always know what they want or need, and circulation will increase through displays and book lists.

Although many libraries are moving to centralized selection for materials, the children's librarian must know the collection and the community's needs in order to provide excellent service to children and families. There are many ways we can save our customers' time and help children become lifelong readers. The next chapter will focus on the major types of services children's librarians provide, most often using the collection as tools for these services.

References

ALA (American Library Association). 1996. Library Bill of Rights. Adopted June 19, 1939, by the ALA Council; amended October 14, 1944; June 18, 1948; February 2, 1961; June 27, 1967; January 23, 1980; inclusion of "age" reaffirmed January 23, 1996. http://www.ala.org/advocacy/intfreedom/librarybill.

ALSC (Association for Library Services to Children). 2014a. "Children's Notable Lists." Accessed June 29, 2014. http://www.ala.org/alsc/awardsgrants/notalists.

ALSC (Association for Library Services to Children). 2014b. "Core Collection of Graphic Novels—2012 Update." Accessed June 29, 2014. http://www.ala.org/alsc/compubs/booklists/grphcnvls.

Hayes, Donald, and Margaret Ahrens. 1988. "Vocabulary Simplification for Children: A Special Case of 'Motherese'?" *Journal of Child Language* 15 (June): 395–410.

Hoffert, Barbara. 2004. "Facing Down the Crunch." *Library Journal* 129, no. 3 (February 15): 38–40.

Jabr, Ferris. 2013. "Do E-readers Inhibit Reading Comprehension?" *Salon* (April 14). http://www.salon.com/2013/04/14/do_e_readers_inhibit_reading_comprehension_partner/.

Larson, Jeanette. 2008. *CREW: A Weeding Manual for Modern Libraries*. Austin, TX: Texas State Library and Archives Commission. http://www.tsl.state.tx.us/ld/pubs/crew/crewmethod08.pdf.

Larson, Jeanette, and Herman L. Totten. 2008. *The Public Library Policy Writer: A Guidebook with Model Policies on CD-ROM*. New York: Neal-Schuman Publishers.

Pierce County Library System. 2014. "100 Books Every Child Should Hear Before Kindergarten." Accessed June 29, 2014. http://www.piercecountylibrary.org/booklists.aspx?id=0&list_id=173&&cat_id=30.

Saldaña, René Jr. 2014. "Forgive Me My Bluntness: I'm a Writer of Color and I'm Right Here in Front of You: I'm the One Sitting Alone at the Table." Accessed September 9, 2014. http://latinosinkidlit.com/2014/09/08/forgive-me-my-bluntness-im-a-writer-of-color-and-im-right-here-in-front-of-you-im-the-one-sitting-alone-at-the-table/.

Scholastic Publishing. 2013. *Kids & Family Reading Report.* 4th ed. Accessed June 24, 2014. http://mediaroom.scholastic.com/files/kfrr2013-noappendix.pdf.

ⓖ Resources Mentioned in This Chapter

Arte Público Press. https://artepublicopress.com/.

AudioFile. http://www.audiofilemagazine.com/.

Bailey, Alan R. 2014. *Building a Core Print Collection for Preschoolers.* Chicago: ALA Editions.

Bannerman, Helen. 1972. *Little Black Sambo.* New York: Platt & Munk.

Barr, Catherine, and John T. Gillespie. 2010. *Best Books for Children Preschool through Grade 8.* Westport, CT: Libraries Unlimited.

Book Links. http://www.booklistonline.com/booklinks.

Booklist. http://booklistonline.com/.

Boyne, John. 2006. *The Boy in the Striped Pajamas: A Fable.* Oxford: David Fickling Books.

Brown, Margaret Wise. 1947. *Goodnight Moon.* New York: Harper & Row.

Bulletin of the Center for Children's Books. http://bccb.lis.illinois.edu/.

Children's Literature Comprehensive Database. http://www.clcd.com.

Comenius, Johann Amos, and John Edward Sadler. 1968. *Orbis Pictus.* London: Oxford University Press.

Crowe, Ellie, and Richard Waldrep. 2007. *Surfer of the Century: The Life of Duke Kahanamoku.* New York: Lee & Low Books.

Cushman, Karen. 2006. *The Loud Silence of Francine Green.* New York: Clarion Books.

Cybil Awards. http://www.cybils.com.

Dahl, Roald, and Joseph Schindelman. 1973. *Charlie and the Chocolate Factory.* New York: Alfred A. Knopf.

dePaola, Tomie. 1978. *Pancakes for Breakfast.* New York: Harcourt Brace Jovanovich.

Duffy, Chris, ed. 2011. *Nursery Rhyme Comics: 50 Timeless Rhymes from 50 Caldecott Cartoonists.* New York: First Second.

Eisner Award. http://www.comic-con.org/awards/eisners-current-info.

Elson, William H., and William S. Gray. 1936. *Dick and Jane.* New York: William Morrow.

Gág, Wanda. 1928. *Millions of Cats.* New York: Coward-McCann.

Galdone, Paul. 2011. *The Three Little Pigs: A Folk Tale Classic.* Boston: Houghton Mifflin Harcourt.

Hawthorne, Karen, and Jane E. Gibson. 2002. *Bulletin Board Power Bridges to Lifelong Learning.* Greenwood Village, CO: Libraries Unlimited.

The Horn Book. http://www.hbook.com/horn-book-magazine-2/.

The Horn Book Guide. http://www.hornbookguide.com.

Horning, Kathleen T. 2010. *From Cover to Cover: Evaluating and Reviewing Children's Books.* New York: Collins.

Horning, Kathleen T. 2014. "Still an All-White World?" *School Library Journal* 60, no. 5 (May): 18.

H.W. Wilson Company. 2010. *Children's Core Collection.* New York: H.W. Wilson Co.

Ketteman, Helen, and Will Terry. 2009. *The Three Little Gators.* Chicago, IL: Albert Whitman.

Kirkus Reviews. https://www.kirkusreviews.com.

Krauss, Ruth, and Crockett Johnson. 2009. *The Carrot Seed.* New York: HarperCollins.

Larson, Hope, Jenn Manley Lee, Andrew Arnold, Hope Larson, and Madeleine L'Engle. 2012. *A Wrinkle in Time: The Graphic Novel.* New York: Farrar, Straus and Giroux.

Lectorum. http://www.lectorum.com.

Lester, Julius, Helen Bannerman, Jerry Pinkney, and Jane Byers Bierhorst. 1996. *Sam and The Tigers: A New Telling of Little Black Sambo*. New York: Dial Books for Young Readers.

Levinson, Cynthia. 2012. *We've Got a Job: The 1963 Birmingham Children's March*. Atlanta, GA: Peachtree Publishers.

Lewis, C. S., and Pauline Baynes. 1994. *The Lion, the Witch, and the Wardrobe*. New York: HarperCollins.

Library Media Connection. http://www.librarymediaconnection.com/.

Lima, Carolyn W., and John A. Lima. 2006. *A to Zoo: Subject Access to Children's Picture Books*. Westport, CT: Libraries Unlimited.

Lobel, Arnold, and Arnold Lobel. 1972. *Frog and Toad Together*. New York: Harper & Row.

Loftin, Nikki. 2012. *The Sinister Sweetness of Splendid Academy*. New York: Razorbill.

Lofting, Hugh, and Michael Hague. 1997. *The Story of Doctor Dolittle*. New York: William Morrow.

Lovelace, Maud Hart, and Lois Lenski. 1940. *Betsy-Tacy*. New York: Crowell.

Lutes, Jason, and Nick Bertozzi. 2007. *Houdini: The Handcuff King*. New York: Hyperion.

Martin, William P. 2015. *The Mother of All Booklists: The 500 Most Recommended Nonfiction Reads for Ages 3 to 103*. Lanham, MD: Rowman & Littlefield.

McDonnell, Patrick. 2011. *Nursery Rhyme Comics: 50 Timeless Rhymes from 50 Celebrated Cartoonists*. New York: First Second.

Minarik, Else Holmelund, and Maurice Sendak. 1957. *Little Bear*. New York: Harper & Row.

Minarik, Else Holmelund, and Maurice Sendak. 1961. *Little Bear's Visit*. New York: Harper & Row.

Mochizuki, Ken, and Dom Lee. 1993. *Baseball Saved Us*. New York: Lee & Low Books.

Myers, Walter Dean, and Ann Grifalconi. 2001. *Patrol: An American Soldier in Vietnam*. New York: HarperCollins.

Nelson, Scott Reynolds, and Marc Aronson. 2008. *Ain't Nothing but a Man: My Quest to Find the Real John Henry*. Washington, DC: National Geographic.

New York Times Book Review. http://www.nytimes.com/pages/books/review/.

Norton, Donna E. 2005. *Multicultural Children's Literature: Through the Eyes of Many Children*. Upper Saddle River, NJ: Pearson/Merrill Prentice Hall.

Obama, Barack, and Loren Long. 2010. *Of Thee I Sing: A Letter to My Daughters*. New York: Alfred A. Knopf.

Publisher's Weekly. http://www.publishersweekly.com/.

Reese, Debbie. *American Indians in Children's Literature* (blog). http://americanindiansinchildrens literature.blogspot.com/.

Rey, H. A. 1941. *Curious George*. Boston: Houghton Mifflin.

Roth, Susan L., Cindy Trumbore, and Christy Hale. 2011. *The Mangrove Tree: Planting Trees to Feed Families*. New York: Lee & Low Books.

Salinas, Bobbi. 1998. *Los tres cerdos/The Three Pigs: Nacho, Tito y Miguel*. Houston, TX: Piñata Pub.

School Library Journal. http://www.slj.com.

Scieszka, Jon. 1989. *The True Story of the Three Little Pigs*. New York: Puffin.

Shen's Books. http://www.shens.com.

Slater, David Michael. 2015. *The Boy and the Book*. Watertown, MA: Charlesbridge.

Slobodkina, Esphyr. 1947. *Caps for Sale: A Tale of a Peddler, Some Monkeys and Their Monkey Business*. New York: W.R. Scott.

Star Bright Books. http://www.starbrightbooks.com.

Dr. Seuss. 1957. *The Cat in the Hat*. New York: Random House.

Tunnell, Michael O., James Jacobs, Terrell A. Young, and Gregory Bryan. 2012. *Children's Literature, Briefly*. Boston: Pearson.

Ward, D. J., and Paul Meisel. 2012. *What Happens to Our Trash?* New York: Collins.

Warner, Gertrude Chandler, and L. Kate Deal. 2012. *The Boxcar Children*. Chicago: Albert Whitman.

White, E. B. 1952. *Charlotte's Web*. New York: Harper & Brothers.

Wiesner, David. 2001. *The Three Pigs*. New York: Clarion Books.

⊚ Additional Readings and Resources

ALA (American Library Association). 1996. *Intellectual Freedom Manual*. Chicago: American Library Association.

ALA (American Library Association). 2014. "Banned Books Week: Celebrating the Freedom to Read." Accessed June 29, 2014. http://www.ala.org/bbooks/bannedbooksweek.

ALSC (Association for Library Services to Children). 2014. *The Newbery and Caldecott Awards: A Guide to the Medal and Honor Books*. Chicago: American Library Association.

Disher, Wayne. 2007. *Crash Course in Collection Development*. Westport, CT: Libraries Unlimited.

Odean, Kathleen. 2004. "Building a Board Book Collection." *Booklist* 101, no. 2: 252–253.

Pinkley, Janet, and Kaela Casey. 2013. "Graphic Novels: A Brief History and Overview for Library Managers." *Library Leadership & Management* 27, no. 3 (May): 1–10.

Stan, Susan. 2014. *Global Voices: Picture Books from around the World*. Chicago: American Library Association.

Library Services for Children

PATRONS COME TO THE LIBRARY for a wide variety of reasons. Even in an increasingly virtual world, many of the services provided for children still take place in the physical library building. Additionally, children's librarians take services out to the community either through virtual and electronic services or through outreach and partnerships programs. These services support the library's mission to inspire and create learners and to facilitate access to information in all formats.

Reference Services

Reference services include the various methods librarians use to assist others in finding information and resources that are needed in response to a specific request. The definition includes both the materials used to find information and the process followed to ensure that the appropriate and accurate answers are found. While reference services are declining in public libraries due to changing technology that makes it easier for patrons to locate answers and resources on their own, "Children evidentially ask for more help at the library reference desk than grownups do" (Walter, 2001: 29). Although Public Library Survey Data does not currently divide reference counts by population serviced, data, when collected, has shown that the rate for children or people asking on behalf of children is higher than the overall average (Walter, 2001). Part of reference services with children involves helping them identify authoritative resources and evaluate the accuracy and reliability of the information.

Much of children's reference questions will originate with school assignments, but many also come from a child's curiosity and desire to learn. Often the help needed is not complex or elaborate, requiring sophisticated search tools and resources. Rather help is needed with simple, straightforward questions that may be related to a homework assignment, a personal interest, or parental needs. Reference work is usually less formal than homework help, discussed later in this chapter, and is provided on demand, rather than at scheduled times. Reference questions are often divided into four categories:

1. Ready Reference—commonly asked questions that can be answered with a small set of standard resources, such as the encyclopedia, an almanac, a dictionary, or an atlas.
2. Research—a more complex transaction that requires the use of multiple resources and back-and-forth communication with the patron about the subject and what is needed to satisfy that need.
3. Reader's Advisory—a type of transaction that focuses on helping children find "a good book" or a book like another that the child has read.
4. Directional—simple answers that help the patron locate a specific area of the library or the collection or that provides information on program schedules, activities, or policies. The Reference and Users Services Association (RUSA), a division of the American Library Association, does not consider directional requests to be reference questions; however, children's librarians spend a lot of time helping children with this type of information and it often leads to more traditional reference requests.

Technology and digital delivery of materials and information has created significant changes in reference services. Although the children's department will have a small collection of basic reference books for ready reference questions—for example, almanacs, dictionaries, and a good encyclopedia—librarians today rely more on licensed databases that provide *The World Book* encyclopedia and other standard tools in electronic formats that are more readily available and continuously revised. In addition to general databases like those provided by EBSCO, there are many databases that provide material aimed directly at the specific needs of students and younger children. Companies also develop kid-friendly interfaces, such as Searchasaurus (http://scdiscus.org/searchasaurus), an EBSCO database that provides full text for elementary-level magazines and several age-appropriate encyclopedias that make it easier for students to search. The database also often spotlights topics that are of current interest for student research. Most public libraries also provide curated access to the Internet through the library's website or by linking to a source like Internet Public Library for Kids, shown in figure 4.1. While children can still search the Internet through various search engines, a preselected set of resources, such as online dictionaries and specialized sites for science information that have been vetted by the librarian, helps students select appropriate tools through a limited list of kid-safe websites.

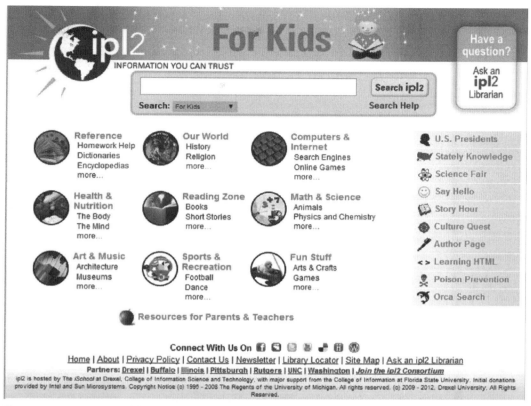

Figure 4.1. Internet Public Library for Kids. *http://www.ipl.org/div/kidspace/*

While the tools may change, librarians are still communicating with patrons and those speaking on behalf of a young patron, using search skills to locate possible sources for the information, determining whether the source has the needed information, and sharing the information with the patron. With children, more so than with adult patrons, the librarian may also be helping them learn how to use the resources and how to evaluate the information for appropriateness and validity.

The Reference Interview

One of the most important skills children's librarians can have with regard to reference work is the ability to figure out what information is needed, at what cognitive level, and how wide and deep the information needs to be for the child asking the question. All of the resources and technology are meaningless unless you know what it is that the patron needs and the level of information needed. When a child wants to know the population of Texas, is she answering a homework question, planning a trip, or writing a report on the Lone Star State? While it is tempting to simply answer the question as it was asked, children often don't fully understand what they are looking for or what information they need to answer the question. They may not even know what question they should be asking. They probably don't have the informational context to know whether the information they find is valid, outdated, or bogus. They may misunderstand unfamiliar words or the assignment and not have asked the teacher for clarification. Knowing if the information is needed for a school assignment or for personal interest helps the librarian assist the patron.

Children may be more reluctant than adults to approach library staff for help. They may not know that they can ask questions or seek assistance or be reluctant to talk to a stranger. Adults can seem aloof or too busy to be interrupted, so it is important for the librarian to be aware of patrons in the children's area and greet them, offering to help and checking back frequently. Whether the child comes to the desk seeking help or responds to an offer to help her find what she is looking for, listen carefully to the statement of need. Children may be shy or struggle to articulate their needs.

The reference interview, which is actually less formal than it sounds, involves talking with the patron about his information needs, asking clarifying questions, discovering how the information will be used, and confirming that the information and answers provided fully satisfy the patron's need. Don't jump to conclusions about the purpose of the information or how it will be used, but also be aware that some questions may be embarrassing for children to ask, either because of the subject or because they think they should already know how to find the answers. A child who asks about child abuse may be writing a report, looking for a novel that includes an abused child, or wanting help for his or her own situation.

Part of the interview may include some discussion of the search strategy you will use, such as talking about subject terms, variations on terminology, and possible resources. Helping the child figure out what words will likely produce good results is important as well. Knowing that using some terms will produce thousands of results means that the search must be more carefully formulated to narrow the topic or further define the intention of the word. For example, a search for Civil War in most databases will bring a lot more than just the U.S. Civil War. Having to cull through hundreds or thousands of search results is frustrating and time-consuming. The librarian can help by using the subject listings or thesaurus in the database to find that a Boolean search for "civil war" AND "United States" is needed. This discussion and negotiation of search terms not only ensures that you understand the child's needs but also helps the child learn research methods. You will also use open and closed questions to help the child focus on his needs and to obtain information needed to help you locate the best resources. Breaking up the questioning as you move through the steps for providing help may also make the transaction less confusing for young patrons.

Children may be reluctant to open up and volunteer their needs. They may also be more easily discouraged or dismissed if the initial response doesn't match their needs. As already noted, catalog and database search terms may be confusing. Pointing a child to the online catalog or the shelves in response to a question about whether the library has any science books usually means that the librarian doesn't discover that the patron is looking for a book on the planets for a school project. Without the librarian's assistance, the child may select a book that is outdated and still shows Pluto as a planet. When the planet mobile she makes includes Pluto, the student will get a poor grade and not know why.

Children may also self-select materials that are above their reading abilities and educational level. Assigned to write a report on the Civil War battle between the *Monitor* and the *Merrimac*, a child who uses the online catalog may be led to a book from a university press that is very academic rather than a book written specifically for young people. Additionally, the online catalog may lead the child to historical fiction books on the topic.

Keep in mind that there may be gender and cultural differences to consider, as well as the needs of children with learning disabilities. Young boys are sometimes less able to focus on passive activities and do better when they are actively involved in the search for information. In some cultures, it is not respectful to disagree with a person who is helping you even when that person is wrong. Non-English speakers may not understand some vocabulary or feel overwhelmed by a lot of questions that seem to imply they don't know what they are looking for. Treat all patrons with respect, no matter how silly the question may seem or how many times you have answered the same question, and treat all questions as confidential. Ask neutral, nonjudgmental questions to clarify the situation and to learn more about how the information will be used.

> Librarian: Hi! May I help you?
> Student: I need to find a book about a scientist.
> Librarian: Great! Are you working on a school assignment or are you looking for something to read for fun?
> Student: My teacher wants me to write a report on a scientist.
> Librarian: Okay. Let's find someone you are interested in learning about. Did your teacher provide any instructions about the assignment?

The interaction in the example allows the librarian to learn that the child needs material for a school project and, once she knows it is for an assignment, whether the child is expected to utilize a variety of resources. The child may even have a copy of the assignment in hand that provides clarification. Once the librarian understands the need, she can ask questions to find out whether the child would prefer to read about Marie Curie, Albert Einstein, or George Washington Carver. Then a visit to the shelves can locate age-appropriate books and a session at the computer databases can locate magazine articles, primary documents, and other resources. End the reference interaction by asking if the patron has enough information and by inviting him or her to return for additional assistance if needed.

Often the most difficult reference interviews will be those that are with surrogates, people asking on behalf of the child who will actually be using the material. The person asking may not know the answers to your questions. All she may know is that she is supposed to find a book or an article or whatever on a specific subject. Do the best you can and be sure that the patron knows she can call or come back if necessary.

Reference Resources

Conducting the best reference interview in the world doesn't finish the job unless you also know how to find the information needed and have access to reliable resources. Part of collection development includes developing and maintaining the children's reference materials. While many standard resources are now available electronically, children's collections still require a basic or core set of print materials that is readily available. Reference materials are often more expensive than materials in the general collection and may need to be updated frequently to remain current. Some items are actually purchased as a subscription so that updates arrive automatically. Keep in mind that children will not immediately understand that reference books are usually for in-house use only or that electronic resources may be available remotely. They also may easily overlook dates that show how current the information is.

While there is no mandatory list of resources for a children's reference collection, and in fact the children's librarian may be using materials from the adult or general reference collection, there are some types of resources that should be readily at hand. Some books in the reference collection will either be duplicated in the circulating collections or be books that are not limited to reference use but that the librarian wants to keep handy.

It is not possible to provide a list of all the basic reference tools that will be useful, but basic reference resources include encyclopedias, almanacs, dictionaries, and atlases. Some of these will be written and published specifically for use by children. Although many basic resources will be available online or through database subscriptions, you will want print copies of at least some of these basic resources. Children's reference collections also usually include books that the librarian will use when helping children and parents locate materials. One example is *A to Zoo: Subject Access to Children's Picture Books* by Carolyn Lima, which allows the librarian to locate pictures books with specific themes or topics. Even if the electronic databases include general encyclopedias, it is recommended that the collection include at least one print general encyclopedia like *The World Book*. This allows easy access if the computers are down and the volumes can be separated for use by multiple children at the same time. Electronic resources may be updated frequently, but some print resources will need to be replaced regularly as well to remain current. Often older copies of almanacs, dictionaries, and other reference materials are moved to the circulating collection when the reference copy is updated.

⊚ Homework Help

According to a 2013 PEW Research Center report, *Library Services in the Digital Age*, people want public libraries to provide homework help in some form. Almost half of library users who visit the library's website are looking for help with homework, and many parents look to the public library for tutoring and other educational support for their children (Zickuhr, Rainee, and Purcell, 2013). While librarians already consider the usefulness of books and other materials in the collection for homework assignments as part of the selection process and may work closely with local schools to ensure material is available for school assignments, formal homework help is an increasingly important service. Many of the children who use the library's homework help program would be coming to the library anyway, and the library provides space and staff, often volunteers or university students, who guide students in successfully completing homework.

Homework help can be similar to reference work except that it is a structured service, often provided in a designated homework center or area with a small collection of tools needed by students, such as dictionaries and thesauri. The main purpose of the homework center is to help students use after-school time in a constructive manner that supports their educational achievement. Wendy Gish (2012), in her article in *Public Libraries*, found that homework help programs are especially beneficial to English language learners and new immigrant families where help at home may be limited by the parents' lack of English language skills.

Specific planning is required to ensure that help is available at appropriate times, and staffing may be adjusted seasonally during testing periods or when major assignments like science fair projects are due. Librarians may also work with the school district to obtain copies of homework assignments and copies of textbooks for students to use in the library. Teachers can support homework help by providing information about assignments to the public librarian. These alerts ensure that the homework help staff and volunteers understand the assignments and have materials available. Paper copies of homework alert forms can be distributed throughout the school year or made available online, such as the one provided by the Keene (New Hampshire) Public Library (http://keenepubliclibrary. org/library/school-assignment-alert#node-174). While they are never used as frequently as public librarians would like, alerts do provide a fast and easy method for teachers to share homework information and may be used more often where formal homework help centers exist.

In addition to live, on-site homework help, public libraries may provide online chatting with students to answer questions about assignments and direct students to appropriate resources. Web pages may be set up to have links to frequently used reference and homework resources and to test preparation sites like Learning Express Library (http://www.learningexpresshub.com/). The library may also pay for help through live online programs like Tutor.com, which provides one-on-one tutoring and guidance on specific subjects and can provide help for students in languages other than English.

Homeschool Support

Homeschooling is a growing trend in the United States, with more than 2 million children homeschooled each year, according to the National Home Education Research Institute (2013). Parents choose homeschooling for a wide range of reasons, but many homeschooling families are avid library users. Librarians may need to reach out to homeschooling families, some of whom are reluctant to publicize their whereabouts, and may need to tailor library policies for them. For example, some libraries have a curfew that restricts school-age children from being in the library during school hours. While the intent of that policy is to minimize truancy and keep students in classes, that shouldn't apply to homeschooled children, who may be in the library during the school day to study or because they are on a break from schooling.

Some of the library's support for homeschoolers may mimic the services provided by a homework center or homework help program. Additional support may be provided through tailored programs that extend the learning capabilities for homeschool families. For example, the public library might serve as the sponsor for a homeschool science fair or provide the voting opportunities for children's choice book award programs like the Texas Bluebonnet Award. Library staff might also conduct lessons on how to use library resources or provide reserved space for group instruction.

Although it is not possible for the public library to provide all of the textbooks homeschooling families might want, and indeed some of the books that are sought are outdated or focused on the beliefs of a specific homeschool organization, homeschool teachers will often ask that the librarian recommend books, pull materials to be used during lessons, provide instruction on how to use specific resources and databases, or ask to use the children's area and computers for study time and research. Homeschool families may also use interlibrary loan to borrow materials. At whatever level of support the library provides, homeschool families tend to be avid library users.

Reader's Advisory

The goal of reader's advisory is to help the patrons find books of interest to them. One of the findings in the Scholastic *Kids & Family Reading Report* indicates that children perceive a major barrier to their doing more leisure reading to be their lack of ability to find books they will like (2013: 44). Children get most of their ideas for books to read from adults, particularly librarians, teachers, and parents, rather than other sources like advertising or reviews. Parents rarely know the range of new books that other readers are enjoying, so young people often ask librarians for suggestions, especially for more books like the one they just read. This personal interaction is critical for children looking for reading ideas, and one thing the public overwhelmingly believes about librarians is that we know books!

Boys do not read as much as girls, as a general rule, and therefore reader's advisory can really help to encourage their reading. According to Michael Sullivan, the reader's advisory service provided must be broader and more flexible to adjust for the overwhelmingly female bias of the library profession (2009: 2). Librarians who provide reader's advisory services—formal or informal guidance about what to read—make a huge difference in the amount of reading that kids do.

Reader's advisory provides a great way to promote the collection, encourage library use, and support the reading habit. Reader's advisory may be provided directly to children or through an intermediary, such as a parent, who is looking for books to bring to a child. There are also indirect methods like booklists and displays that bring books to the attention of readers. Another form of reader's advisory is booktalking, which is reader's advisory provided to a group and will be discussed in a later section.

Direct Reader's Advisory

A child may approach the librarian and ask for help finding something to read. While reader's advisory is primarily used for leisure reading, a child may have been assigned to find a book to read for a class. The first step the librarian will take is to get some idea about the child's likes and dislikes. Does the child want a fiction book or a nonfiction title? What was the last book the child read? Does the child prefer, or need, a specific genre? Are there authors whose books the child has enjoyed reading? Are there other specifications, such as length of the book, if this is for an assignment?

You are not recommending the books, per se, as much as you are suggesting them based on the patron's interests. Books you are suggesting may or may not be to your own reading tastes but are your suggestions for books that match the reader's interest. As you browse the shelves with the patron, be sure to mention why you are suggesting the book and allow for feedback from the child to further refine your suggestions.

When a parent or caregiver seeks reader's advisory help on behalf of a child, the same questions may be asked, although the responses are being filtered through an intermediary who may or may not have the answers. Parents and other adults may also have very limited knowledge about current reading fads and interests or may not know their child's interests as well as they thought. Be prepared to offer some choices based on knowledge of what other kids are currently reading and suggest that the parent take a few extra titles.

It is also important to get some idea about the child's reading level and proficiency so that an appropriate book is identified. Parents may overestimate or underestimate their child's abilities. Depending on the subject and motivation, a child may read a book that is more difficult than her or his level. For example, a beginning reader who is a dinosaur aficionado has no trouble reading complex scientific names but might still stumble and be discouraged by a long chapter book. Asking about the last books a child read can help the librarian ascertain an approximate reading level. It is also appropriate to encourage the child to read a couple of paragraphs to see if the level is comfortable, and some librarians use the "five finger test." This works best with books that have a reasonable amount of text and few or no pictures on the page. The child reads a page from the book and folds down one finger when a difficult word is encountered. The book is probably too difficult if five fingers go down and too easy if only one or two difficult words are encountered. It is usually not a problem to read a book that is too easy if the child is reading for pleasure, but a book that is too difficult may frustrate the reader and diminish the child's interest in reading.

A lot of reader's advisory recommendations come from the librarian's personal reading, so it is important for children's librarians to regularly read new and classic books. Of course, it is not feasible for any librarian to have read every book in the collection, but over time it is possible to accrue a nice repertoire of titles from which you can pull suggestions. Children, more so than adults, want personal input and a brief description of the book. They will often ask if the librarian has read the book, while adults are more willing to accept a recommendation based on reviews or what others have said about the book. It's not necessary to have read every book you recommend, and never lie about that, but do let the child know why you are suggesting that particular book.

In addition to reading books, be sure to look at the carts of returned books. This provides insight into what kids are checking out. Peruse the shelves when you have a few minutes to see what catches your eye. Read the jackets' information, especially if you are not a regular reader of the type of books you are exploring.

Librarians rely on the reviews being read for collection development to gain a working knowledge of new books. Even if the children's librarian is not directly involved in the selection process, review journals and articles about children's literature are an important part of professional reading. It's easy to peruse review journals, making note of books that sound particularly interesting or that would fill an interest for a young patron. Many librarians keep notecards, notebooks, or online notes about books they have read or that might be recommended to readers.

When a patron is looking for more books like _____ (you can fill in the blank; it could be Harry Potter, the Hunger Games, Lemony Snicket, or any of a multitude of other titles), librarians can also use online catalogs and databases to identify potential candidates. The subject tracings in a catalog record can be helpful but are often too broad. For example, a librarian looking for books similar to the Enola Holmes mystery series can easily find other titles that deal with Sherlock Holmes by using the subject heading "Holmes, Sherlock (Fictitious Character)—Fiction," but they include many adult books. Some free online resources can suggest additional books. The What's Next database compiled and maintained by the Kent District Library in Michigan (http://ww2.kdl.org/libcat/WhatsNextNEW.asp) and Mid-Continent Public Library's (Missouri) *Juvenile Series and Sequels* (http://www.mcpl.lib.mo.us/readers/series/juv/) helps librarians and patrons find more books that are like ones that they already have read. Subscription databases like Children's Core Collection and Fiction Connection offer a lot of support for reader's advisory and may include reviews of the books and a link to display similar books. Of course, these databases won't tell the librarian if the titles are owned by the local library.

Printed volumes, including *A to Zoo*, *Best Books for Children: Preschool through Grade 6*, and *Book Crush: For Kids and Teens* (Pearl, 2007), offer indexes, cross references, and lists to help the librarian point the reader in the right direction. *A to Zoo* is particularly helpful in locating picture books that match specific topic criterion such as books about new siblings, toys, or emotions. New guides, such as *Popular Picks for Young Readers* (Foote, 2014) or *Popular Series Fiction* (Thomas and Barr, 2014), come out fairly regularly, but even slightly dated resources like *Across Cultures: A Guide to Multicultural Literature for Children* (East and Thomas, 2007) will be useful until you find that the library doesn't own a good selection of the titles included. Also check to see if the author of an older book included in these guides has written more recent titles. Librarians often annotate these printed volumes to indicate titles that are owned by the library both to help with reader's advisory and to use as a collection development tool, looking for titles to add to the collection.

Indirect Reader's Advisory

Reader's advisory is also provided when librarians create bibliographies, bookmarks, displays, and bulletin boards to promote specific books. Bibliographies and bookmarks that promote genres or specific types of reading material may also be purchased from vendors, including the American Library Association and Demco. Some publishers offer free posters that promote new books, classics, or books in series. Publishing and word processing software have made it easy to create bibliographies and brochures that are tailored to local interests and needs, with many ready-to-use templates that allow the user to fill in the blanks. Attractive brochures can be printed to hand to patrons who need help finding funny books, books with quirky girl characters, materials at a particular reading level, or audiobooks for family listening. The possibilities are as wide as your imagination, and creating these booklists and brochures provides a good way to meet repetitive requests for the same type of materials.

Displays are another easy way to provide ongoing reader's advisory and promote specific areas of the collection while making it convenient for patrons to find something

Figure 4.2. Mystery Book Display. *Display by Laura Harper, Joliet Public Library, Black Road Branch, Illinois*

new and interesting. Often displays are tied to holidays, local interests, or simply new titles. Joliet (Illinois) Public Library created an eye-catching mystery book display, shown in figure 4.2, to attract attention to the genre by including a Clue game board and other realia with the books. Although this display is in a glass case, an accompanying bibliography provided by the library will lead readers to other books and materials. The easiest display is to leave a book cart in the children's department with books that are waiting to be reshelved. Many patrons want to read what others have read.

It is interesting to look at the ways that technology and e-books impact reader's advisory services. Although e-book reading is not as prevalent for children, the number of kids reading books on e-readers is growing. Helping a child to identify titles to borrow electronically from the library is similar to helping him or her locate good titles from the physical collection but may be a little more frustrating because the librarian is often less familiar with what is available in the e-book collection.

Electronic Reader's Advisory

Librarians are also using technology and social media to connect readers and good books. Look at sites like Goodreads.com or Shelfari.com to see what other libraries are doing. There are online book clubs, peer and librarian reviews, recommended lists, and more. The key is finding a social media site that library patrons are using and are willing to connect on. Depending on the site, it may be possible to have multiple accounts so that postings are tailored to specific interests. Keep in mind that often social media reader's advisory will be directed more toward parents and caregivers as many sites don't allow children under the age of 13 to have accounts. Along with listservs like ALSC-L, PUBYAC, and

Child_lit, social media provide opportunities for the children's librarian to get help from colleagues when trying to identify a book, often referred to as a "stumper," that a patron has described. Based only on vague descriptions, other librarians and children's literature specialists help to identify the needed title, often within minutes of posting.

Book trailers, short movies about a book, have become a popular method for recommending good books. Like movie trailers, book trailers are a short commercial for a book, intended to entice readers. Some librarians have young people create the trailers

CHECK IT OUT!

Sam, a mouse, lives in the library behind the reference books. At night he uses the library's resources to read so much that, with his head full of information, Sam decides to write his own book. *Library Mouse* is an inspirational story to share during school visits to the library!

Figure 4.3. *Library Mouse. Courtesy of Harry N. Abrams; © 2007 by Daniel Kirk*

during library programs and then upload the video to YouTube or another file sharing service and provide a link to them from the library's website. Moviemaking programs like Animoto, Windows Live Movie Maker, or iMovie allow librarians and children to easily create short trailers. Keep in mind that copyright regulations usually will mean that trailers cannot include images from the book being promoted, but there are copyright-free or licensed images that can be used. Some libraries also provide links to trailers created by the authors and illustrators of books that are being recommended or that have been created by other moviemakers. For an excellent example of a book trailer created by a fourth-grade class see the one for *We've Got a Job* by Cynthia Levinson (http://www.cynthialevinson.com/publications/books-for-young-readers/).

Booktalking

Booktalking is a way of providing reader's advisory to a group of children, often as part of a program. It can be a very effective method for encouraging reluctant readers to try something new as well as a way to recommend new titles and genres for avid readers. Many librarians provide booktalks during class visits or after library tours. Think of booktalks, and their new "kissing cousin" the book trailer, as sneak previews or commercials for the books being recommended.

The booktalker's enthusiasm and creativity are key elements for a successful booktalk. Although there are booktalks available written by other librarians, it is important that the booktalker has read the book, enjoyed—or at least appreciated—it, and is recommending it. The booktalker is *selling* the book, and while it is possible to sell books in a genre that is not a personal favorite, the salesperson has to be able to express enthusiasm for the item being sold. Written booktalks can help librarians learn how to create original booktalks and serve as a shortcut for programs. However, prewritten talks should not be relied on in lieu of actually reading the book even when the librarian is choosing books outside his own personal reading interests. Use these as a template or starter but tailor the booktalk to make it your own. A sample booktalk is provided for *The True Meaning of Smekday* on page 82, and more are available on websites like Booktalks Quick and Simple (http://nancykeane.com/booktalks/). There are also collections of booktalks in books like *Booktalking around the World: Great Global Reads for Ages 9–14* by Sonja Cole.

Booktalks can be thematic, for example, grouping mysteries or books about heroes or good dog books together. They can also be broad based, focusing on "new books" or "contemporary topics." Because booktalks are presented to groups, remember to offer variety as not every book will, or should, appeal to everyone in the audience. Select books that will match varied interests. The presenter is speaking to the audience, often with very limited information about the group or their interests and without any opportunity for the interview that can be conducted with direct reader's advisory.

Look for books with attractive jackets to show the audience. Include some titles that are of high interest for children of lower reading abilities as well as a title or two for avid readers that might expand their boundaries and diversify their interests. Mix in some nonfiction and poetry if appropriate. Consider whether the books feature only girl protagonists or are all very similar, and modify the selections to provide diversity.

Plan to feature about ten to twelve books and to limit each talk to about 90 seconds. When possible, select titles where multiple copies of the book are available so that more than one child can choose the book. Prepare talks for enough books ahead of time to allow for tailoring the program to match books that are currently available and can be

The True Meaning of Smekday by Adam Rex
(Created by Amy Seto Musser)

It all started when 11-year-old Gratuity's mother was abducted by aliens and made to fold laundry. Then the aliens, called the Boov, invaded Earth. Smart and independent, Gratuity, called Tip by her friends, manages to stay in her mother's apartment alone until Moving Day, the day the Boov have chosen for all humans in the United States to be relocated to Florida. Tip decides to drive her mother's car to Florida and unexpectedly finds herself on a road trip with one of the Boov.

"You do not to say it right," he said finally.

"Say what?"

"'Boov.' The way you says it, it is too short. You must to draw it out, like as a long breath. 'Bo-o-ov.'"

After a moment I swallowed my anger and gave it a try.

"Booov."

"No. Bo-o-ov."

"Bo-o-o-o-ov."

The Boov frowned. "Now you sound like sheep."

I shook my head. "Fine. So what's your name? I'll call you that."

"Ah, no," the Boov replied. "For humansgirl to correctly be pronouncing my name, you would need two heads. But, as a human name, I have to chosen 'J.Lo.'"

I stifled a laugh. "J.Lo? Your Earth name is J.Lo?"

"Ah-ah," J.Lo corrected. "Not 'Earth.' 'Smekland.'"

"What do you mean, 'Smekland'?"

"That is the thing what we have named this planet. Smekland. As to tribute to our glorious leader, Captain Smek."

"Wait." I shook my head. "Whoa. You can't just rename the planet."

"Peoples who discover places gets to name it."

"But it's *called* Earth. It's *always* been called Earth."

J.Lo smiled condescendingly. I wanted to hit him.

"You humans live too much in the pastime. We did land onto Smekland a long time ago."

"You landed last Christmas!"

"Ah-ah. Not 'Christmas.' 'Smekday.'"

"Smekday?"

"Smekday."

But Gratuity and J. Lo's adventures have just begun. Did I mention it's up to them to save the world? That there is more than one race of invading aliens? That J.Lo loves to eat cans of cola and dental floss? That in addition to boys and girls, the Boovish genders include boygirls, girlboys, boyboys, boyboygirls, and boyboyboys? All this and more in the hilarious book, *The True Meaning of Smekday* by Adam Rex.

displayed during the talk. It's frustrating to hear about a book and then seek it out only to find it is checked out already. For larger groups, it is also acceptable to have additional titles in a series, or similar titles, available even though those books are not specifically being booktalked. Ideally every child will find a book to read by the end of the booktalk.

Booktalks are *not* book reviews. The booktalker only talks about the positive elements of the book. If the book is too flawed for you to recommend for leisure reading, select another book. A good booktalker can talk about a book she didn't especially enjoy for her own reading by focusing on the positive aspects and concluding with a line like "If you enjoy books about boy wizards, you will love this book." Librarians often provide a list of all the books, sometimes as a checklist, so that children can mark the ones they want to read.

Think of booktalks as commercials where the booktalker tells enough about the plot, action, characters, and theme to entice someone in the audience to read the book. Always start by showing the book, holding it up for all to see. State the title and author of the book and tell a little bit about it. It is acceptable to read a paragraph or two, but never give away too much and *never* reveal the ending! Leave the audience eager to find out what happens or to read more.

After the booktalk has been written, practice reading it aloud. Remember, this is part performance, and the booktalk should express drama, enthusiasm, mood, and personality. Watch for places that are rough to read or where the words don't flow nicely. The tone of the talk can be formal or informal and language is often rather casual, and some booktalkers will have an appropriate prop or other item to show. It is also acceptable and expected to express emotions and enthusiasm for the book, even indicating "This is one of my very favorite books," or "This book makes me cry, in a good way, whenever I read it." In preparation for the actual booktalk, be sure to read the talk and practice enough times to almost know it by heart. To help with memory, many booktalkers will print out the script and tape it to the back of the book. Hold up the book while presenting the talk and the script is then visible if cueing is needed. At the end of the talk, repeat the title and author and invite the audience to "check it out." Keep copies of scripts to reuse at future booktalk programs.

Partnerships

Children's librarians serve children who are also served by a wide range of other organizations and businesses. This means that partnerships are essential to the success of library programs and services and open up a vast array of additional opportunities to help children and families achieve their academic, intellectual, and personal goals. The library gains a lot from working with other organizations that work with children and families, and those organizations and businesses, in turn, can support library programs. Additionally, library programs and services can be brought to other locations, expanding the reach of these services as well as attracting new patrons and library users.

Libraries frequently partner with

- Agencies that serve new immigrants
- Boys' and girls' clubs
- Community agencies that work with special needs children and their families
- Early child care providers and organizations that support quality child care

- Health and welfare organizations
- Juvenile correctional facilities
- Local businesses
- Museums and cultural organizations
- Public and private schools

Partnership implies a somewhat equitable arrangement, whereby each partner both gives and gains something from the relationship. Many organizations value a partnership with the library because libraries have great reputations and a high level of credibility. Libraries also usually have good infrastructure support—the collection, staff, the building—and a good track record for successfully carrying out projects.

Libraries frequently gain advocates for programs and the ability to reach new audiences via partnerships. For example, the Head Start teachers will tell parents about the library storytimes and encourage participation by parents who don't currently visit the library. Libraries gain credibility as part of the education community from this type of partnership, with children's librarians serving as good role models for storytime presentations.

Sometimes a partnership means that the library will gain additional funds or resources, or avoid having to directly pay for services needed for successful programs. For example, Austin Public Library partnered with the Texas School for the Deaf to offer a program with sign language interpreters and deaf storytellers who presented storytime with the librarian at the library. The school benefited from a library program that met the needs of their students and families (who also enjoyed a trip to the library), sign language students in the community had opportunities to practice their skills and observe master interpreters in action, and the library was able to serve an audience that was otherwise underserved and saved the cost of hiring sign interpreters. Hearing children and their families also appreciated the opportunity to learn sign language in a fun setting. Both organizations were credited as the sponsors for the program.

Building relationships for a successful partnership takes time and effort. It is important for all parties to know and understand what is expected from each partner and for everyone to be frank and direct about concerns. Every partnership does not need to be "equal," but the partnership experience should help to fulfill the needs and mission of each of the partners.

⑥ Outreach Services

Often the children who regularly visit the public library come from middle-class families with parents who have grown up visiting libraries themselves. While these children and their families are vital to the library's success, children who don't have the opportunity to visit the library on a regular basis are most in need of the librarian's efforts. Through outreach programs, librarians bring library services to potential users outside of the library building. In most cases the ultimate goal is to bring those new users into the library, but that may not happen for years. For example, librarians often will conduct storytimes for children at child care centers in low-income areas of the community. These children need early literacy experiences, but their parents, who may themselves have low literacy skills, are working and don't have the time to come to library storytimes. Often new immigrant families are not even aware of the library and its services.

Figure 4.4. Storytime Kit. *Courtesy of Austin Public Library, Texas*

Outreach programming may range from the bookmobile that visits housing projects and child care centers weekly, to monthly programs on early literacy at the Women, Infants, and Children (WIC) clinic or an occasional program for children living at the women's shelter. A number of librarians have taken storytimes to local shopping centers to reach families that might not ordinarily visit the library or bring library programs to youth detention centers.

To provide early literacy programs for children in low-income child care centers, librarians may create storytime kits that include books, puppets, and other materials needed for an off-site storytime. Regular library staff may present the storytimes, but many libraries also use trained volunteers and interns who can then visit the child care center weekly. The kit seen in figure 4.4 has everything that is needed for a dinosaur storytime. Several age-appropriate books are included so that the librarian or volunteer can select two or three to share. Printed cards provide the words and actions for fingerplays and rhymes, as well as tips for enhancing the program. It is good practice to provide stickers or a handout that alerts parents that their child had a library experience and encourages the parents to visit the library. For many child care centers, the librarian also serves as a role model for staff who are not trained in early literacy activities and who may themselves not understand the importance of reading to children.

Libraries may also provide long-term loan of tailored collections for child care centers, preschools, and home daycares. Boxes, or buckets, may contain 20-30 items including books, music CDs, board books, and book and CD kits. These may be delivered during the off-site storytime program and then swapped for another set on the next visit.

⊚ Class Visits

Class visits can be either in-library programming, where a class or two comes to the library for a tour and educational program, or an outreach service in which the librarian visits the school. Although class visits may include a tour of the library, showing children the various departments and helping them feel comfortable with the library as a place, they often include some educational activities such as learning how to use the library catalog, using library resources, or enjoying hearing a story or viewing a puppet show. Teachers may approach the public library to schedule a field trip, but this is also a great opportunity for the children's librarian to invite classes to visit.

When classes visit the library as a field trip, teachers may have a specific educational goal in mind. When scheduling the visit be sure that the expectations are clearly outlined so that preparations can be made. If you will be demonstrating how to use the library's catalog or online databases, you will want to be sure you reserve some computers. Books and other resources may need to be pulled to facilitate research on a specific topic or to booktalk and share for students to use for silent reading. Programming may include scavenger hunts to reinforce library skills that were learned during the tour, storytelling or a puppet show that provides a taste of ongoing programs held at the library, or booktalks to encourage students to check out books. Often library card applications are sent home with students in advance so that library cards can be issued during the visit. Field trips require advance preparation by the school as well, including transportation and chaperones, so be sure to confirm that the time is set aside and staff is scheduled appropriately. It's a good idea to always confirm the arrangements and then reconfirm a day or two ahead.

Librarians may visit schools to promote programs like summer reading clubs, to be a special guest to talk about careers or be a guest reader for a literacy day celebration, or to provide instruction on how to use library resources. Visits may be coordinated through the school librarian and held in the library or visits may be at the invitation of a classroom teacher. Librarians may also be invited to the school to speak at a PTA (Parent Teacher Association) meeting or to speak at a teachers' meeting about library resources that are available to educators and students.

As more and more public schools lack school librarians or are staffed by part-time librarians or paraprofessionals, the public children's librarian plays an increasingly important role in encouraging children to read and to help them learn to use library resources. The declining number of schools with on-site, full-time librarians means less exposure to research tools and less support for learning how to use the library. Rightly or wrongly, more of the burden for library education is falling to public librarians in many school districts.

⊚ Literacy Partners

Over the past couple of decades, based in part on research conducted on early brain development as well as research on the importance of ensuring that children have access to books as a means of combating illiteracy, many programs have been developed that are carried out within or through other organizations, such as hospitals and health clinics, arts organizations, and homeless shelters. Libraries are natural partners for many of these programs, some of which are held in the partner location, such as by providing kits for new parents after childbirth before the mother leaves the hospital. Others are held in the public library with the library staff providing training for parents and others who work with young children.

Librarians and library associations have been involved in the development of programs like Mother Goose on the Loose (http://www.mgol.net) or Every Child Ready to Read (http://everychildreadytoread.org), which are licensed for use with parenting groups and child care provider organizations. Libraries also may have developed their own local literacy initiatives, such as the King County (Washington) Library System's Take Time to Read program (http://www.kcls.org/taketimetoread/) that seeks partnerships with local organizations. Other programs, such as Reading is Fundamental (http://www.rif.org/) or First Book (http://www.firstbook.org/), were created and are managed by nonprofit organizations. First Book works through community organizations like libraries to put books into low-income homes where children often have no age-appropriate books. Regardless of their genesis, these programs work well for public libraries.

The American Academy of Pediatrics officially weighed in on the importance of early literacy when it announced a new policy in June 2014 asking doctors to talk with parents about "the importance of reading out loud, singing and talking during an infant's first days" during pediatric visits (Motoko, 2014). This validates programs like Reach Out and Read's (http://www.reachoutandread.org) RX for Reading project that began in 1989. Reach Out and Read is a pediatric-based program conducted in the offices of pediatricians during well-baby visits. The doctor actually writes out a prescription for reading, emphasizing the importance of parents and caregivers reading with young children every day. Libraries can partner with the project by providing books for the waiting room or offering storytimes at clinics.

There are many national programs and initiatives that may have branches within the community but additionally there are local groups, so look around the area served by the library for these partnership and outreach opportunities. Working with various parts of the community, libraries are in the forefront of building literate communities, and these programs bring the community into the library.

◉ Key Points

The services that libraries provide to children and their families play an important role in the educational system as well as in developing lifelong readers and library users. While the tools used and the format of the services change with technology, the basics of providing the services have remained constant. Even with almost universal access to the Internet, children need help locating accurate and timely information. Virtual services allow many patrons to access services from their home, school, or office, but many services are best provided face-to-face. Libraries should reach out to bring new patrons into the library and partner with community organizations to reach those most in need of library services and resources.

- Children use references services more than adults in most libraries.
- Although many reference resources are now provided in electronic formats, a basic ready reference collection is essential to providing good service.
- There are many resources in print and electronic format to help the children's librarian provide reader's advisory services that encourage children to read for enjoyment and recreation.

- Partnerships and outreach reinforce the public library's educational roles.
- Early literacy services support early learning and school readiness.

Library services for children are often very similar to the services provided to adults and teens. Although children may need more assistance in selecting good reading material or in locating facts and information than adults, the skills and resources are not unique to children's librarianship. The next chapter will look at early literacy programs and the important role storytimes play in early education.

References

Gish, Wendy. 2012. "Homework Help Helps." *Public Libraries* 51, no. 5 (September/October): 8–9.

Motoko, Rich. 2014. "Pediatrics Group to Recommend Reading Aloud to Children from Birth." *New York Times*, June 24. http://www.nytimes.com/2014/06/24/us/pediatrics-group-to-recommend-reading-aloud-to-children-from-birth.html?_r=0.

National Home Education Research Institute. 2013. Accessed March 30, 2014. http://www.nheri.org/.

Scholastic Publishing. 2013. *Kids & Family Reading Report*. 4th ed. Accessed June 24, 2014. http://mediaroom.scholastic.com/files/kfrr2013-wappendix.pdf.

Sullivan, Michael. 2009. *Serving Boys through Readers' Advisory*. Chicago, IL: ALA Editions.

Walter, Virginia A. 2001. *Children and Libraries: Getting It Right*. Chicago, IL: American Library Association.

Zickuhr, Kathryn, Lee Rainee, and Kristen Purcell. 2013. *Library Services in the Digital Age*. Accessed January 22, 2014. http://libraries.pewinternet.org/files/legacy-pdf/PIP_Library%20services_Report_012213.pdf.

Resources Mentioned in This Chapter

ALSC-L. http://www.ala.org/alsc/compubs/alsc20/alscdisclist.

Barr, Catherine. 2013. *Best Books for Children: Preschool Through Grade 6*. Santa Barbara, CA: Libraries Unlimited.

Booktalks Quick and Simple. http://nancykeane.com/booktalks/.

Child_lit. https://email.rutgers.edu/mailman/listinfo/child_lit.

Cole, Sonja. 2010. *Booktalking around the World: Great Global Reads for Ages 9–14*. Santa Barbara, CA: Libraries Unlimited.

East, Kathy, and Rebecca L. Thomas. 2007. *Across Cultures: A Guide to Multicultural Literature for Children*. Westport, CT: Libraries Unlimited.

Every Child Ready to Read. http://everychildreadytoread.org.

First Book. http://www.firstbook.org/.

Foote, Diane. 2014. *Popular Picks for Young Readers*. Chicago: American Library Association.

H.W. Wilson Company. 2010. *Children's Core Collection*. New York: H.W. Wilson Co.

Internet Public Library for Kids. http://www.ipl.org/div/kidspace/.

Kent District Library. *What's Next*. http://ww2.kdl.org/libcat/WhatsNextNEW.asp.

Kirk, Daniel. 2007. *Library Mouse*. New York: Abrams Books for Young Readers.

Learning Express Library. http://www.learningexpresshub.com/.

Lima, Carolyn, and John A. Lima. 2006. *A to Zoo: Subject Access to Children's Picture Books*. Westport, CT: Libraries Unlimited.

Mid-Continent Public Library. *Juvenile Series and Sequels.* http://www.mcpl.lib.mo.us/readers/series/juv/.

Mother Goose on the Loose. http://www.mgol.net.

Pearl, Nancy. 2007. *Book Crush: For Kids and Teens.* Seattle, WA: Sasquatch Books.

PUBYAC. http://www.pubyac.org/.

Reach Out and Read. http://www.reachoutandread.org.

Reading Is Fundamental. http://www.rif.org/.

R.R. Bowker Company. 2000. *Fiction Connection.* New Providence, NJ: R. R. Bowker.

Searchasaurus. http://scdiscus.org/searchasaurus.

Take Time to Read. http://www.kcls.org/taketimetoread/.

Thomas, Rebecca L., and Catherine Barr. 2014. *Popular Series Fiction for K–6 Readers: A Reading and Selection Guide.* Santa Barbara, CA: Libraries Unlimited.

World Book, Inc. 2014. *The World Book.* Chicago: World Book, Inc.

⑥ Additional Readings and Resources

Furness, Adrienne. 2008. *Helping Homeschoolers in the Library.* Chicago, IL: ALA Editions.

Harper, Meghan. 2011. *Reference Sources and Services for Youth.* Chicago, IL: Neal-Schuman Publishers.

Harrod, Kerol, and Carol Smallwood. 2014. *Library Youth Outreach: 26 Ways to Connect with Children, Young Adults and Their Families.* Jefferson, NC: McFarland.

Intner, Carol F. 2011. *Homework Help from the Library: In Person and Online.* Chicago: American Library Association.

Knoer, Susan. 2011. *Reference Interview Today.* Oxford, England: ABC-CLIO.

Mediavilla, Cindy. 2001. *Creating the Full-Service Homework Center in Your Library.* Chicago, IL: American Library Association.

Naidoo, Jamie Campbell. 2014. *Diversity Programming for Digital Youth: Promoting Cultural Competence in the Children's Library.* Santa Barbara, CA: Libraries Unlimited.

Pattison, Darcy. 2012. *The Book Trailer Manual.* Little Rock, AR: Mims House.

Peck, Penny. 2010. *Readers' Advisory for Children and 'Tweens.* Santa Barbara, CA: Libraries Unlimited.

CHAPTER 5

Early Literacy Programs for Children and Families

Storytime Programs

PUBLIC LIBRARY STORYTIMES are a cherished memory for many adults. In many libraries, storytimes are the highest profile part of the children's librarian's job. For many children, it is the first sustained interaction they have with a non-parental adult. There are many factors that go into planning storytime programs, and a number of anticipated outcomes are expected. In addition to sharing great books with children and helping them learn to behave as members of an audience, the public library storytime can set the stage for lifelong learning and library use, playing an important part in the education process.

Storytime is more than simply picking up some books and reading them to a group of children. The storytime presenter carefully selects books that are good to read to a group, books that not only are good stories but that also have excellent illustrations that reinforce the story and are large enough to be viewed by the group. The librarian is also modeling appropriate reading methods for parents and caregivers. Storytime includes activities that reinforce the stories told and encourage children to develop motor skills through crafts and interactive activities. The variety of stories selected reflects the diversity of the world around us, and stories encourage children to be curious about places and faces they may never see. Storytime also allows the librarian to be a performer and to encourage participation in creative dramatics, storytelling, and use of language.

School teachers and librarians also share books with children in a storytime setting, and many schools have established prekindergarten programs that also help establish a solid basis for learning. The major difference between storytime activities in a school setting and those in a public library primarily have to do with the audience. Classes have a limited number of students and some consistency in the class membership from week to week. Because the same children are together as a group on a regular basis, the teacher or librarian often knows the children quite well and interacts with the students more frequently and in different settings. While some school-based storytimes are offered for the pleasure of enjoying a good story, the particular books shared may be selected to support specific curriculum objectives and the development of specific skills required by state standards. While public library storytimes support the development of early literacy and learning skills, the emphasis is less on curriculum and more on enjoying literature.

Many public library storytimes must include children of different age levels and who are in different stages of child development. However, some libraries are able to hold programs designed specifically for a narrower target audience. While the basic structure for the program will be similar, different approaches work better to support the development of specific early literacy skills for different ages and levels of development.

Registration is one of the major questions bandied about when children's librarians talk about storytime. Having families sign up ahead of time may create more of a sense that storytime is something special, available to a limited number of people. However, registrations also can create a barrier to families that would benefit the most from participating in storytime. This may include situations where parents are new immigrants, unfamiliar with public library services, or where parents have limited language skills and don't know that they need to register in advance. Attendance will also vary from week to week because things come up with children. An empty seat in the storytime room goes unfilled when participation is limited to those who registered. Registration may also be considered when storytime becomes so popular that attendance grows to an unwieldy size. Rather than starting to register attendees, consider adding a second session. Repeating a program that has already been planned requires less preparation than planning a different program. Libraries that can't offer a second storytime but don't want to require registration may use tickets to control access and encourage attendees to arrive early (figure 5.1).

Some libraries offer storytime every week without breaks other than holidays when the library is closed. Especially when registration is used, storytime may be broken up into discrete series of sessions that start and end, allowing a different group of families to register. That helps offer the programming to more families but breaks up the continuity of learning since the same child is unlikely to get into back-to-back storytime sessions. There are no cut-and-dried answers, so look at what will best meet the needs of the community.

Planning Storytimes

Although storytime is sometimes called story hour, most last about 30 minutes. Programs for younger children, toddlers, and infants may be as short as 20 minutes, while programs

Figure 5.1. Storytime Sign. *Photo courtesy of Joanna Taylor with the Las Vegas-Clark County Library District, Nevada*

Thirty-minute program for preschool children
Theme: Cats and Kittens Everywhere

Opening Ritual Song: If You Want to Hear a Story (traditional)

Sing to the tune of "If You're Happy and You Know It"

> If you want to hear a story, clap your hands!
> If you want to hear a story, clap your hands!
> If you want to hear a story,
> if you want to hear a story,
> if you want to hear a story, clap your hands!

Other verses (add as many as desired until children are ready to settle down):

"nod your head"

"rub your tummy"

"pat your back"

Final verse:
> If you want to hear a story, sit right down.

Book 1: *Kitten's First Full Moon* by Kevin Henkes

This simple book with black-and-white illustrations tells the story of a young kitten who confuses the full moon for a bowl of milk.

Fingerplay: Five Little Kittens (traditional)

Ask the children to count along as you count down kittens on your hand and act out the motions. Act out actions in parentheses.

> Five little kittens, sleeping on a chair. (*Pretend to sleep; hands by head.*)
> One rolled off, leaving four there.
> Four little kittens, one climbed a tree. (*Act like you are climbing a tree, hand over hand.*)
> To look in a bird's nest; then there were three.
> Three little kittens, wondered what to do. (*Hold finger by cheek expressing wonder.*)
> One saw a mouse; then there were two.
> Two little kittens, playing near a wall. (*Pretend to throw a ball.*)
> One little kitten chased a red ball.
> One little kitten, with fur soft as silk. (*Pretend to rub fur.*)
> Left all alone to drink a dish of milk. (*Rub your belly.*)

Book 2: *Pete the Cat: I Love My White Shoes* by James Dean

This story tells about a jazzy cool cat who loves his new shoes. As Pete walks along singing he steps in various things that change the color of his white shoes. No matter what color his shoes are, Pete continues along singing and humming!

Movement Song: I Love My White Shoes

Download the song from http://assetlibrary.supadu.com/images/ckfinder/687/images/Pete-the-Cat/audio/pete-the-cat.mp3. Invite the children to sing along as they walk in place, stopping at the appropriate points. Hold up paper sneakers in each color as Pete steps in messes that change the color of his shoes to start the next verse.

Alternate Format Story: *Millions of Cats* by Wanda Gag

Read or tell the story *Millions of Cats* by Wanda Gag. Provide stick or paper bag cat puppets for the children to hold up as they repeat the lines:

> Cats here, cats there,
> Cats and kittens everywhere,
> Hundreds of cats,
> Thousands of cats,
> Millions and billions and trillions of cats.

Early Literacy Tip for Caregivers

Providing an alternate way for children to tell a story allows them to express themselves using language and they learn the rhythm of language.

Closing

Recite the ritual closing rhyme, encouraging the children to learn and speak the words. A ritual closing song or rhyme signals that storytime is ending.

> *We've Listened* (traditional)
> We've listened to stories
> And sat with our friends,
> But now we are finished
> And it is the end.

Ending the Program

Remind the children and caregivers that you welcome them back next time. Point out the display of books for checkout. Ask the children to line up and offer to stamp their hand with a rubber stamp or sticker.

　　Optional activity: Some storytimes end with an open period for children and caregivers to share a book or an art or craft activity and interact with other children and the librarian.

for older children may run longer or include crafts or other activities that extend the program to an hour for those with the attention span to stay engaged. While there are differences, which will be discussed later in this chapter, in programs for various aged children, there are no hard-and-fast rules for storytime. Most public library storytimes follow a basic pattern—similar to the one shown on pages 94–95—that includes a welcoming ritual, a mix of two or three stories, and stretchers or activities that engage the audience and allow them to move around to get out the wiggles. The stretchers, activities, and techniques incorporated into storytimes as adjuncts to the books or as fillers between books can range from rhymes and songs to magic and puppetry. Some of these are discussed later in this chapter, but you are also encouraged to look at books like the now dated but still very useful *New Handbook for Storytellers* by Caroline Feller Bauer or the newer book *The Handbook for Storytime Programs* by Judy Freeman and Caroline Feller Bauer.

Many librarians use a theme or concept to organize the program, selecting books, finger rhymes, songs, and activities that address the theme. These themes vary widely but should be ones that will appeal to children. Tried-and-true themes are broad enough to encompass a range of stories and children's preferences. A theme that is too narrow, such as hamsters rather than pets, may lead to expressions of disinterest from some children before they have a chance to be introduced to the books. While there is nothing sacred about having a theme, and some storytimes may appear to have no theme other than "favorite stories," a theme helps to create a cohesive program and provides structure. Additionally, parents sometimes want to know the theme ahead of time so that they can decide on the suitability of the program for their child. This is especially true for holiday themes—some religions do not celebrate secular holidays, including birthdays—or themes related to magic and fantasy, but can also be true for subjects, such as weather or clowns, that might be frightening for a particular child. Without discounting some themes, such as trains or dinosaurs, which may be perceived as being of interest only to boys, try to use themes that are inclusive of both genders; instead of princess stories have a royalty theme, for example. Keep in mind that themes for younger children should focus primarily on things that are familiar to them and their immediate world, while themes for older preschoolers can include elements of fantasy and travel. Some suggestions for storytime themes are listed below.

Many children find comfort in the rituals of storytime programs. Welcoming activities can set the mood for the program, helping children settle down while signaling that the program is about to begin. These activities help children learn that it is time to sit

POPULAR STORYTIME THEMES

- Trains
- Colors
- Seasons
- Pets
- Monkeys
- Farm animals
- Ducks and pond life
- Bears
- Food

and pay attention, an important skill for school. To enhance the early literacy concepts, many presenters also provide a brief introduction for parents/caregivers that explains or describes the early literacy skills that will be highlighted in the program. Some librarians use a mascot such as a hand puppet or stuffed animal to introduce the program and to gently remind children to sit flat on their bottoms, turn on their listening ears, and such when the program begins and, if needed, during the program. A classic source for storytime rhymes, including thematic rhymes, is *Ring a Ring o' Roses* (Flint Public Library, 2008). Updated regularly, this inexpensive book includes a variety of rhymes, including some in Spanish. While *Ring a Ring o' Roses* is an essential source for any children's librarian, there are many other sources for these storytime fillers and stretchers in books and online. Some of the different storytime features are described later in this chapter, but each storytime should include some activities that happen between readings to allow children to express themselves, move about, experience language in different ways, and refocus on the program.

Books should be the main component of public library storytime, but reading aloud to a group of children requires careful selection of appropriate books that are suitable for group use (figure 5.2). This is very different from selecting a book to read to an individual child who is sitting close up or in a parent's lap. First, the book must be large enough for group viewing, and the illustrations should be large and clear. If children can't see the pictures, or need to closely examine small components, they will either lose interest or be on top of each other trying to get close to the presenter. It is critical to select a story that the presenter enjoys and finds engaging. If multiple readings become boring, or if there are parts of the story that the presenter would prefer to omit for any reason, select a different book.

Figure 5.2. Storytime Group. *Courtesy Tom Green County Library System, San Angelo, Texas; Sally Meyers, children's librarian*

After selecting the books, practice reading until the story can almost be told without looking at the text. It is not necessary to dramatize the story with accents and voices, but the presenter's voice should be expressive and modulated in tone. Speak clearly and practice projecting so that children in the back of the group will hear. Read the book silently three or four times to learn the pacing of the story and then practice reading it aloud another two or three times. Sometimes a book that seems great when read silently bombs when the words are read aloud. The story may be too complicated or include long sentences or words that trip up the reader's tongue.

Also practice reading while holding the book level and moving the book, panning it, slowly from left to right and back again, so that all can see the pictures. Read at a slower than normal pace so that the children have time to hear the words and process what they hear. With practice, storytime presenters learn to just glance at the page to recall the words. Skilled presenters are careful not to turn the book toward themselves in order to read the page, showing the pictures after reading the text. Doing so leaves the audience feeling left out, and they will become restless. Remember that the practice is worth the effort, as the stories will be used year after year with a new crop of children.

Brain Development and Storytime

While public library storytimes are focused on sharing the joy of books and reading, the activities play a key role in the development of a child's brain. The human brain continues to develop after birth, and the first three years are a period of incredible, and critical, growth. Although a child's brain continues to grow for many years beyond three, by age five 93% of brain development has occurred (Marsico Institute for Early Learning and Literacy, 2013). During this initial period, the brain produces billions of cells and trillions of connections, or synapses, between these cells. These synapses need stimulation to connect into networks, or they are pruned and discarded. These neural connections are stimulated by sensory experiences, including seeing, hearing, touching, and tasting. According to studies summarized by Reach Out and Read (2012), "early foundational language skills help start children on a path of success when they enter school." The silly songs, finger rhymes, colors in picture books, and other things librarians include in storytimes provide this stimulation, helping the brain prepare for future learning successes.

Additionally, the library storytime can encourage parents to read to their children regularly and model early literacy skills. Although studies show that reading aloud helps stimulate brain development, less than half of infants and toddlers are read to regularly. Children are not born knowing how to handle a book. Seeing how others hold a book, and how in Western culture we read from left to right, prepares a child for learning to read.

Storytime programming also helps to expand a child's attention span and learn to behave as part of a group and a member of an audience. Library programming that reaches low-income families is especially important because knowing the alphabet and having high levels of direct contact with books are major predictors of academic success. More than 35% of all children enter school at risk for academic difficulties, but the rich vocabulary shared through books and activities at storytime expands the words that a child has heard before entering school. Children from low-income families generally start first grade with less than 25 hours of one-on-one reading, while children from middle-class families enter with more than 1,000 hours (Adams, 1990). Storytime programs encourage parents and caregivers to borrow books to use at home, providing further help in the development of early literacy skills.

Early Literacy Skills

The public library plays a major role in preparing young children for school and learning to read. While the programs are generally not structured as classroom lessons and the opportunities for interaction are limited, sporadic, and episodic, the role of the public library in early childhood education is well established.

The storytime program should be engaging and entertaining, but elements of the programs—how the librarian interacts with the children, the way the books and stories are presented, and the methods used to enhance the storytime activities—will vary depending on the ages of the participants. Variations will be outlined later in the chapter, but each storytime program can provide children with the skills needed to be successful readers and learners.

Most children's librarians have not received any formal training in early childhood education, and undergraduate degrees are often in areas other than child development. Intuitively, accidentally, or because librarians recognized results, storytimes often included activities that resulted in skills that research has now validated as being beneficial. Recognizing that public libraries reach a lot of preschool children and their parents and that storytime is an excellent opportunity to offer early literacy programming, the Public Library Association and the Association for Library Services to Children, both divisions of the American Library Association, created the Every Child Ready to Read @ Your Library program (http://www.everychildreadytoread.org/). Since 2000, librarians have used a variety of components to share early literacy information with parents and caregivers, to provide language rich environments, and to enhance storytime programs with components that foster early literacy skills. The original Every Child Ready to Read program focuses on six early literacy skills that provide the building blocks for reading. These skills are incorporated in practices in the updated version of the program, but it is helpful to understand how storytime supports these skills before looking at them in

Figure 5.3. Early Literacy Skills. *Photo courtesy of Joanna Taylor with the Las Vegas-Clark County Library District, Nevada*

EARLY LITERACY SKILLS FROM EVERY CHILD READY TO READ

Vocabulary
Print motivation
Narrative skills
Letter knowledge
Print awareness
Phonological awareness

practice. To remind parents about these skills, they are often displayed in the storytime room (figure 5.3) and the presenter points out the skills and ways to reinforce them as part of the program.

Early literacy is not about teaching children to read but rather about providing the building blocks that are the foundation for reading. Every Child Ready to Read identifies three areas of reading instruction that are necessary for children to become fluent readers: alphabetics (including phonemic awareness and phonics), fluency, and comprehension (including vocabulary and text). Library storytime and other early literacy programs can support these areas by helping young children develop specific skills that lay the foundation for reading fluency. The early literacy skills needed to be ready to learn to read include phonological awareness, print awareness, print motivation, letter knowledge, vocabulary, and narrative skills.

Every storytime should support *print motivation*, an interest in and enjoyment of books. Children experience the joy of books and stories and are encouraged to interact with books. Closely linked is *print awareness*—noticing print around us and understanding how a book works. In storytime, the librarian often points to words on the page and is modeling how, in Western culture, text is read from left to right. *Letter knowledge* teaches a child that letters are symbols that connect print with sound. In order to learn to read, a child must be able to recognize differences between specific letters as well as differences between capital and lowercase versions of the same letter. Singing "The Alphabet Song," labeling items around the storytime room, and reading alphabet concept books help children learn their letters. *Phonological awareness* is the ability to distinguish the sounds that make up words and provide the tools needed to decipher words that are being read. This skill is supported by rhymes and songs, especially those that allow the child to play with words and manipulate them. *Vocabulary* means knowing the names of things and being able to label them. Various studies link the size of a child's vocabulary—the number of words she or he has heard—at the start of formal schooling to reading achievement. Further, children who enter school with limited vocabulary knowledge struggle to catch up with their peers (Baker, Simmons, and Kame'enui, 1997). Sharing a wide variety of different books, singing songs, and reciting poetry exposes children to a rich vocabulary, including words that they may not hear at home. When children are encouraged to describe things and to tell stories, they strengthen their *narrative skills* and utilize the vocabulary they have heard. Using puppets and flannel boards to allow children to retell a familiar tale and providing take-home activities to remind the children about the stories they heard encourages their oral language abilities.

Saroj Nadkarni Ghoting and Pamela Martin-Díaz (2006) clearly outline the components of a good early literacy storytime in their book *Early Literacy Storytimes @ Your*

Library: Partnering with Caregivers for Success (2006). Their work includes detailed scripts to help the librarian share information about early literacy skills with parents and caregivers and examples of model programs.

The second iteration of the original Every Child Ready to Read program is outlined in *Storytimes for Everyone! Developing Young Children's Language and Literacy* (Ghoting and Martin-Díaz, 2013) and builds on these six early literacy skills (listed on page 100) by focusing on five practices that by their nature will include those skills. These five practices are

1. Talking
2. Singing
3. Reading
4. Writing
5. Playing

This approach to early literacy programs shifts the focus from the resulting skills to the activities that develop those skills, recognizing the overlap between skills that are enhanced through various actions and activities. "Talking with children is the key to developing their oral language" (Ghoting and Martin-Díaz, 2013: 15). Storytime activities that encourage children to participate in telling the story or to talk about what they heard encourages early literacy. Singing adds to the development of vocabulary, and in fact, research has shown that it is easier to memorize something that is sung. There is a direct link between music and phonological awareness because music is broken into smaller sounds (notes). Reading is often mentioned as the single-most important activity that anyone can do with a child to help prepare the child to be successful in school. Studies show that there is a correlation between the availability of books and a print-rich environment, the amount of time spent reading to children, and how often children play with books (pretend reading) and being a proficient reader. Writing may just be scribbling for young children, but this supports the development of fine motor skills as children begin to understand the connection between symbols and sounds that create words. Play is "internally motivated" (Ghoting and Martin-Díaz, 2013), and dramatic play helps children develop thinking skills and use their imagination.

You will want to be familiar with both the skills and the activities to incorporate early literacy elements into your storytimes. Another element involves coaching parents and caregivers about the connection between the activities used in storytime and the development of early literacy skills while encouraging similar activities at home. It is obvious how some storytime activities support these skills, but additional ideas are available in Ghoting and Martin-Díaz's books as well as through websites and blogs, such as Ghoting's blog, *Storytime Share* (http://www.earlylit.net/storytimeshare/). These ideas can also be incorporated into handouts that are shared with parents and caregivers that encourage them to continue using and advancing these skills and activities at home. How the elements are incorporated into your program, and how much of each, will depend on the ages of the children in the specific program.

⑥ Lapsit Storytime

Lapsit programs are held for caregivers and babies, generally around 3 months old to about 12 to 15 months old, with the child sitting in the caregiver's lap. Babies require close contact, and this interaction with the parent or caregiver supports the social and emotional development that serves as the foundation for other learning experiences. The librarian is more of a facilitator than a presenter of lapsit programming. If enough copies of a book are available, the presenter may read the book aloud, modeling reading for the caregivers while they turn the pages and point to objects on the page for their baby. Different books may be distributed for the caregiver to share one-on-one. This close reading is important because the baby's eyesight is still developing until about eight months of age, and babies can only focus on objects that are within 8 to 12 inches. For the same reason, select books that have simple shapes and bright bold colors that the baby's eyes can see. Mix in books that are illustrated with photographs, especially pictures of babies and parents.

Part of brain development relies on tasting and babies will stick books in their mouths, so board books, made of durable laminated cardboard, work well in lapsit storytime and can be cleaned between readers. The presenter can, of course, use other books, including big books, oversized books that are easier for a group to view, but board books are a staple of lapsit programming.

In addition to books, lapsit programs are filled with simple rhymes, music to sing and move to, fingerplay, and activities that engage the child, such as bouncing, peek-a-boo, and bubble blowing. Having a cohesive theme is less important than having repetition and helping children, and their parents, develop familiarity with songs and books. A standard structure for lapsit programming might include a welcoming song that is repeated each session, two or three short rhymes or songs that may be repeated several times with the rhythm being clapped, a book followed by two or three more songs or rhymes, a movement activity, a second book, and the closing song. With lapsit programming the activities move rapidly from one to another, but it is also important to be flexible and make adjustments to reflect the group's needs and the mood of the day.

Lapsit programs are generally about 20 minutes long with additional time allowed for socializing and interaction between caregivers and babies. Because each child has a caregiver, it may be tempting to work with large groups; however, lapsit programs are most effective when the group is small, limited to 6 to 10 pairs. This allows for fewer distractions and more interaction between the librarian and the caregiver. Before long the babies will be talkers and ready for a longer, more involved program.

Best Practices for Lapsit Programs

- Hold the program in a separate room. This reduces distractions and provides a safe environment.
- Limit attendance to infants and their caregivers, if possible. Older siblings will be distracted and distracting. If parents must bring siblings, offer an alternative program for them in another area.
- Use a lot of rhymes and songs, including books that are based on nursery rhymes and songs.
- Post the words to rhymes and songs on a white board or flip chart. If possible, provide caregivers with a handout to take home so that they can continue sharing the songs and rhymes with their baby.
- Limit the reading part of the program to one or two books. Remember that the baby's attention span is very short.

- Repeat the same welcoming song each week and include many of the same rhymes and songs that have been used previously. Repetition is important for babies.
- Expect some wandering. It's all right to allow babies to crawl or toddle around the room as long they are safe.
- Provide plenty of books for parents to check out for reading at home.

Board Books for Babies and Toddlers

A major component of lapsit programming is the board book, usually the first books presented to most babies. They are generally eight pages and are printed on heavy cardboard with a washable laminated coating. They are small enough to be held by a baby's little hands and some may even be cut into shapes like animals, fruit, or vehicles.

Babies should respond positively to the books they see so selecting engaging books is important. While some board books are edited versions of longer picture books, such as *The Carrot Seed* by Ruth Krauss, many more are created specifically for baby's interests. Be aware that some board books are published more for their commercial value and may be attractive to adults but uninteresting and unsuited for babies.

Look for board books with minimal text—a few words on each page—and large, plain typeface. Simple pictures on a plain background provide contrast that is appropriate for baby eyes. Familiar items and objects, such as faces, toys, and animals work well, as do books about concepts like colors and shapes that allow the reader to label objects for the baby. Lists of good board books are readily available in resources like *Great Books for Babies and Toddlers: More Than 500 Recommended Books for Your Child's First Three Years* by Kathleen Odean, and authors and illustrators like Tana Hoban, Byron Barton, and Rosemary Wells can be counted on to provide some tried-and-true selections. Some board books are available in Spanish and other languages. Star Bright Books (http://www .starbrightbooks.org/) offers an excellent assortment of board books in multiple languages with many featuring children from diverse cultures.

Toys for Babies and Toddlers

To some extent board books and soft books are toys for babies; they play with them while using small muscles and learning to manipulate pages. But many libraries also provide developmentally appropriate puzzles with large pieces, big blocks, and stuffed animals for babies to play with in the library. These items may also be incorporated into lapsit and toddler programs.

Busy boxes and sensory tables set out in the children's area offer opportunities to develop hand-eye coordination and fine motor skills. The toys should be safe, sturdy, and clean. As with board books, purchase items that can be washed or wiped down. Purchasing from educational and library supply companies usually means you will get sturdier pieces that last a long time.

Libraries, such as Cuyahoga County Public Library (Ohio), Springfield-Greene County Library (Missouri), and Salinas Public Library (California), also offer educational and developmental toys and musical instruments for circulation. The USA Toy Library Association (http://www.usatla.org/USA_Toy_Library_Association/Toy_ Library_Locations.html) maintains a list of toy lending libraries, many of which are in public libraries. (Often toy libraries that are not in a public library charge an annual membership fee.) Having toys available is also frequently an important service for children with learning and other disabilities. Palm Harbor (Florida) Public Library has an extensive collection of adaptive toys for children with disabilities.

Toy lending collections allow parents and caregivers to have access to a wide variety of educational toys without spending a lot of money as babies and toddlers quickly progress to new ones that use more challenging skills. The collections can be time intensive to maintain. When puzzles are checked out, pieces have to be accounted for on return. Sanitizing is important, and libraries that do not have a washing machine for cloth books, puppets, and other items made from fabric often choose not to include these items in the collection. Plastic toys can be washed in a soapy solution or sprayed with a child-safe disinfectant. Sources for toys for the library collection include Childcraft, Demco, Fisher-Price, and teacher supply stores like Lakeshore Learning.

Toddler Storytime

Storytimes for toddlers are generally planned for children about 15 months to 30 months. Toddlers are talking and are able to interact with the presenter and are curious and willing to try new things. Toddler storytimes can be a little longer, running up to 30 minutes in length. While they tend to wander around the program room, toddlers are also soaking up the vocabulary and concepts shared in storytime. Beginning to really be able to participate in the program, toddlers quickly learn the words to songs and rhymes and can play with sounds. The books shared will still be short, and early literacy skills can be reinforced through retellings of stories using flannel boards, puppets, and props.

Stories should have plots that are straightforward and involve only a few characters. Select books that encourage interaction, such as helping to make animal sounds. Point to key words on the page and cue the children to repeat phrases in cumulative tales like *Jump Frog, Jump* by Robert Kalan. Books like this may also have predictive illustrations that encourage the children to look closely to predict what the next animal will be in the sequence or surmise what might happen next. Clear illustrations against uncluttered backgrounds make it easier for toddlers to follow the story. It's also important to read clearly and at a relaxed pace, panning the book slowly while reading it so that every child sees the pictures. Involvement with the story adds to the child's love of books and stories and sets the stage for becoming lifelong readers.

Add longer books in to the program so that toddlers start to increase their attention span but intersperse the books with activities that release their energy. Interspersing songs and rhymes between stories refocuses toddlers on the program and allows them to play with words while learning concepts and following instructions. Fine motor skills are still developing so avoid fingerplay that requires tiny movements. Storytime may include a craft that serves as a memento or reminder of the program, but it should be simple and not require toddlers to use scissors or handle very small objects like wiggle eyes. Toddlers put a lot of things in their mouths but also can't manipulate small objects. Glue sticks, crayons, and stickers are staples of toddler craft times.

Toddlers are beginning to behave as a group, although the presenter will be a magnet for their interest. It's not uncommon to find a child playing with your shoelaces, mesmerized by your jewelry, or wanting to tell you about her or his new puppy. Children may also need to be reminded to keep to their own space. Some programs use carpet squares or mats to help maintain distance between each child in the group.

Best Practices for Toddler Programs

- Hold the program in a separate room. Toddlers like to wander. A caregiver or assistant can help redirect the toddler back to the group.
- Allow older siblings to attend if necessary, although they may find the program elements too simple and babyish.
- Use a lot of songs and repeat the same songs often.
- Post the words to rhymes and songs on a white board or flip chart, and if possible, provide caregivers with a handout to take home so that the toddler can learn the words.
- Use a theme to create a cohesive program that occurs between rituals. This helps cue the toddler when storytime is beginning and ending.
- Use no more than three books for most programs. If more stories are desired, tell them using a flannel board or puppets.
- Display books for parents to check out for reading at home.

Preschool Storytime

The public library storytime that comes to mind for most people is the preschool storytime for children ages three to five years old. These children are becoming increasingly independent and often attend storytime alone while their parent or caregiver waits in the library. Their speech ability is advancing and they are able to sit longer and listen to longer, more intricate stories. Often they will participate in the storytelling, whether invited to or not. The librarian may be the first non-parental adult with whom the child is building a relationship.

Storytimes can be structured in a variety of ways, and some decisions will be based on the goals of the program, available staffing, size of the group, and other factors such as the size and shape of the program room and whether the storytime space is out in the children's area or a separate room (figure 5.4). Librarians have to decide whether parents are required to stay with their child. Not having parents in the storytime room provides an independent experience for the child and conversation material for later, an important consideration when the child is with a stay-at-home parent all day. However, more and more today, parents are encouraged to stay so that they can help with their child and so that they can be involved in the development of early literacy skills. Although certainly handouts can be distributed with early literacy tips, it is more effective when parents and caregivers see the librarian modeling reading, hear and see how early literacy tips are shared, and participate in learning songs and rhymes.

In order to be ready to learn to read, and be ready for school, children need to know the alphabet by heart, recognize letters, have a good listening and speaking vocabulary, and be able to comprehend the stories they hear, including being able to predict actions, make connections between the story and their own lives or other stories they have heard, and answer simple questions about the story. Many other school readiness skills, such as using scissors and tracing shapes, impulse control, and being able to follow simple instructions, are also developed through storytime activities.

Most preschool storytimes are 30 to 40 minutes long, although some also allow extra time at the end for a craft or shared reading and browsing for books. Ritual beginnings—setting out mats, putting on name tags, a welcoming song or rhyme, or interaction with a puppet—make the program special and help children recognize that storytime is about

Figure 5.4. Storytime Room. *Photo courtesy of Joanna Taylor with the Las Vegas-Clark County Library District, Nevada*

to begin. The librarian should introduce herself and welcome the participants. This is also a good time to share a little bit of information about the early literacy skills that will be incorporated into the program, reinforcing the library's role in early childhood education. Two popular storytime starter rhymes are provided on page 107, but there are as many available as there are librarians.

Usually the preschool storytime program will include three books, but one or two more short books can be included. In general, it should not take more than about seven or eight minutes to read any book; longer stories are better suited for one-on-one reading or for reading to older children. Program themes work especially well with preschool storytimes and can help to ensure that a wide variety of different books, with different illustration styles and a rich range of vocabulary, are included.

Stories can be longer and plots can be more intricate. Keep in mind that the subject or theme of some picture books makes them more suited to school-aged children. Books like *Smoky Night* by Eve Bunting or Chris Van Allsburg's *Jumanji* are picture books by format, but the stories are too complex or mature for preschoolers in a group. It's still important to select books with good, clear illustrations, but the illustrations may be more detailed and sophisticated. Avoid using very small books like *Chicken Soup with Rice* by Maurice Sendak unless a big book is unavailable. The book is too small to share with a group. Many of these stories that were published in small format books are available on video or can be shared through a flannel board story or other oral or dramatic retellings. Preschool children also can enjoy retellings of folk and fairy tales, including some fractured fairytales or parodies of familiar stories. *Bubba the Cowboy Prince* by Helen Ketteman or *Rubia and the Three Osos* by Susan Middleton Elya will be easily recognized as versions of Cinderella and Goldilocks and the Three Bears, respectively. Include some nonfiction books like *A Butterfly Is Patient* by Dianna Hutts Aston or *Biggest, Strongest,*

Fastest by Steve Jenkins. Filled with factual information presented in a highly shareable format, nonfiction books often introduce vocabulary words not used in every day speaking and focus on subjects of interest to young children.

Best Practices for Preschool Programs

- Be sure that the room is set up to support storytime. Preschoolers will sit on the carpet and may stretch out on the floor. Parents and caregivers will appreciate chairs at the back of the room.
- Remind parents that they should participate as much as possible. They may also be learning the songs and rhymes, but are also modeling group participation skills for their child.
- Be prepared for behavior issues. Preschoolers can be temperamental and moody. Alter the program to use more activities and movement if the room is overflowing with energy.
- Encourage parents to take an unhappy child out of the program for a few minutes to calm down or return another day.
- Post the words to rhymes and songs on a white board or flip chart, and if possible, provide a handout that includes the words and also includes ideas for additional activities that support early literacy skills.
- Display books for use at home, and encourage parents to read different stories and to read each story several times.
- Suggest ways that parents and caregivers can engage their child in readings. Research has indicated that children benefit most from one-on-one reading when

A large format book like *How Rocket Learned to Read* by Tad Hills encourages preschool children to learn the alphabet and be eager to learn to read. It's a perfect book to share!

Figure 5.5. *How Rocket Learned to Read. Written and Illustrated by Tad Hills. Schwartz & Wade Books, ©2010*

they are actively involved in the story, answering questions and predicting action rather than passively listening (McGee and Schickedanz, 2007).

Storytime Features

Fingerplays and Action Rhymes

Fingerplays are short rhymes, four to eight stanzas, with actions. As the words are spoken, actions, gestures, movements, or pantomimes are performed. This engages children, helping them become active listeners who are following directions and playing with words while also developing fine motor skills and releasing some energy so that they can again focus on sitting and listening. Longer action rhymes usually involve larger body movements and actions like marching in place, stretching, or bending. In addition to supporting phonological awareness, fingerplays and action rhymes increase vocabulary and often introduce or reinforce concepts like body parts or counting.

Many fingerplays have no set melody but are spoken in a rhythmic, sing-song voice. Others, such as "I'm a Little Teapot" or "The Itsy-Bitsy Spider," have distinctive tunes. Fingerplays or rhymes are available from many cultures and in many languages. Some are based on nursery rhymes, while others are created specifically for a theme or concept. Some allow the children to add words and create new actions.

Some picture books are available based on the rhymes that are frequently shared in storytimes, allowing for an alternate presentation of the element. There are, for example, many illustrated versions of the very popular song "The Wheels on the Bus." Paul O. Zelinsky's version, with moveable parts, has become a classic. Pairing a reading of that book with a performance of the action rhyme reinforces the early literacy skills, and children can be encouraged to add additional verses. Another popular option is to pair the traditional action rhyme with a reading of a variant version, such as *The Seals on the Bus* by Lenny Hortis.

In addition to books like *Ring a Ring o' Roses*, mentioned earlier, there are many books of fingerplays and rhymes available for storytime use. Consider adding a few to the youth services professional collection so that they are readily available. One of the newer large compendiums is *1,000 Fingerplays and Action Rhymes: A Sourcebook and DVD* by Barbara A. Scott (2010), but many older books are still available. The Internet also offers a huge assortment of rhymes and fingerplays to match almost any program theme. Larger public libraries, such as King County (Washington), have posted rhymes online (http://wiki. kcls.org/tellmeastory/index.php/Main_Page), sometimes with video to show the actions, as part of parent and educator resources.

Music

Music makes storytime lively and adds to the educational experience by encouraging children to join in. Songs help children remember and retain concepts and develop gross and fine motor skills that support learning to read. Music also provides great opportunities to learn new words, including words in other languages. Some librarians begin and end the program with music, signaling the start and end of the program. A song like "Buenos días" can be shared in Spanish and English and is quickly learned. Sung as a

---

"BUENOS DÍAS"

Sing to the tune of "Are You Sleeping?" or "Frère Jacques."

Buenos días, buenos días
¿Cómo estás?, ¿Cómo estás?
Yo muy bien gracias, yo muy bien gracias.
¿Y usted? ¿Y usted?

round, the verses can be repeated, getting quieter and quieter until the group has settled down to listen. Soft music can help relax a group of toddlers, while energetic music allows preschoolers to shake their wiggles out. There are also many book versions of songs that include illustrations to highlight the words of the song. Some may even include a CD recording of the song that can be played before or after reading the book. Rosemary Wells collected and illustrated the Broadway musical tunes of Richard Rodgers and Oscar Hammerstein II in *Getting to Know You*, while "This Old Man" gets a jazzy makeover in *This Jazz Man* by Karen Ehrhardt.

One advantage to working with children is that they enjoy singing and making music without regard to voice quality—theirs or yours. Even those who can't carry a tune can enjoy singing along. Recorded music can be used for convenience, to introduce the songs of various children's performers or as an alternative to a cappella singing without having to play an instrument. There are songs and music to enrich any program, and performers range from solo acts to large groups, singing songs in every musical genre. Some songs are familiar nursery songs and rhymes set to music, while others are original songs. Sharing recorded music also promotes the library's audiovisual collection, and parents should be encouraged to borrow circulating materials or download music from the library's database.

Movement songs, such as the "Hokey Pokey" or "If You're Happy and You Know It," allow the children to move about in an organized fashion as a break from sitting still. Playing instruments and tapping out the beat of a song helps with recognizing rhythm and supports the early literacy skill of phonological awareness, recognizing the smaller sounds that make up words. Often musical instruments will be included in the program, allowing children to use simple percussion instruments like bells, shakers, and rhythm sticks to follow the beat. Child-friendly instruments can be purchased from educational supply stores like Lakeshore Learning (http://www.lakeshorelearning.com/). With older preschool children, instruments might be made as part of the program. Shakers can be created from plastic eggs, while empty oatmeal containers become great drums. A handful of uncooked rice in a paper towel tube can become a rain stick to accompany a story about the rain forest.

Award-Winning Children's Performers

- Bill Harley
- Cathy Fink and Marcy Marxer
- Tom Chapin
- Joe McDermott
- Laurie Berkner

Piggyback Songs

Because music strengthens the ability to learn concepts, piggyback songs are a popular part of storytime programs. Piggyback songs add new lyrics that have been tailored to fit a particular theme or concept to an existing, and usually very familiar, melody. Many are available on the Internet, in songbooks, and on recordings. There are even picture books, such as *The Croaky Pokey* by Ethan Long, which uses the "Hokey Pokey" with an amphibious twist, or *There Was an Old Pirate Who Swallowed a Fish* by Jennifer Ward, where a pirate ends up eating his own ship! Many librarians have noted that almost any words can be used with tunes like "The Hokey Pokey," "I'm a Little Teapot," "Old McDonald," and "B-I-N-G-O."

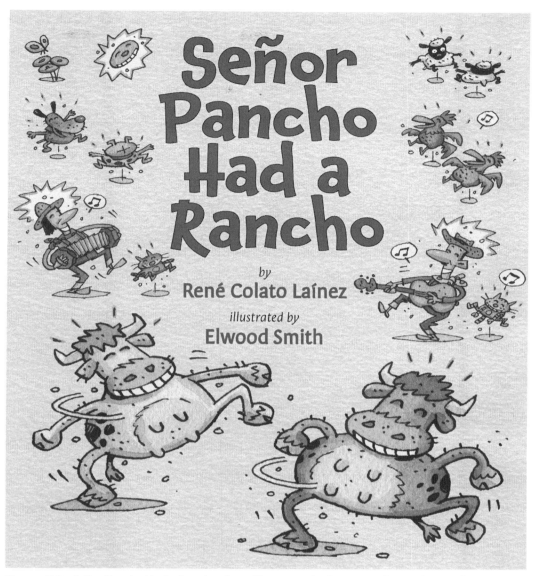

Figure 5.6. *Señor Pancho Had a Rancho. Cover illustration for* Señor Pancho Had a Rancho *copyright © 2013 by Elwood Smith. Used by permission of Holiday House.*

SAMPLE PIGGYBACK SONG

Hello song (sing to the tune of "Are You Sleeping?" or "Frère Jacques")

Hello, children. Hello, children. (*Substitute each child's name if desired for additional verses.*)
How are you? How are you?
We're so glad to see you.
We're so glad to see you.
Here today, here today.

Children, and parents or caregivers, are often already familiar with and comfortable singing "Frère Jacques," "The Farmer in the Dell," or "Mary Had a Little Lamb," so they can readily join in to sing a hello song as the opening storytime ritual, a song to learn colors, or, like *Señor Pancho Had a Rancho* by René Colato Laínez (figure 5.6), a song with Spanish and English words for animals.

While it's generally easy to find piggyback songs to suit the program's needs, many librarians write their own. Katie Fitzgerald, formerly a librarian in the Washington, DC, system, offers some tips on her blog, *Story Time Secrets* (http://storytimesecrets.blogspot.com/), which are provided in the following list.

Writing a Piggyback Song

1. Stick to the rhythm of the original song.
2. Use imperfect rhymes sparingly.
3. Don't overuse tunes.
4. Have a purpose.

For older children, piggyback songs provide a way for them to play with language, making up their own additional verses or retelling the story with flannel board pieces.

Storytelling without a Book

There are many elements that can be included in storytimes, but a couple of others that are integral to public library programs allow the presenter to share a story without also sharing a book. True storytelling, based on the oral tradition, involves memorizing a story and knowing it so well that it is presented in a theatrical way without reading or showing illustrations. In fact, the story may not be based on a book; or, if the story is one that has also been retold in a published book, the storyteller will adapt it to make it her own. Public libraries sometimes hire professional storytellers, although they are probably best reserved for programs for older children and families. Younger children can pay attention to dramatic tellings for short periods, but most are not able to focus for a full storytelling concert. Librarians who are interested in storytelling can successfully incorporate a shorter story, especially a fairy tale or other story that may already be familiar to the preschoolers, as one element of a storytime.

Flannel Boards

Flannel boards allow the librarian to share a story or rhyme in a different way, often including members of the audience in the presentation and the sequencing of pieces being placed on the flannel board. The set shown in figure 5.7 can be used for retelling classic tales like *Stone Soup* or contemporary stories like *The Wolf's Chicken Stew* by Keiko Kasza.

Although the format refers to flannel, there are actually many ways to create flannel board stories. Pieces are prepared ahead of time to show the major characters and items in a story. As the story or rhyme is recited the pieces are placed on a board. The board is covered in flannel and figures made from felt or with Velcro backing will stick to it. Similarly a metal board can be used with magnetic pieces. Both the flannel board and the story pieces can be purchased through teacher supply stores, but both are also easily made. A great use for discarded books is to cut out pictures to create flannel board pieces. Glue the pictures to tag board and add a small piece of Velcro to the back of each. Store the set in

Figure 5.7. Flannel Board Pieces. *Courtesy Tom Green County Library System, San Angelo, Texas; Sally Meyers, Children's Librarian*

a manila envelope for an inexpensive, custom story set. Alternately, pieces can be cut from felt using a die-cut machine, or die-cut pieces can be purchased from a teacher store or from companies like Little Folk Visuals (http://www.littlefolkvisuals.com) or Lakeshore Learning. Blogs like *Miss Meg's Storytime* include flannel board ideas and patterns in the Flannel Friday section (http://missmegsstorytime.com/category/flannel-friday/).

While the method seems rather old school in a world filled with technology, children are fascinated by the magic of the flannel board. The pieces are held up for the audience to see while the presenter speaks a line or two of the story, then places the piece on the board. Hearing the words while looking at the item reinforces vocabulary, but children also begin to understand the sequence of events as the pieces are placed on the board in order. The telling can become a hands-on learning experience by distributing the pieces to members of the group and having them come up at the appropriate time to place the piece on the board.

Puppets

Puppets have many uses in storytime, which may be the only place children regularly see, and interact, with them in today's high-technology environment. As was mentioned previously, some librarians use a puppet as a mascot to introduce storytime and gently remind children about storytime etiquette and behavior. Check sources like Folkmanis (http://www.folkmanis.com/) for high-quality puppets that make great mascots.

Short puppet shows can be incorporated into a storytime but should be based on familiar folktales or follow simple plots. Folkmanis provides free copies of short scripts for two puppets that can easily be performed without a stage. Lakeshore Learning (http://www.lakeshorelearning.com/) and other teacher supply stores offer an array of puppet types and kits that include all of the puppets for a program.

More commonly, puppets are used in storytimes to help with songs and rhymes. The presenter may use a glove puppet, sometimes called a mitt puppet, with Velcro pieces to

Figure 5.8. Glove Puppet. *Courtesy Tom Green County Library System, San Angelo, Texas; Sally Meyers, children's librarian*

share a finger rhyme like "Five Little Monkeys," using a crocodile hand puppet or an uncovered hand to "snap" the monkeys one by one. These glove puppets can be purchased but are easily made with inexpensive knit gloves, craft pompom balls, and adhesive Velcro pieces. Small finger puppets that actually fit over each finger can be held up and then folded down when singing songs like "Old McDonald Had a Farm." Other puppets, such as a spider, can be used when singing "The Itsy Bitsy Spider" or held for emphasis when reading a book about an animal or character that might not be immediately familiar to the children. The one shown in figure 5.8 is used by librarian Sally Meyers, Tom Green County (Texas) Library, for her welcoming song "The More We Get Together," but it can also be used for many other songs and rhymes.

Children can be encouraged to participate in the story through the use of stick puppets or paper bag puppets that are either premade or that they make for themselves, with help from a caregiver, during a craft part of the program. Stick puppets are usually made by coloring a cardboard character and adhering it with tape or glue to a craft or Popsicle stick. Paper bag puppets, similarly, are created by coloring the pieces of the character and gluing the parts to a lunch-sized paper bag. Many craft sites for preschool children offer free downloadable patterns. Additionally, these are inexpensive and easy to make at home, allowing the children to put on their own shows.

Props and Realia

Props can also be used to help focus children's attention and clarify vocabulary during storytime. If a book like *The Giant Carrot* by Jan Peck, a retelling of a Russian folktale,

Figure 5.9. Giant Carrot Prop. *Photo by Konrad Odell*

is being shared, a plastic or plush carrot (figure 5.9) can be displayed for the children to touch. Smaller items can be passed around the group. A large plastic egg, a fire fighter's hat, or a tiara are just a few props that are commonly used to highlight stories, rhymes, and books and add to the magic of a program.

Key Points

Early literacy programs in public libraries are among the most popular and valued of our services. Reading to young children is vital to their educational development and encourages them to become lifelong readers. Planning these programs varies by age and often includes providing literacy tips and modeling reading techniques for parents and caregivers. Reading aloud to a group of children is different from reading one-on-one and requires planning, practice, and the inclusion of activities that help refocus attention and reinforce the material presented. Storytime is also one of the most enjoyable parts of a children's librarian's job!

- A child's brain is developing the most rapidly during the first three years of life.
- Early literacy skills and practices can easily be incorporated into storytimes.
- Storytimes include more than reading books aloud.
- Best practices suggest that librarians employ music, poetry, flannel boards, and other techniques to engage children in early literacy learning.

Programming starts with infants and preschool children but continues through the elementary grades. While the objectives of most programs are educational and intended to help children discover library resources and read, they are also fun and entertaining. In the next chapter we will look at the variety of programs libraries offer for school-age children.

References

Adams, Marilyn Jager. 1990. *Beginning to Read: Thinking and Learning about Print*. Cambridge, MA: MIT Press.

Baker, Scott K., Deborah C. Simmons, and Edward J. Kame'enui. 1997. "Vocabulary Acquisition: Research Bases." In *What Reading Research Tells Us about Children with Diverse Learning Needs: Bases and Basics*, edited by Deborah C. Simmons and Edward J. Kame'enui, 183–217. Mahwah, NJ: Erlbaum.

Bauer, Caroline Feller. 1995. *New Handbook for Storytellers*. Chicago: ALA Editions.

Flint Public Library. 2008. *Ring a Ring o' Roses: Fingerplays for Preschool Children*. Flint, MI: Flint Public Library.

Freeman, Judy, and Caroline Feller Bauer. 2015. *The Handbook for Storytime Programs*. Chicago: ALA Editions.

Ghoting, Saroj Nadkarni, and Pamela Martin-Díaz. 2006. *Early Literacy Storytimes @ Your Library: Partnering with Caregivers for Success*. Chicago: American Library Association.

Ghoting, Saroj Nadkarni, and Pamela Martin-Díaz. 2013. *Storytimes For Everyone!: Developing Young Children's Language and Literacy*. Chicago: American Library Association.

Marsico Institute for Early Learning and Literacy. 2013. Home page. Marsico Institute. University of Denver. Morgridge College of Education. Accessed June 11, 2013. http://www.du.edu/marsicoinstitute/.

McGee, Lea M., and Judith A. Schickedanz. 2007. "Repeated Interactive Read-Alouds in Preschool and Kindergarten." *Reading Teacher* 60, no. 8: 742–751.

Miss Meg's Storytime. http://missmegsstorytime.com/.

Reach Out and Read. 2012. "Research Findings." http://www.reachoutandread.org/why-we-work/research-findings.

Resources Mentioned in This Chapter

Aston, Dianna Hutts. 2011. *A Butterfly Is Patient*. San Francisco: Chronicle Books.

Bunting, Eve. 1994. *Smoky Night*. San Diego: Harcourt.

Ehrhardt, Karen. 2006. *This Jazz Man*. Orlando: Harcourt.

Elya, Susan Middleton. 2010. *Rubia and the Three Osos*. New York: Disney/Hyperion.

Hills, Tad. 2010. *How Rocket Learned to Read*. New York: Schwartz & Wade.

Hortis, Lenny. 2000. *The Seals on the Bus*. New York: Henry Holt.

Jenkins, Steve. 1995. *Biggest, Strongest, Fastest*. New York: Ticknor & Fields.

Kalan, Robert. 1991. *Jump Frog, Jump*. New York: Greenwillow.

Kasza, Keiko. 1987. *The Wolf's Chicken Stew*. New York: Putnam.

Ketteman, Helen. 1997. *Bubba the Cowboy Prince*. New York: Scholastic.

Krauss, Ruth. 1945. *The Carrot Seed*. New York: Harper.

Laínez, René Colato. 2013. *Señor Pancho Had a Rancho*. New York: Holiday House.

Long, Ethan. 2011. *The Croaky Pokey*. New York: Holiday House.

Odean, Kathleen. 2003. *Great Books for Babies and Toddlers: More Than 500 Recommended Books for Your Child's First Three Years*. New York: Ballantine.

Peck, Jan. 1998. *The Giant Carrot*. New York: Dial.

Scott, Barbara A. 2010. *1,000 Fingerplays and Action Rhymes: A Sourcebook and DVD*. Chicago: American Library Association.

Sendak, Maurice. 1962. *Chicken Soup with Rice*. New York: Harper.

Storytime Secrets. http://storytimesecrets.blogspot.com/.

USA Toy Library Association. http://www.usatla.org/.

Van Allsburg, Chris. 1981. *Jumanji*. Boston: Houghton Mifflin.

Ward, Jennifer. 2012. *There Was an Old Pirate Who Swallowed a Fish*. New York: Two Lions.

Wells, Rosemary. 2002. *Getting to Know You*. New York: Harper Mifflin.

Zelinsky, Paul O. 1990. *The Wheels on the Bus*. New York: Dutton.

Additional Readings and Resources

Bauer, Caroline Feller. 1993. *New Handbook for Storytellers*. Chicago: American Library Association.

Carlson, Ann. Spanish Translation by Ana-Elba Pavo. 2005. *Flannelboard Stories for Infants and Toddlers*. Bilingual ed. Chicago: American Library Association.

Cottrell, Megan. 2013. "Toy Libraries: A Place to Play." *American Libraries* 44, nos. 11/12 (November/December): 14–15.

Diamant-Cohen, Betsy, Melanie A. Hetrick, and Celia Yitzhak. 2013. *Transforming Preschool Storytime: A Modern Vision and a Year of Programs*. Chicago: American Library Association.

Feinberg, Sandra. 2007. *The Family-Centered Library Handbook*. New York: Neal-Schuman Publishers.

Freeman, Judy, and Caroline Feller Bauer. 2015. *The Handbook for Storytime Programs*. Chicago: American Library Association.

Hennepin County Library. "Birth to Six." http://www.hclib.org/BirthTo6/.

MacMillan, Kathy, and Christine Kirker. 2014. *Baby Storytime Magic: Active Early Literacy through Bounces, Rhymes, Tickles and More*. Chicago: American Library Association.

MacMillan, Kathy, and Christine Kirker. 2012. *Multicultural Storytime Magic*. Chicago: American Library Association.

Marks, Robbie Bravman. 2006. *Early Literacy Programs and Practices at Colorado Public Libraries*. Colorado Department of Education. http://www.lrs.org/documents/closer_look/early_lit.pdf.

Nash, Madeline J. 1997. "Fertile Minds." *Time* 149, no. 5 (February 3): 48–53.

Odean, Kathleen. 2005. "Choosing Effective Board Books." *Book Links* 14, no. 3 (January): 49–52.

Orozco, José Luis, and Elisa Kleven. 1997. *Diez deditos = Ten Little Fingers: And Other Play Rhymes and Action Songs from Latin America*. New York: Dutton Children's Books.

CHAPTER 6

Programs for Elementary Children

IN THIS CHAPTER

▷ Using programs to bring children and families into the library

▷ Encouraging reading and book discussion through educational programs

▷ Introducing children to ideas, new topics, and people through enrichment programs

▷ Working with children who spend a great deal of their out-of-school time in the library

▷ Distinguishing library programs through connections to reading and books, library resources, and formal and informal learning

---

About Programming for Children

CHILDREN'S LIBRARIANS PROVIDE a lot more programming than librarians serving other age groups generally do. A great deal of the programming is targeted to school-age children who visit the library outside of school hours and during the summer. Some programming may be provided during the traditional school day for homeschooling families or during class trips to the library, but most takes place after school, during holiday breaks, and over the summer.

Out-of-school time makes up a large part of every child's day. This time includes the hours after school, on weekends, and during the summer and other school holidays. While many young people are enrolled in organized activities, such as afterschool child care, or are with their parents or grandparents, as many as 25% of school-age children are home alone. While other community organizations offer programs that provide enriching experiences for children, it is the intentional outcomes and the connection to reading, books, and other sources of information that separate library programs from

CHECK IT OUT!

Tomás and the Library Lady by Pat Mora and Raúl Colón is a picture book biography of Tomás Rivera that demonstrates how the library and a special relationship a young boy had with the librarian help the impoverished child of migrant workers become a successful author and educator.

Figure 6.1. *Tomás and the Library Lady. Copyright Pat Mora; illustrations by Raul Colón. Knopf Books for Young Readers, 1997.*

other afterschool activities. Year-round programming for children also contributes to the library's visibility in the community, enhances community support, and can increase library use and circulation of materials. Although it can appear to other staff that children's librarians are simply having fun, these programs have serious objectives, require careful planning, and can provide excellent outcomes for the library and the participants. Programs in the public library also enhance the library's role as a place for lifelong learning and as a community hub.

Broadly, programs for elementary students can be classified as educational or enrichment. Some library programs, such as providing space and materials to play chess or other board games, may appear to be purely recreational, but even those programs provide an educational or enrichment component.

Often the best library programs will encompass factors that educate children while also enriching their lives and providing fun. In fact, "brain research suggests that fun is not just beneficial to learning but, by many reports, required for authentic learning and long-term memory" (Slade, 2010). Some librarians also distinguish between literature-based and non-literature-based programming. While programs may be based on books, such as holding a Harry Potter party or hosting a book discussion, books and other materials should be available and displayed for checkout at virtually every program, making every program literature based. Remember that part of the librarian's job is to encourage reading and use of library materials.

⑥ Educational Programming

Book Discussion Groups

Book discussion groups, sometimes labeled book clubs, bring people together to talk about books. They help create a community of readers and foster the library's role as a community space and place. Children are motivated to read more when they have opportunities to share their reading with others and to voice their opinion about their reading in a comfortable environment. They also encourage communication between generations and with peers.

Book groups can vary in audience and purpose, ranging from homeschool families looking for opportunities for kids to interact with other kids, to mother/daughter book clubs, to groups especially for boys. They may focus on a theme, such as a graphic novel book club or a mystery book discussion group. Many public libraries are also offering online book discussion groups or a combination where the group interacts online between monthly get-togethers.

The target ages for these programs in the children's department will most commonly be tweens, children ages 9 or 10 and up, and teens, so that the participants have the maturity and skills required to read a book and then talk about it. Decide how frequently the group will meet and any parameters that need to be in place. Many groups meet once a month to allow time to read in between, but during the summer a group might meet weekly.

Usually these are informal gatherings that have few rules or requirements. Everyone is simply talking about a book, hearing opinions from others, and exploring issues related to the story. Ideally everyone has read the book beforehand but that is not always the case, especially when working with young people. Keep the group small so that everyone will have a chance to talk. Popular topics for series book discussion include the Wimpy Kid books, the Percy Jackson titles, and the Magic Tree House, in part because, although the participants may not have read every book in the series, they will have read some. Sometimes the program will include food related to the book or an art or craft activity that ties back to the story or characters. A new facet to book groups includes inviting the author to hold a virtual visit with the group through electronic media like Skype or online chatting.

Think about how books will be selected. Some libraries encourage the group participants to make the selections and vote on the reading choice. Although some participants may purchase their own copy of the book, the library needs to have multiple copies available, so titles that are available in paperback work best. This is another reason focusing on a series is popular!

The librarian will guide the discussion but let the kids take control. Keep in mind that not everyone participating will have actually read the book, so it is a good idea to have a few questions ready to start the conversation or to move it along if there is a lull. Many publishers offer discussion guides for books they publish and larger libraries may even post their own guides on their website.

Some book discussion programs are ongoing, meeting regularly and open to all, with participants coming and going depending on their schedules and interests. They generally run from an hour to 90 minutes, with about 15 minutes for relaxing, introductions, and getting settled. The discussion may last 30 to 45 minutes with some additional time for snacks or an activity. Remember that a major purpose for the book groups is to encourage more reading, so be sure to display related books for check out at the end of the session. And, of course, remind the participants that they are welcome at the next meeting.

After-School Clubs

Clubs can focus on a multitude of subjects, including writing, science, the arts, cooking, or a series of books. Many libraries set up clubs as a series of weekly or biweekly interconnected programs that build on skills and activities from previous weeks. Although clubs offer consistent, consecutive programming, as opposed to one-shot events, the same children may or may not attend each week. Registering participants and limiting the number that can enroll encourages attendance and makes it easier to prepare materials, although some libraries have open enrollment and make adjustments for new children who show up.

The clubs often have catchy names like Library Animators or After-School Cool Club. Some are simply called After-School Fun. Meetings generally last 45 minutes and

IDEAS FOR LIBRARY CLUBS

- Anime
- Art
- Board games
- Chess
- Comedy
- Legos
- Photography
- Writing

activities may include reading a picture book that is intended for older kids, a hands-on activity related to the club's theme, and a snack. As with all programming, books and other media should be displayed for checkout.

Some people may ask what connection there is between libraries and play activities like games, anime, or Legos. Research demonstrates a strong connection between play and literacy. "Play paves the way for learning" (Klebanoff, 2009: 24). Literacy and library resources are easily incorporated into play programs by reading part of a book, sharing poetry, and displaying books for checkout.

Participation in library-based clubs supports developmental assets like positive peer influence and constructive use of time. Often the participants are able to play a major role in planning the weekly activities and can assume leadership roles while working with other club members. The activities, and participation in the club, provide a stimulating environment for learning while also engaging them in activities and interactions that are enjoyable and relaxing. They also drive traffic to the children's department and stimulate circulation.

Recreational and Enrichment Programs

After-School Programs

After-school, or more accurately, out-of-school, time makes up a large part of every child's day. This time includes the hours after school, on weekends, and during the summer and other school holidays. Because so many children are on their own for a few hours, and many will be in the library anyway, they offer a built-in audience for library programs.

Although public libraries practically invented after-school programs, possibly out of the need to provide something for latchkey children to do, some librarians express concern that this programming is costly and takes staff away from other library services. While staff time, fees for presenters, supplies, and space needs certainly must be considered, they can be factored into budgets. Many programs require little or no expense beyond staff time.

Other staff and administrators may oppose the programs because they believe that promoting reading is the responsibility of the school system or that public library programs are redundant (for example, parks and recreation offers art programs) or are duplicating the work of other organizations, including for-profit and nonprofit businesses such as movie theaters, the symphony, and martial arts studios. However, both literature-based and non-literature-based programs offer opportunities for children to explore new interests and discover library resources. The families of many of the children who attend public library programs, such as puppet shows and art activities, may not be able to afford to pay for those programs elsewhere.

After-school programs provide opportunities for children to learn something new, discover library resources, and expand their interests. Most often participation is voluntary on the part of the participants; unlike school they are not required by the institution to be present. It is the intentional outcomes and the connection to independent learning, reading, books, and other sources of information that separate library programs for other after-school activities. Programs attract many library users and nonusers to the library and, once in the library, the library staff can offer additional library services or increase the patron's awareness of services.

Arts and Crafts and Hands-On Programming

There is a strong sentiment, held by many educators, parents, and child development specialists, that children in our society are not sufficiently exposed to the arts—both decorative and performance arts. Many schools have been forced to cut or severely reduce arts programs, and an emphasis on testing and core requirements often leaves little time or money for the arts. Arts and craft activities provided in public libraries may supplement a reading program or presentation or be offered as a stand-alone program. These programs expose children to the arts and may offer children hands-on opportunities to learn how to manipulate clay, create origami characters, take photographs, or try various drawing techniques.

A recent type of programming, often aimed at tweens and younger teens, revolves around games and game playing. Again this can appear to have little relationship to libraries and learning, but in fact, game playing "contributes to early literacy development by increasing attention span, memory, creativity, and language and vocabulary skills. It also lays the foundation for logical mathematical thinking, scientific reasoning, and problem solving" (Klebanoff, 2009: 24).

Other hands-on programs such as Lego labs, which allow participants to hone engineering skills and stretch their imagination, and bring boys, a hard-to-reach group, into the library. By displaying books about Legos, engineering, building, and bridges, reading is encouraged and circulation increases. Free-play board games are a little old school by some thinking but offer opportunities for critical thinking, reading game cards, and interacting with peers. Some libraries sponsor family games nights that bring families into the library for an enriching experience. Chess, a game that exercises both sides of the brain and teaches strategic thinking, has enjoyed a resurgence among young people in libraries. Every type of game and play, whether on a computer, a board, or with pieces, probably has several books written about it and strategies for improving skills—books that kids can be encouraged to read. The library collection probably even includes fiction titles like *Chasing Vermeer* by Blue Balliett, in which puzzles like pentominoes play an important part in the plot, or *Alex and the Wednesday Chess Club* by Janet Wong. Books that feature games can be read aloud or booktalked as part of the program and offered for borrowing.

The advent of Makerspace programs is revolutionizing programming in many libraries, turning the program room into community centers for creating. The high-interest, hands-on content encourages science learning. Often also called DIY (or do-it-yourself) centers, creative spaces, media labs, or hacker fairs, participants make something but are also encouraged to attempt additional inventing and tinkering. The library provides space, online and analog, or physical, tools, computer hardware and software and, in some cases, 3D printers and scanners. Makerspaces can come in a variety of sizes and shapes, depending on the space and resources available at the library. Regardless of the space, the program brings patrons of all ages into the library for a collaborative learning experience.

Libraries with limited space or staff may provide "make-and-take" art projects that allow participants to stop by during a period of time and enjoy creating something to take home. For example, parents might assist their child to make a paper bag rabbit puppet for Easter or a dreidel for Hanukkah. Set up a table with the required materials—construction paper, crayons, glue sticks, and decorative items like wiggle eyes for puppets

MAKE-IT TAKE-IT CRAFT

Supplies needed:

8 1/2 × 11 pieces of paper to make an origami boat

Photocopies of cow, donkey, sheep, pig, and a tiny mouse patterns

Plastic drinking straws cut into three-inch pieces

Safety scissors, scotch tape, and crayons

Steps:

Fold the origami boat.

Color the animals and cut them out.

Tape a piece of straw on back of animals.

Retell the story while placing each animal in the boat.

Figure 6.2. *Who Sank the Boat? Tom Green County Library System, San Angelo, Texas; Sally Meyers, children's librarian*

or stickers—and post a sheet with instructions. Display books for checkout nearby. An easy way to count participation for statistics is to count the number of items that can be made with the materials provided. Few children will make more than one craft.

Include a "take, then make" craft in storytimes for older children for an easy and stress-free way to extend the program at home. Prepare kits ahead of time (the preparation work is a great job for teen volunteers) by placing the parts for stick puppets or pieces to create a mask in a plastic zip-lock baggie with instructions for parents and caregivers to help the child make at home. For example, the items in figure 6.2 are used to make stick puppet figures and an origami boat so that children can retell the story *Who Sank the Boat?* by Pamela Allen or make up new ones. This type of play activity helps children learn to follow instructions, use tools that enhance hand-eye coordination, and use small muscles. The best crafts also allow for creativity and originality, so these take-home crafts should be as open and flexible as possible.

Puppet Shows

Puppetry is another art that is maintained in our society primarily through public libraries. While puppetry is often incorporated into preschool storytimes, school-age children also enjoy watching a good puppet show or helping to create a puppet show for presentation to others (figure 6.3).

Public libraries provide a forum for shows by professional puppet troupes but some also establish their own puppet team, scripting and producing their own shows. Resources like *One-Person Puppet Plays* by Denise Anton Wright or *Worlds of Shadow: Teaching with Shadow Puppetry* by David Wisniewski and Donna Wisniewski provide guidance and scripts. *Practical Puppetry A to Z* by Carol R. Exner covers everything from various types of puppets to building your own stage or creating body puppets and aprons to perform without a stage. Puppets can be purchased commercially from companies like Folkmanis (http://www.folkmanis.com), although many librarians prefer to make their own. A practical tip shared by many librarians suggests that Goodwill and other thrift stores often have puppets at heavily discounted prices. School supply stores like Lakeshore Learning (http://www.lakeshorelearning.com) sell specialty puppets like community helpers, as well as washable puppets for kids to use.

When space permits some libraries set up a kid-sized puppet stage in the children's department and provide hand puppets for ad hoc use by patrons. Plans for building your

Figure 6.3. Puppet Show. *Library Larry Live at Denton Public Library, Texas; photo courtesy of Kerol Harrod*

own stage from PVC piping are available from a number of sources, including a set of plans from Puppets in Education at http://www.play-script-and-song.com/pipe-puppet -stage.html. Display books of children's scripts in case the children want to check some out or use the scripts to present their own puppet show. Combine this opportunity with a craft program where the children can make their own puppets.

Movies

Showing movies may seem out of character for a library. After all, children can readily see movies at home or in theaters. Library programming that features or includes film offers the opportunity to view movies as part of a group, to discuss the movie, learn about books and other library resources on the same subject as the movie, and create crafts or art activities that were inspired by the film.

While children may have easy access to commercially produced films that are shown on television or can be purchased at Walmart, there are many outstanding movies that receive limited distribution. Films that are based on children's books provide a great bridge to reading the book. Educational or informational films provide an interesting supplement to a program on the same subject. For example, show a nature film on sharks and then make a shark craft as in figure 6.4. Movies also offer good entertainment for library parties or "shut-in" programs.

Some libraries host film festivals that last throughout the day or feature movies over a period of several weeks. Organizations like the Coalition for Quality Children's Media and their Kids First! program (http://www.kidsfirst.org/about-us/) work with libraries and other organizations to review films, host festivals, and help to put films by small producers into the hands of viewers. They also welcome kid reviewers. Libraries can encourage young filmmakers by hosting programs that help children create and show their own movies. Software programs like iMovie or Animoto can be used to create movies with or without original camera images. Another popular film program encourages participants to create

Figure 6.4. Tween Movie Advertisement. *Courtesy Pflugerville Public Library, Texas*

book trailers for their favorite books. These short commercials can then be shown on the library's website to encourage others to read a book.

For most commercial movies to be shown in the library, you will need a public performance license. If you rent a film from a commercial company for public performance the cost of the license is usually included in the fee. This is different from renting a movie from Netflix or your local video store. Licenses are also rarely included in the purchase of DVDs or streaming film for the library to circulate to patrons. An annual blanket movie license is generally priced based on the number of registered patrons. Be sure to check that the license covers the major studios that you want to use as not every studio participates in the licensing process. Movie Licensing USA (http://www.movlic.com) is one company that works with a lot of libraries and schools.

Older movies, such as Laurel and Hardy, may be in the public domain. You still need to have a copy to show, of course, but sites like Desert Island Films (http://www.desertislandfilms.com) can help you determine if the film you want to show is free of copyright restrictions. Some libraries still have access to old 16 mm films and projectors and this "old-school" technology can be used for an interesting program featuring classic comedies and other movies from the early days of cinema.

Presenters and Special Guests

Presenters, performers, and speakers bring the world to the library. These programs can focus on almost any topic and discipline. They can consist of lecture and demonstration, or they might include an interactive component where the children attending the program get to try something new, enjoy a brief lesson, or handle objects and artifacts. The primary considerations are to select a subject that will be of interest to the children in attendance and to pick a presenter who is skilled in presenting to a group of children.

Artists can discuss their craft and their career, giving children insight into potential paths for formal and informal study. Dance groups might provide a sample of their art or teach specific styles. Singers and performers often talk about their instruments and may even bring instruments for the children to play as they take part in performing a piece of music. For many children, the performance by a noted children's singer or by a theater troupe will be their first experience with live performance, and they learn to be members of a theatrical audience.

Art and music programs can introduce diverse cultures to children. For example, Taiko drummers bring part of Japanese culture to children at the library. After the performance participants can browse through fiction and nonfiction books about Japan and Japanese culture and about music and drumming. They may also check out musical recordings for family listening. Performers like Kim Lehman, storyteller and musician, seen in figure 6.5, performed at the Murphy Memorial Library in Livingston (Texas) but also talked to the children about how to play an instrument and demonstrate techniques for creating music.

Many of the programs are educational, with organizations like Mad Science (http://www.madscience.org/) showing the audience how cool science can be. The audience is entertained while they are also learning how science works in the real world. Author programs may include a writing component that encourages children to create poetry or write a short story. Cooking programs may have a chef teaching children about nutrition and food sources while demonstrating how to make after-school snacks. Anthropologists

Figure 6.5. Kim Lehman Performing.
Photo by Nita Kuehn

and geologists bring bones to talk about fossils and dinosaurs, while ornithologists show off the birds kids can see in their neighborhood.

Magic shows are popular in libraries and the best magicians wow the kids while entertaining adults. Many magicians who work with libraries and schools incorporate reading and the magic of books into the program. Often the magicians learned their first tricks from magic books, so be sure to display materials from the collection.

A major difference between presenter-led programs and the other programming that the librarian and her staff lead is in control. Once the librarian has introduced the guest presenter or speaker, that person is in control of the content and quality of the program. Therefore, it is critical that the librarian has done all the appropriate planning and preparation to ensure that the program works well.

Presenters may be paid or they may be volunteers, depending on the program and the community. Publicly funded organizations and nonprofits, like museums, symphonies, and theaters, may have an outreach component that brings programming to groups of children in schools and libraries. High school teachers or university professors often volunteer their time to talk about a topic they normally teach. Hobbyists, like stamp collectors or birders, may offer to share their interests with children in the library. Businesses, such as a karate studio or a photography store, might be willing to offer a short class or demonstration for the advertising potential and community goodwill.

Volunteers can add a lot to programs but be sure that the expectations for the program are clearly understood. Not everyone is experienced with working with children or comfortable in handling potential problems like inattentiveness or distractions that may arise. Be clear about the content and how much time the presenter will have for the program. Discuss how the children generally behave and interact with each other and the presenter. Have an agenda that outlines what will happen when and talk about circumstances where staff will step in to assist. Often volunteer presenters are not comfortable stopping to ask a disruptive patron to step out of the room. Additionally be up front about any library regulations about advertising or selling during and after programs. It may be permissible for the yoga studio to leave flyers on a table but not okay for them to collect names and contact information for follow-up on classes.

Sometimes when services are being donated, the presenter may not be as committed to showing up if a scheduling conflict arises or they are distracted by other things in their lives. As part of the invitation and confirmation process, be sure that the volunteer understands that the program will be advertised to the community and the volunteer will be playing an essential role. Confirm the arrangements at least 24 hours in advance and provide clear directions on where to come when they arrive at the library, who to see, where to park, and so on. It is easy to assume that the presenter knows what to do because he is also a library patron, but the volunteer may not realize that there is a separate children's program room. Always provide an emergency number so that the volunteer can reach staff in case of a last minute problem. It's also a good idea to have the presenter's emergency number in case he doesn't show up or the library unexpectedly closes. Lastly, remember that the volunteer is doing this out of community spirit and to support the library, so be sure to say thank you and recognize the support in some way, even if only with a certificate of appreciation.

Paid performers and presenters are usually professionals who earn all or part of their living by traveling from venue to venue. Many target their talents to groups in schools and public libraries and gain a following for their work. These may include magicians, singers, clowns, puppeteers, storytellers, and animal acts.

If possible, observe a performance before hiring that performer. If that is not possible, the performer may have video available that provides a sample of a program. Also ask for references or check with other libraries that have used the presenter in the past. Fees are generally set but may be negotiable and often depend on several factors, including the number of performances being scheduled, whether other performances can be booked in the area for the same time period, and the number of children the library anticipates will be attending. Be sure that the performer is aware of any city or county purchasing rules—such as having to register as a vendor—and whether payment is made immediately following the program or is mailed later. These professionals are comfortable discussing financial arrangements, so avoid embarrassment by understanding what will happen and when.

PRESENTER PROGRAM CHECKLIST

Prior to Program

____ Contact potential program presenter and get information/references.

____ Discuss costs, fees, and supplies or equipment that is needed.

____ Check references (other libraries that may have had this program/presenter).

____ Check room availability and reserve room desired.

____ Set a date for program and confirm with presenter.

____ Send confirmation letter—including date, time, length of program, target audience, payment agreed on, room setup, and equipment needed.

____ For paid presenters, request payment check in advance to be ready for date of program.

____ Check equipment to make sure it is working properly.

____ Contact program presenter a day or two before to confirm and remind about any arrangements, directions, where to find you. Provide emergency contact information.

____ If refreshments are being served, purchase food, drink, paper goods.

Day of Program

____ Make sure room is set up (chairs, tables, equipment, refreshments).

____ Be sure an appropriate person is available to help with equipment.

____ Display library flyers, information on upcoming programs.

____ Display books and other materials related to the program for patrons to check out.

____ Provide evaluation forms for patrons to fill out (supply pencils for patrons).

____ Greet presenter and help set up equipment, if needed.

____ Give payment check to presenter (if applicable).

____ Announce that there is a program beginning shortly.

At the Program

____ Greet patrons.

____ Introduce presenter.

____ Assist presenter if needed (lights, handouts, equipment, etc.).

____ Conclude program by thanking the presenter and audience.

____ Announce next scheduled program.

____ Ask patrons to complete the evaluation form.

____ Remind patrons that there are books and other materials for checkout.

After Program

____ Put away library equipment and all other items used.

____ Write a thank-you letter to presenter.

____ Review program evaluations.

Be sure that the program expectations match the library's expectations. Often professional presenters have a menu of options. A clown may have a program that is strictly for entertainment while also offering a literature-based program that motivates children to read. If the library is expecting an interactive element, such as face painting or demonstrating clowning techniques for the children to learn, be sure that the presenter understands this and is in agreement. Performers need some idea of how many children are expected to attend so that they know the size of the audience but also how the performance space will be arranged. Are the children seated on the floor or in chairs? Is the area separate from the rest of the library or out in the open? Remember that the performer may need setup time or time to prepare before children arrive.

The librarian should introduce the program and establish behavior expectations. Even when the librarian is not presenting the program, it is essential that she remain in the room and available to handle any issues that arise. The librarian, not the presenter, would deal with seating latecomers, children leaving and returning, or parents who need to pick up a child before the end of the program. The librarian will also close out the program by thanking the presenter and reminding children to check out the display of books related to the program as they leave. The checklist on page 131 will help you remember all of the various details for programming with presenters and special guests.

Key Points

Public libraries practically invented programming for children and families. These programs can be educational or more recreational, but they provide safe, high-quality activities for children during out-of-school hours. They also enhance the library's role as an educational organization and often enhance formal education.

- Programming is a vital part of the services provided by children's librarians.
- The type and format of library programs is wide and varied but may include librarian-led programs or paid presenters.
- Some programs, such as puppet shows, are not commonly offered elsewhere in the community.
- It takes time and careful planning to develop enriching and educational programs that are also enjoyable and attract children and families to the library.
- Programs should include information about supplemental or related materials and books to enhance learning.

Library programs can be scheduled anytime there might be an audience and participants. They reach all of the ages the children's librarian works with at different times. In the next chapter we will look at programming that is targeted specifically at very young children and the development of early literacy skills.

References

Klebanoff, Abbe. 2009. "Block Party: Legos in the Library." *School Library Journal* 55, no. 7 (July): 24–26.

Slade, Sean. 2010. "Why Fun Is Important in Learning." *Washington Post: The Answer Sheet* (blog), June 4. http://voices.washingtonpost.com/answer-sheet/learning/why-fun-matters-in-education.html.

⟲ Resources Mentioned in This Chapter

Allen, Pamela. 1983. *Who Sank the Boat?* New York: Coward-McCann.

Balliett, Blue. 2004. *Chasing Vermeer*. New York: Scholastic.

Exner, Carol R. 2005. *Practical Puppetry A to Z*. Jefferson, NC: McFarland.

Mad Science. http://www.madscience.org/.

Mora, Pat, and Raúl Colón. 1997. *Tomás and the Library Lady*. New York: Knopf.

Puppets in Education. http://www.play-script-and-song.com/pipe-puppet-stage.html.

Wisniewski, David, and Donna Wisniewski. 1997. *Worlds of Shadow: Teaching with Shadow Puppetry*. Englewood, CO: Teacher Ideas Press.

Wong, Janet. 2004. *Alex and the Wednesday Chess Club*. New York: Margaret K. McElderry Books.

Wright, Denise Anton. 1990. *One-Person Puppet Plays*. Englewood, CO: Teacher Ideas Press.

⟲ Additional Readings and Resources

Burke, John. 2014. *Makerspaces: A Practical Guide for Librarians*. Lanham, MD: Rowman & Littlefield.

Diamant-Cohen, Betsy. 2010. *Children's Services: Partnerships for Success*. Chicago: American Library Association.

Healy, Anna. 2002. "Giving Readers a Voice." *Book Links* 11, no. 4: 28j.

"How to Host a Lego Club." November 2, 2012. *The Show Me Librarian* (blog). Accessed July 29, 2014. http://showmelibrarian.blogspot.com/2012/11/how-to-host-lego-club.html.

Johnstad, Kristin, James Conway, and Yvonne Pearson. 2004. *More Than Just a Place to Go: How Developmental Assets Can Strengthen Your Youth Program*. Minneapolis: Search Institute.

Littlejohn, Carol. 2011. *Book Clubbing! Successful Book Clubs for Young People*. Santa Barbara, CA: ABC-CLIO.

Makerspace Playbook. 2013. http://makerspace.com/.

Nespeca, Sue McCleaf. 2012. *The Importance of Play, Particularly Constructive Play, in Public Library Programming*. Chicago: Association for Library Services to Children. http://www.ala.org/alsc/importance_of_play.

Reading Initiatives and Celebrations

◎ The Power of Reading

ONE OF THE PRINCIPLES of children's librarianship is the power of reading. Children's librarians believe in the importance of reading and the value of reading and the ability of reading to change lives. While reading is clearly an important skill for academic success, it is also important as a skill for grasping abstract concepts and the development of imagination and understanding, and as a path to entertainment and enrichment. It's a bit of a cliché, but books take the reader to places they may never be able to visit.

Studies like Stephen Krashen's *Every Person a Reader* emphasize the importance of free-choice reading, allowing the reader to select books without regard to reading level, subject, or topic, or other factors that might limit or restrict reading in the classroom. In his studies of factors that make children good readers, Krashen (1996) concludes that there is no difference in reading test scores between children who are taught reading skills and have them drilled into them and children who are given carte blanche to read for pleasure. Programs like First Book, described later in this chapter, point to one of the public library's greatest strengths, access to books, as a major factor in reading development. More than half of low-income families have no books for children in their homes. Library reading programs encourage families to avail themselves of the many books in the collection and encourage one-on-one reading time, another essential element in the development of good reading skills.

Public library reading initiatives also encourage children to read novels. A great deal of emphasis in schools is on nonfiction reading, and while that genre, especially narrative nonfiction, can also be enjoyable reading, studies show that reading novels is equally important. Reading fiction increases emotional intelligence, helping us understand and appreciate complex relationships and developing understanding that can support decision making (Kreamer, 2012).

It has been said that teachers teach children how to read; librarians teach children to love reading. While that is clearly an oversimplification, as teachers and school librarians and parents also help children develop a love of reading, public library programs like the summer reading clubs and book-related celebrations encourage what author Pat Mora calls *bookjoy*, "the private pleasure of settling down with a good book" (Mora, 2014).

⟳ Summer Reading Programs

According to the American Library Association, over 95% of public libraries offer a summer reading program. This makes it one of the most prevalent programs, equaling or surpassing storytimes. Because so much time and staff effort is involved, it is important to know why the summer reading program is a vital part of public library services.

Research has shown that a child loses an average of three months of learning over the summer vacation. Repeatedly, studies have shown that regardless of a child's family background, the single best predictor of loss or gain of academic skills over the summer is whether a child reads during vacation. Since few schools are in session over the summer, most of the encouragement for summer reading comes from public library summer reading programs or clubs.

The classic study *Summer Learning and the Effects of Schooling* (Heyns, 1978) confirmed many of the assumptions long held by children's librarians, and additional studies have further defined the important role of public library summer reading programs. Heyns's specific findings include the following:

- The number of books read during the summer is consistently related to academic gains.
- Children in every income group who read six or more books over the summer gained more in reading achievement than children who did not.
- The use of the public library during the summer is more predictive of vocabulary gains than attending summer school.
- "More than any other public institution, including the schools, the public library contributed to the intellectual growth of children during the summer" (Heyns, 1978: 77).

A more recent study completed in 2010 by Dominican University researchers reaffirmed the positive effects of summer reading and public library initiatives, particularly on student achievement (Roman, Carran, and Fiore, 2010). While many children love to read and will read over the summer regardless of library programs, prizes, and certificates, many children need the incentives and recognition that come with a formal initiative. All children will benefit from summer reading, but there are groups of children who benefit greatly from the extra attention provided by the public library. Many children live in families where reading is not recognized as an important skill or a leisure activity. Many children have problems reading or have physical or mental challenges that make reading difficult, and they benefit greatly from extra practice and encouragement. The Dominican study also found that public libraries need to do more to help boys become involved in reading so that they keep up with their female peers academically (Roman, Carran, and Fiore, 2010).

The public library benefits from summer reading programs because of increased circulation of materials (in many libraries more than half of the circulation of juvenile materials may occur during the summer), opportunities to reaffirm the library's role in community education, and partnerships that are built with other community organizations that serve children during the school holiday. Long-term benefits include attracting new patrons to the library and helping children become lifelong readers and regular library users.

⊚ Developing a Summer Reading Program

For many libraries a summer reading program is as basic as simply encouraging children to read for pleasure while keeping a record of their reading. Although experts generally agree that summer reading should be about enjoyment and not testing, often children who achieve a reading goal are recognized with a certificate and, perhaps, small prizes. The library may also schedule literature-related or educational programs to motivate reading and expand interests. In some libraries the program is truly a "summer reading club" where children join and attend regular meetings and programs, although even libraries with clubs don't usually require that children attend programs in order to participate in the reading part of the summer reading initiative.

The programs that occur during or in conjunction with the summer reading program are very similar to the programs offered after school during the school year. Many libraries continue to host storytimes for preschool children and encourage pre-readers to participate in a read-to-me program. They may also offer read-aloud programs for older children to listen to stories or book discussion groups. Setting up a summer reading program is much like preparing for any other major program except that it likely will operate for six to nine weeks and include a variety of different types of activities and events under the umbrella of the summer reading program. Often the summer reading program begins with a big kick-off event and concludes with a celebration where certificates are presented and everyone who achieved reading goals enjoys a presentation, activities, and snacks.

Planning for Summer Programs

It is best to begin planning for summer reading programs or clubs early, often just a few months after the previous program ends. Begin by establishing the program's goals and objectives for the library's program. While summer reading programs across the country are very similar, each library has different primary goals for the community. Even a few stated goals and objectives make it easier to plan the program, communicate the program's needs to administration and funders, and promote the program to the community. The specific goals and objectives may be similar to those provided here but should reflect the local concerns and needs. They will also provide a framework for the types of activities, rules or guidelines, methods for recognition of participants, and motivation for creating the programs and activities. For example, setting a group goal that encourages working cooperatively might mean that the program recognizes all participants who help achieve a community goal of reading for 2,000 hours in June.

Objectives are measurable results that the program will strive to achieve. For example, this year the library might establish an objective to increase circulation of children's materials during June by 10% over the previous year as one indication that the goal to attract new users has been met. Another objective might be to add one activity program each week to increase attendance at children's programs and encourage regular visits to the library.

Summer library programming, including summer reading, also must fit within the library's mission and long-range planning. Usually summer programming will easily fit within the library's mission related to lifelong learning and reading as a leisure activity. Since the programs bring in participants from different areas of the community, summer programming also fits long-range plans that include service to diverse communities. It also supports long-range plans to increase circulation and the use of current popular materials, plans to improve the use of the library as a commons or gathering place in the community, and lifelong learning. The process described in the Public Library Association's *Planning for Results* uses different catchphrases, referred to as service responses, to describe potential services or services related to specific community segments, and most of them can include services and programs for young people. While some, such as "Create Young Readers: Early Literacy," obviously support youth services, others, such as "Learn to Read and Write: Adult, Teen, and Family Literacy" or "Stimulate Imagination: Reading, Viewing, and Listening for Pleasure," will support summer reading programs and other youth programming.

Additionally, by building a library community or a community of literacy, library programs support the developmental assets needed for children to become healthy, productive adults. The Search Institute identifies 40 building blocks that help children as they grow up. The assets are different for each of four age groups, but all are relevant to library service for young people. Take time to review the developmental assets and be prepared to identify those that are supported by library services and programs. Concise two-page documents are provided by the Search Institute at http://www.search -institute.org.

Look at all of the assets, but just as an example, the assets for middle childhood (ages 8–12) include several related to empowerment and to constructive use of time. Library programs support these assets in several ways, including

- Community values youth—child feels valued and appreciated by adults in the community
- Creative activities—child participates in music, art, drama, or creative writing two or more times per week
- Child programs—child participates two or more times per week in cocurricular school activities or structured community programs for children

Best practices indicate that it is important for the children's librarian to know how summer programming and the summer reading club fits with the library's long-range plan and goals. At any time, administrators or funders may question the amount of time and expense allocated to what may be interpreted as children "just having fun" or the library duplicating services provided by the parks or recreation department. Not that there should be anything wrong with just having fun, but librarians must be able to articulate the value of summer activities, including how they support child development. Being able to include some of this information in grant applications or in letters requesting funding or donations may be the difference between success and failure.

Themes

Most libraries develop their reading program for a specific year around a theme that changes each year's focus. Using a theme may not be everyone's cup of tea, but it provides a framework for clearly branded activities for the six to nine weeks of summer reading. Themes are usually broad in interest with short, catchy slogans that reflect the theme. Often the slogans are translated into Spanish or another language that is prevalent in the community. Be cautious and get expert help with these translations as literal translations can be problematic or embarrassing. Additionally, while the theme or topic may be the same, often there will be a different slogan and programming emphasis for teens. If you are producing your own summer reading program, rather than purchasing prepared materials, consider adapting themes such as those provided below or using them as inspiration for your own slogans and themes. Of course, themes can also be recycled every 10 years or so since there will be a new group of young people in the library. The Nebraska

SAMPLE SUMMER READING SLOGANS

Every Hero Has a Story (CSLP, 2015)

Get a Clue . . . at the Library (Texas, 2012)

Go for the Gold . . . Read! (Louisiana, 1996)

Lions & Tigers & Books (Arizona, 1982)

On Your Mark, Get Set, Read (CSLP, 2016)

Paws to Read (iRead, 2014)

Reading Road Trip (Nebraska, 2001)

Reading: The Sport of Champions (Texas, 2006)

Library Commission hosts a web page (http://nlc.nebraska.gov/youth/summerreading/manuals.aspx) with information about statewide themes (including examples from states as well as from the Cooperative Summer Library Program and iRead) and bibliographic information for the planning manuals. Often these manuals can be borrowed from the sponsoring state or are available online, although art may be restricted to use by libraries in the particular state.

Although many libraries continue to create their own theme, slogan, and materials, there are companies and consortia that develop these items. Today most states, plus some of the U.S. territories, participate to some degree in the Collaborative Summer Library Program (CSLP) (http://www.cslpreads.org/), although membership may change annually. This grassroots program sets annual themes and all public libraries are included in their state's membership that allows the use of the theme and materials, including purchasing thematic incentives, promotional materials, and other supporting items like program manuals and clip art. Public libraries may receive some items at no cost from state or regional associations or the state library or may purchase all materials with local funds. Another commercially produced program is provided by iRead (http://www.ireadprogram.org/), based in Illinois. Available to any library, the program started as a cooperative effort by Illinois librarians to create high-quality materials to support summer reading programs. The catalog includes not only thematic manuals to help librarians plan and execute local programs but also related incentives and small prizes.

Because of bulk ordering and the cooperative creation of materials like the planning manual, costs may be lower for libraries that join iRead or CSLP. However, some libraries or regional collaborative groups prefer to develop their own theme and produce their own materials. It may be less expensive for larger systems to print their own reading logs and certificates and they may prefer to use a local artist to create promotional materials. While the American Library Association (http://www.ala.org) doesn't set specific themes for summer, they do create posters, bookmarks, incentives, and other items that can support an independently developed theme.

Regardless of how the theme is selected, it should be geared toward attracting the target audience. The slogans that embody the theme usually directly or indirectly encourage reading. For example, the 2014 CSLP theme focused on science and the slogan was "Fizz, Boom, Read!" "Paws to Read" was the slogan for the 2014 iRead theme focusing on pets and animals. The program guides or manuals provide guidance on how to develop a summer program with activities, bibliographies, crafts, decorations, snacks, and more tied in to the theme. The art related to the theme is often prepared by well-known children's book illustrators. The manual will include copyright guidelines for acceptable and appropriate use of the clip art and other materials produced for the theme, including rights to print materials locally if that is more cost-effective.

Registration

Many summer reading programs begin by having the children formally register. This may include obtaining the child's name, grade, and school. This information allows the librarian to gather statistics and to determine where additional promotion may be needed the next year. If one school has a low registration rate, more work may need to be done to encourage participation.

Registration may be ongoing, anytime up to the last day of the summer schedule, although some libraries have a formal deadline for registration a few weeks after school lets out. Some libraries use paper registration forms, but many are moving to online or computerized registrations. The latter makes it easier to compile statistics and may allow families to register without coming into the library. Products like Evanced (http://evancedsolutions.com/products/summerreader/) track registrations and participation and may even link to the library's integrated library system or with social media to allow participants to post book reviews or otherwise be more actively engaged with the program. The online programs are also very useful for multibranch systems where participants may report their participation at any of several locations. In addition to packaged products and subscription services, there are open source and homegrown programs for tracking registration, progress, and completions.

Obtaining contact information like parents' e-mail addresses or a phone number can also help with promoting continued participation in the program. If parents agree, regular e-mail messages can be sent to encourage completion of reading goals or to remind children about upcoming programs and presenters.

It's tempting to use the registration information to share participants' names with their schools, but privacy laws and regulations may not permit this. To share names with schools, it is critical that parents or guardians give approval; otherwise confidentiality laws related to patron records and use of the library may restrict sharing. An easy way to handle this is to encourage the children to bring their certificates to school with them in the fall. Alternately some libraries include the permission as part of the registration process, allowing parents or guardians to give permission while providing the other information needed by the library. Of course, for older children, parents may not be present when they register, and some parents may prefer that information about their children not be shared with the schools or other entities.

Tracking Participation

While there are various ways to track participation, the majority of public libraries have the participants record either the titles of books read or the amount of time the child spends reading. A variation that has some growing popularity involves counting the number of pages read. Each system has strengths and challenges. Counting titles is easy, and many children enjoy keeping a log of the books they read, but this method can be unfair. Reading a lengthy book like *The Lightning Thief* by Rick Riordan counts the same as a short, very quickly read book like *The Hamster of the Baskervilles*, a Chet Gecko mystery by Bruce Hale. Very proficient readers will reach their reading goal very quickly because they tend to be fast readers and may already be highly motivated to spend leisure time reading. Counting pages helps to compensate for the differences in the length of books but can be cumbersome to record on reading logs, and inevitably some questions arise about how to count pages of picture books, which are short on text and often unnumbered.

Counting time spent reading has the advantage of leveling the field for struggling readers, who require more time than proficient readers to get through the book. These struggling readers are the very children who most need to read for fun and benefit from practicing their reading skills every day. Reading for even 15 minutes a day may have more impact for that child than struggling to read a book a day. Additionally, making time to read regularly encourages people to develop the reading habit and become life-long readers. For many children, especially boys, magazines are the preferred reading choice. Reading magazines, short stories, and even picture books can be claimed as reading time.

Another popular measuring device is to allow the child to set a goal through a contract. The child sets her own threshold for completion and is challenging herself to read a certain number of hours or books. This supports developmental assets like setting goals and self-motivation.

Each library will set its own parameters for participation and method of tracking progress. While reading logs that count time or titles are most common, some libraries turn the tracking into a game, allowing various challenges for participants. These may include encouraging participants to read specific types of books or from different genres, trying something other than a book, such as listening to an audiobook, using a specific library service, or participating in programs.

What Counts as Reading?

While the main point of summer reading programs is to encourage children to read, keep in mind that reading comes in a variety of forms. Especially when working with children with learning disabilities or reluctant readers, librarians are encouraged to interpret reading as broadly as possible.

Many libraries permit summer readers to include audiobooks. While there has been some debate about whether listening is really reading or if it is "cheating," most educators now agree that there are proven literacy benefits gained by listening. Some children will listen to an audiobook while also following along on the written page, and the benefits of hearing the words that are being decoded are clear. It is harder for a person to read a word that they have never heard. Even when not following along with the book, listening to literature works very well for struggling readers and for readers who are not proficient English-language readers. Mary Burkey, author of *Audiobooks for Youth*, calls audiobooks "sound literature" and reminds librarians and educators that "audiobooks communicate through sound, requiring a different set of literacy skills than print media, yet engaging many of the same comprehension skills as reading" (Burkey, 2013: 15). Audiobooks also provide an opportunity for the entire family to enjoy a book together while on summer vacation trips, and listening allows a child to continue participating in the summer reading program while away from home. This can have the additional benefit of increasing library circulation or encouraging use of downloadable audiobooks through the library.

If the program is based on time spent reading, magazines are a popular reading format, especially for boys. The library might spotlight titles from the collection or purchase popular culture magazines from a local newsstand. Magazines like *National Geographic Kids* or *Cricket* are just as enjoyable and challenging as books.

Graphic novels or comic books may encourage boys to spend time reading, and the vocabulary and story arcs are frequently quite sophisticated. Even some video or computer games require substantial reading and may be just the incentive some kids need to keep reading. The librarian can always point out books related to the subject in an effort to include books in the child's regular pleasure reading.

If the library offers a "read-to-me" summer program encouraging reading aloud to pre-readers, consider allowing an independent reader to count picture books read to younger children. Picture books have vocabulary on par with many chapter books, and independent readers benefit from reading aloud to someone else while the younger child gets to count the reading time as well.

Incentives

Probably no other topic can generate more debate than a discussion about how to reward the children who read in the summer reading program. Many librarians consider reading to be its own reward, and of course it is. However we live in a society that encourages recognition and that uses prizes and incentives to increase motivation and participation. Some children need the extra carrot of a prize to persevere through a six- to nine-week program.

Incentives may be provided as a means to encourage participants to keep returning to the library throughout the summer. Motivation to continue reading and participating in activities may be provided by offering "book bucks" on each visit that can be exchanged for little gifts like free food coupons from local businesses, bookmarks, or small toys. Younger children enjoy the opportunity to shop and to save their play money for something they really want. Some libraries provide items like bookmarks, pencils, erasers, and such that fit in with the theme of the summer reading program at various intervals to encourage children to keep moving toward their reading goals. Companies like JanWay (http://www.janway.com/) offer preprinted and custom-printed items ranging from buttons and patches to key chains and tote bags.

Incentives for completing the program can be as simple as a certificate signed by the library director and other community leaders or a handshake and pat on the back from the librarian. Often certificates are presented with a lot of fanfare at an event or celebration for the participants and their families. Some libraries go to the other extreme and offer a large prize, often a computer or a bicycle, to the child who reads the most. As with many things, the best choice probably lies in the middle. Library "lock-ins" or lunch with the librarian provide a unique experience for kids who reach goals. Some libraries, such as Jefferson County (Washington), use the summer reading program to create a community of readers by encouraging the participants to help create something through their reading. In 2009, the project fit the art theme of the program and had children replicate art masterpieces like the *Mona Lisa* by adding squares to a numbered grid for each book read (figure 7.1). The incentive to keep reading was the ability to add more squares to finish the masterpiece. For another summer, readers were challenged to read a year's worth of reading in one summer by creating a timepiece in the library (Ashenfelter, 2012).

The certificates provided by many programs are often beautiful and may have been created by children's book illustrators. A grand ceremony where certificates are presented can be a memorable event for many families, and seasoned librarians all have stories about family photos taken during the ceremony and cherished certificates being framed and treasured for years.

A favored reward, where funds are available, is to let each child who completes the program select a paperback book as a prize. Gently used books from bookstores like Half-Price Books can serve nicely, but new books are also available through companies like Scholastic that hold warehouse sales or online vendors like Book Depot (http://www.bookdepot.com) that sell quantities of remaindered or overstocked books at deep discounts. First Book (http://www.firstbook.org) also offers free or deeply discounted new books for use with low-income and disadvantaged families.

Each library must decide how to handle incentives. Local policies may prohibit giving away items, or administrative philosophy may influence decisions. Whenever possible, the best practice is to keep the rewards in line with the goal of summer reading—reading is fun—and the prizes small so that every participant gets something. Best practices suggest

Figure 7.1. Summer Reading Club *Mona Lisa* Art. *Conceived and created by Martha Ashenfelter, librarian, and Drew Elicker, artist*

that coupons from local businesses should provide something that is truly free, as opposed to a discount or free-with-purchase offer. It's hardly a prize if parents have to purchase something in order for their child to get the gift. If competition is the way the library wants to go, try to keep it fair to all readers, perhaps by offering every reader the chance to earn tickets for the big prize drawing. A fun way to encourage competition that is gaining favor is to have the children strive to reach a group goal. For every book read something is placed on the bulletin board or, if funding is available, a small donation is made to a charity.

Promoting Summer Reading

As with all other programs and services, the library will likely need to promote its summer reading program. While some kids, and their parents, will remember that the library offers something special during the summer, most children will need to be reminded. Other families may not realize that there are fun, educational programs that are free at the library.

Utilize all the same promotional tools used for other programs, including press releases, social media, flyers, and posters. The program manual for the year provided through CLSP and iRead usually includes templates and samples that can be tailored for local use. Be sure that the appropriate dates, including the year, and the library contact information are on items being distributed in the community. Flyers have a way of getting misplaced and may not reappear for a year or two!

One popular and effective method for promoting the summer reading club is a visit to the local schools. The librarian can request time to visit classes, either individually or in a larger assembly, to encourage kids to come to the library, and to provide handouts to be sent home to parents. While this is a very effective promotion method in many communities, it is also time-consuming. If possible, enlist the aid of teachers, especially for those grades where it is important that children practice reading over the summer. Teachers may be willing to give out flyers during the final parent/teacher conference of the year and talk with parents about the importance of summer reading.

Evaluation

An aspect of summer reading programs that may be overlooked is evaluation. Keep in mind that evaluation is part of the planning process and should be based on the goals and objectives for the program. It is critical for staff to know how the program will be evaluated so that they know what data to collect. For outcomes measurements, surveys may need to be administered at key points throughout the summer and these, of course, need to be developed in advance.

While some evaluation is ongoing over the summer—for example, assessing why the audience wasn't as large as expected for a magic program or considering how to increase registrations that are lower than expected during the first week—much of the formal evaluation happens after the program has ended. Evaluation is also the first step in planning for the next summer. Knowing what worked and what needs improvement helps set the stage for the work that will begin after a short breather, but the evaluation may also need to be reported to administration and funders. While it is certainly appropriate to take a short break after all the hard work and intensity of the summer, best practices require that evaluation be done soon enough that memories are fresh and problems or concerns don't fade away.

Statistics play a large role in evaluation and are referred to as outputs. They are the things that are counted as the result of the summer program and can be compared to previous years and to projected expectations. How many books or other items circulated? Did participation increase as much as expected? Did as many children finish as were projected? Did participation by one grade level or a particular school lag behind the others? Knowing answers to these questions can help determine what changes might be needed for promotion efforts in the future or help staff figure out how to do something differently.

Of equal importance are outcome measurements, which may require that the library formally survey parents and participants or use other methods to determine whether the program made a difference and by how much. Outcomes measurements reflect changes in a participant's behavior, attitude, or knowledge. For example, if one objective is to increase attendance at programs by new library users, the librarian might ask for a show of hands to indicate who in the audience is a first-time attendee at the program. Surveys or questionnaires can ask parents to evaluate their child's feelings about reading as an enjoyable activity. Outcomes-based evaluation can sound more onerous than it is, and there are many guides to help plan the process and allow the children's librarian to answer the question "So what happened?" when it comes to the importance of summer reading.

⑥ One Book, One Community

The One Book, One Community reading initiative began in 1998 when Nancy Pearl, then director of the Washington Center for the Book, started the program If All Seattle Read the Same Book. For a set period of time, the library asks the community to read a specific book and come together to discuss the book and participate in related programming. The idea quickly spread, and by 2005 similar One Book programs were being held in all 50 states. The actual name of the program may be tailored locally and the concept has expanded to include either a book that can be read and enjoyed by adults and school-age children, fostering intergenerational discussions and programs, or partnering a children's book with an adult book.

While many cities select a fiction title, others choose nonfiction. Literature is broadly defined and may lead to reading one of the classics or a more contemporary book. The concept expanded further when some libraries began to incorporate a book for young people into the programming, either by focusing on a book that would be accessible and appeal to the whole family, such as *The Wizard of Oz*, or by adding a complementary book to the adult selection. For example, if adults are reading *The No. 1 Ladies' Detective Agency* by Alexander McCall Smith, children might read *The Great Cake Mystery: Precious Ramotswe's Very First Case* by the same author. Or combine themes by linking *The Grapes of Wrath* with young people reading Karen Hesse's *Out of the Dust*.

The American Library Association offers a free online planning guide to help develop local programs (http://www.ala.org/programming/onebook). Similar programs, such as the Big Read (http://neabigread.org/), also offer free resources to support community book discussions for many books that would be appropriate for children. Regardless of the book selected, community-wide book discussion programs that include books for young people offer fantastic opportunities to partner with the local schools, as well as with other community organizations that work with children. They also promote the library as a part of the cultural and literary foundations of the community and bring new users into the building.

Some schools may partner with the community to host One Book, One School programs. Each library sets its own goals for the program, typically focusing on building a sense of community, promoting literacy and reading for pleasure, and increasing library use. These programs also position the library as part of the cultural fabric of the community; a place to come for humanities programming and a venue for conversation and discussion about literary works. Some books are selected to foster discussion about a topic of interest or concern in the community, such as racism, justice, or education, while others may offer an opportunity to revisit a classic of literature or enjoy a recent best seller.

Planning a One Book program usually begins with selection of the book. The main point is to select a book that works well for book discussions and programming and that will appeal to the target audience. A book like *The Wizard of Oz* is a popular choice for all ages in part because there are various ancillary books available, including some for very young children, and the book offers great potential for related programming. *Three Cups of Tea* by Greg Mortenson allows the same story to be shared by adults, children, and preschoolers through various versions of the book, including a young reader's edition for elementary ages and *Listen to the Wind: The Story of Dr. Greg and Three Cups of Tea*, a picture book by Greg Mortenson and Susan L. Roth.

The book should be complex enough to provide room for discussion about the topic and offer opportunities for programming. Publishers often have discussion or program guides for books that are popular selections for One Book initiatives. Programs related to the young reader's edition of *Three Cups of Tea*, for example, might include a presentation on mountain climbing conducted by a representative from a local sporting goods store, a guest speaker talking about humanitarian efforts and the education system in different countries, and opportunities to learn about the cultures, people, and food of Pakistan and Afghanistan. Given the controversy surrounding how much of the story the author fabricated, the library might also hold a discussion about memoir writing, plagiarism, and the role of fictionalization in nonfiction books. Whatever the library plans to do, offer variety, stimulating discussion, and opportunities to talk about books.

El día de los niños/El día de los libros (Children's Day/Book Day)

As celebrated by librarians, El día de los niños/El día de los libros, or Children's Day/ Book Day, is a bilingual reading initiative. An enhancement of the various internationally celebrated days that bring attention to the importance of children, this celebration, often referred to simply as Día, is the brainchild of author/poet Pat Mora. In 1997, libraries began offering programs that focused on bilingualism and cultural literacy. The celebration culminates on or around April 30, but the initiative encourages activities and events throughout the year. Although the name of the initiative is in Spanish, Día emphasizes the importance of literacy for children from all linguistic and cultural backgrounds and encourages libraries to focus on languages that are important, both currently and historically, in their community. Libraries have hosted Día programs that feature Korean, Persian, Portuguese, Polish, and many other languages.

Librarians determine the extent and scope of local programming. Using April 30 as a target date for culminating the year's activities, libraries may incorporate bilingual literacy into world-language storytimes, develop afterschool programs focusing on a specific language and culture, or feature authors, illustrators, and storytellers at family programming. The variety of programming opportunities is very broad, and the focus of Día can be incorporated into almost any regular programming.

Children's librarians often shy away from programs that include material in a language they don't speak. Día programming ideas include many that allow librarians to celebrate any language and showcase books and other materials in the collection that are bilingual or available in that language. Kenton County (Kentucky) Public Library presents a single

In *Book Fiesta!* (figure 7.2), Pat Mora, the founder of Día, and Rafael López tell a story that is perfect for sharing anytime during the year but especially around April 30. Spanish and English text and bright illustrations support this celebration of bilingual literacy.

Figure 7.2. *Book Fiesta! Used by permission of HarperCollins Publisher*

book in multiple languages by inviting native speakers to read a page in their language, with each reader sequentially reading the same page in additional languages. *El día de los niños/El día de los libros: Building a Culture of Literacy in Your Community through Día* by Jeanette Larson (2011) and the Association for Library Services to Children's Día website (http://dia.ala.org/), provide support for planning and executing bilingual programming for Día.

Children's Book Week

The longest-running national literacy initiative in the United States, Children's Book Week is sponsored by Every Child a Reader, a nonprofit literacy organization (http://

www.ecarfoundation.org/), and the Children's Book Council, a nonprofit trade association for publishers (http://www.cbcbooks.org/). Originally held each year in November, the celebration was moved to May beginning in 2008. As of 2015, Children's Book Week will start on the Monday of the first full week in May and run through Sunday.

During Children's Book Week, book and reading events take place across the nation in libraries, bookstores, homes, and schools—all places where children can connect with books. The Children's Book Council provides free posters and templates for printable bookmarks, created by some of children's literature's best illustrators. Schools may host Children's Choice Book Awards selection activities throughout the year culminating with the announcement of the winners during Children's Book Week. Children of all ages select the winning books, and public libraries can support the voting process by making copies of nominated books available.

Other library activities include read-ins with local celebrities reading from their favorite books, poster design contests, and book exchanges. Local authors can be invited to talk about their books and the writing process. Some libraries host book drives to collect books for children's shelters and hospitals. All of the activities are designed to highlight the fun of reading and the importance of books in our lives.

Children Reading to Dogs (and other animals)

The main goal of literacy programs that encourage children to read to an animal is to provide a relaxed, nonjudgmental environment for the practice of reading. As the child relaxes with a reading dog, she becomes more confident reading aloud. Usually the reading slots are about 15 minutes, and the child may select any book to read. Librarians may display some books, often with pet themes or even books like those by Dori Hillestad Butler. Her Buddy File books (see figure 7.3) feature a reading program dog. The whole first chapter of *The Case of the Library Monster*, pages 7–18, illustrates, from the dog's point of view, what it is like to be a reading program dog. It's a great read aloud for librarians who are explaining the program or for a child to read to their dog.

These programs may have names, such as Paws to Read, Tail Waggin' Tutors, and Reading to Rover, among others. The programs are usually virtually free, with dog and handler volunteers (see figure 7.4) providing the service. Children sign up for time slots for their reading. The handler knows when to allow a break for the dog. It's best to provide a quiet area where child and dog can read without interruptions or distractions. Parents and other caregivers should stay away from the reading pair so as not to interfere with the supportive environment the child and dog enjoy. Children involved often comment about how the dog doesn't laugh or try to correct them if they mess up on words. Dogs don't rush them or become impatient if the readers take too long to finish a sentence. Of course, not all children are comfortable being around dogs. Since the program is voluntary, many children who have never interacted with a dog become accustomed to them by being with these well-trained, gentle dogs.

It is important to use dogs and volunteers who have completed therapy dog training. Several recognized therapy animal organizations place dogs in library reading programs. Usually that means that the dogs have gone through rigorous testing to ensure that they are comfortable in various situations, including noisy environments with children and adults who may make sudden and unexpected moves. The therapy organization also usually provides liability insurance for their teams. R.E.A.D, Reading Education Assistance

Figure 7.3. *The Buddy Files #5: The Case of the Library Monster. Cover illustration by Jeremy Tugeau, published by Albert Whitman & Company*

Figure 7.4. Tail Waggin' Tutors. *Whitaker and Jon Luc, Tail Waggin' Tutors, Lewiston Public Library, New York.*

Dogs, the first recognized dog therapy program was started by Intermountain Therapy Animals in 1999. Their website, http://www.therapyanimals.org/R.E.A.D.html, provides a great deal of information on programs, research that supports pet therapy programs, and links for affiliate programs in many states.

Even More Celebrations

This chapter has considered a few of the major national events that are held in public libraries to promote reading and literacy and, with the exception of the One Book program, events that are primarily intended for children. In addition, a quick search will uncover a multitude of even more celebrations and initiatives. There is something to be celebrated in almost every month and for every interest! Some celebrations may be localized or unique and original to a specific library. Many have been going on for decades while some are new or just catching on.

September offers opportunities to highlight the value of a free public library card during Library Card Sign-up Month. The American Library Association provides sample public service announcements, logos, and more (http://www.ala.org/conferencesevents/celebrationweeks/card) for libraries to use in reminding parents that a library card is an essential school supply.

Picture Book Month (see figure 7.5) was started by storyteller Dianne de las Casas to celebrate the book format that is often a child's first experience of looking at and reading art. Picture books also help prepare children to learn to read. The website, http://picture bookmonth.com/, provides printable certificates of participation; promotional materials,

Figure 7.5. Picture Book Month Logo. *Courtesy of Picture Book Month*

including templates for shelf talkers that allow staff to recommend books; and activity ideas for programs focused on the importance of picture books.

Other celebrations include Banned Books Week, which provides an opportunity to celebrate our freedom to read and the importance of books and open access to information; National Library Week; and Read across America, a day to celebrate reading and the birthday of Dr. Seuss. There is even a day to celebrate games, International Games Day. April is Drop Everything and Read (DEAR) Month, with April 12 labeled DEAR Day. Ideas for this celebration are available at http://www.dropeverythingandread.com/ and encourage participants to take time to read every day.

All of these library and literacy celebrations have online information and resources to help with planning and additional days, weeks, and months for celebrations can be identified through resources like *Chase's Calendar of Events*. It's easy to find plenty of reasons to celebrate literacy, libraries, books, and reading.

⊚ Key Points

While summer reading programming may be the most commonly recognized in libraries, many other reading initiatives and celebrations encourage children to enjoy reading. Notably these programs also help to build a community of readers and bring children and families to the library.

- Summer reading programs help prevent summer slide in learning.
- Planning a quality summer reading program takes effort.
- Community-wide programs, such as One Book, One Community, enhance the library's role as part of the educational community.
- Multicultural programming, such as Día, emphasizes the importance of literacy for children from all linguistic and cultural backgrounds.
- Programs that celebrate books, libraries, and literacy promote lifelong learning, reading, and library use.

Each of the programs and services covered so far requires administration and management. Although children's librarians may not be responsible for the development of budgets, they need to know how budgets come to be. You will help develop library policies and supervise other staff and volunteers. You may need to write grants or assist with fund-raising efforts for your programs. These and other topics dealing with management of the children's department are covered in the final chapter.

⊚ References

Ashenfelter, Martha. 2012. "Bringing Community to the Summer Reading Program." *Alki* 28, no. 3 (November): 20–21.

Burkey, Mary. 2013. *Audiobooks for Youth*. Chicago: American Library Association.

Heyns, Barbara. 1978. *Summer Learning and the Effects of Schooling*. New York: Academic Press.

Krashen, Stephen D. 1996. *Every Person a Reader: An Alternative to the California Task Force Report on Reading*. Culver City, CA: Language Education Associates.

Kreamer, Anne. 2012. "The Business Case for Reading Novels." HBR Blog Network. January 12. http://blogs.hbr.org/2012/01/the-business-case-for-reading/.

Mora, Pat. 2014. *Bookjoy* (blog). http://www.patmora.com/blog/. Accessed November 21, 2014.

Roman, Susan, Deborah T. Carran, and Carole D. Fiore. 2010. *The Dominican Study: Public Library Summer Reading Programs Close The Reading Gap*. River Forest, IL: Dominican University, Graduate School of Library & Information Science.

⊚ Resources Mentioned in This Chapter

American Library Association. http://www.ala.org.

American Library Association. Celebration Weeks & Promotional Events 2014–2015. http://www.ala.org/conferencesevents/celebrationweeks.

Association for Library Services to Children. Día! Diversity in Action. http://dia.ala.org/.

Baum, L. Frank. 1900. *The Wizard of Oz*. Chicago: George M. Hill Co.

Book Depot. http://www.bookdepot.com.

Butler, Dori Hillestad. 2011. *The Buddy Files #5: The Case of the Library Monster*. Chicago: Albert Whitman.

Chase's Calendar of Events. http://www.mhprofessional.com/templates/chases/.

The Children's Book Council. http://www.cbcbooks.org/.

Children's Book Week. http://www.ecarfoundation.org/childrens-book-week.

Collaborative Summer Library Program. http://www.cslpreads.org.

Cricket. 1973. La Salle, IL: Open Court.

D.E.A.R. http://www.dropeverythingandread.com/.

Evanced. http://evancedsolutions.com/products/summerreader.

First Book. http://www.firstbook.org.

Hale, Bruce. 2002. *The Hamster of the Baskervilles*. San Diego: Harcourt.

Hesse, Karen. 1997. *Out of the Dust*. New York: Scholastic Press.

iRead. http://www.ireadprogram.org.

JanWay. http://www.janway.com.

Larson, Jeanette. 2011. *El día de los niños/El día de los libros: Building a Culture of Literacy in Your Community through Día*. Chicago: American Library Association.

Mora, Pat, and Rafael López. 2009. *Book fiesta! Celebrate Children's Day/Book Day = Celebremos el día de los niños/el día de los libros*. New York: Rayo.

Mortenson, Greg, and David Oliver Relin. 2007. *Three Cups of Tea: One Man's Mission to Promote Peace—One School at a Time*. New York: Penguin Books.

Mortenson, Greg, and Susan L. Roth. 2009. *Listen to the Wind: The Story of Dr. Greg and Three Cups of Tea*. New York: Dial Books for Young Readers.

National Geographic Society (U.S.). 2002. *National Geographic Kids*. Washington, DC: National Geographic Society.

Nebraska Library Commission. "Summer Reading Program Manuals from Other States." http://nlc.nebraska.gov/youth/summerreading/manuals.aspx.

One Book, One Community program of the American Library Association. http://www.ala.org/programming/onebook.

Picture Book Month. http://picturebookmonth.com.

Riordan, Rick. 2005. *The Lightning Thief*. New York: Hyperion Books.

Roman, Susan, Deborah T. Carran, and Carole D. Fiore. 2010. *The Dominican Study: Public Library Summer Reading Programs Close the Reading Gap*. River Forest, IL: Dominican University, Graduate School of Library & Information Science.

Search Institute. http://www.search-institute.org/.

Smith, Alexander McCall. 2012. *The Great Cake Mystery: Precious Ramotswe's Very First Case*. New York: Alfred A. Knopf.

Smith, Alexander McCall. 1998. *The No. 1 Ladies' Detective Agency*. New York: Random House.

Steinbeck, John. 1939. *The Grapes of Wrath*. New York: Viking.

Additional Readings and Resources

Ash-Geisler, Viki. 1993. *Marketing the Texas Reading Club: A Guide for Youth Services Specialists*. Austin: Library Development Division, Texas State Library.

Celano, Donna, and Susan B. Neuman. *2001. The Role of Public Libraries in Children's Literacy Development: An Evaluation Report*. Harrisburg: Pennsylvania Library Association.

Dresang, Eliza T., Melissa Gross, and Leslie Edmonds Holt. 2006. *Dynamic Youth Services through Outcome-Based Planning and Evaluation*. Chicago: American Library Association.

Fiore, Carole D. 2005. *Fiore's Summer Library Reading Program Handbook*. New York: Neal-Schuman Publishers.

Francis, Alison. 2009. "Thursdays with MacGyver." *Children & Libraries* 7, no. 2 (Summer): 50+.

Matthews, Joe. 2010. "Evaluating Summer Reading Programs: Suggested Improvements." *Public Libraries* 49, no.4 (July/August): 34–40.

Nelson, Sandra. 2008. *Strategic Planning for Results*. Chicago: American Library Association.

Stauffer, Suzanne M. 2009. "Summer Reading Incentives: Positive or Pernicious?" *Children and Libraries* 12, no. 2 (Summer/Fall): 53–55.

Management of the Children's Department

Administration and Management

AS THE YOUTH SERVICES LIBRARIAN, you will be responsible for the administration of services for children: the activities related to running the department. It takes monetary and human capital to provide programs and services for children in a public library. Many people enter youth services because they love working with children and youth and find great satisfaction in the creative side of the programs and services provided by public libraries. However, it's important for every children's librarian to also have an understanding of, and to actively participate in, the management of the library's services for young people and families.

All youth services staff perform some managerial functions, at least to some degree, because they plan programs and services, participate in the development of long- and short-term goals, and evaluate programs and services. You are responsible for library assets, may be spending tax dollars, and are making decisions as to the disposition of assets that are no longer useful. You will develop, revise, and interpret policies, and, often, are called upon to supervise and train staff and volunteers.

Depending on the size of the library and the way it is administered, the children's librarian's involvement in setting budgets, writing grants, and establishing policies will vary from minimal to quite extensive. It is tempting to think that this work and these issues could be left entirely to the library director or the head of public services. After all, the children's librarian needs her time for the work with children. But if youth librarians don't understand management responsibilities and issues, then the fate of children's services and programs will rest with others who may or may not understand children's librarianship.

Children's librarians may chafe at the idea of "running a library like a business" and prefer to avoid the business and political parts of librarianship, but it is essential that every librarian be able to articulate the value of the services and programs provided and be able to explain why things are done the way they are. Funders, administrators, and the community want to know how the library's services and programs make a difference for children and families. These services and programs are too important to assume that others know or understand why it is worth the effort and the public or private funding of them.

Being an effective librarian working with children and families requires a broad range of experience and professional skills. Children's librarians must first be fully knowledgeable in the theories, practices, and emerging trends of public librarianship. Additionally, the children's librarian will also have specialized knowledge of the particular needs of young library users. The Association for Library Services to Children has outlined competencies (see appendix A) needed to be an effective youth librarian (ALSC, 2014). Among other skills, the administrative and management competencies include long-range planning, understanding the budget and being able to analyze the costs of library services, evaluating services and documenting needs, marketing services to the targeted audiences, and being able to develop and enact policies and procedures. You are also expected to continue learning and improving your own skills, and support the development of skills by other staff and volunteers, through professional development and continuing education.

Policies

Every library has policies that guide the provision of services. A policy is a set of guidelines that defines managerial actions and decisions. While policies may be implied or oral, best practices emphasize having written policies that ensure the effective and efficient running of libraries. Policies are based on the library's priorities and guide the thinking behind the actions necessary for libraries to achieve their goals and objectives.

Policies may be broad, addressing basic principles of service, or specific, dealing with a targeted group of users or set of activities. For example, the library may have a broad policy on materials selection that dictates how materials are purchased, received as gifts, or otherwise acquired by the library. There may also be a specific policy that addresses services to homeschool families that makes reference to the types of materials that will or will not be provided for use by this subgroup.

Policies are guides to actions and differ from procedures, which provide a step-by-step outline of how to actually do a task or provide the service. Each policy will generally start with a statement about the policy and the library's need for it, along with references to any regulations or laws that impact the policy. The policy will indicate how specific situations are to be handled by staff and may include procedures or steps to be followed in making decisions about the issues or in resolving problems.

When developing new policies or revising existing policies, sufficient time should be allowed to consider why the policy is needed, the issues related to the policy, and the manner in which the policy will be implemented. Take time to reread the policy several times and to have others read it. Check to ensure that the policy can be carried out fairly and consistently and that nothing in it appears to be arbitrary or discriminatory. Once the policy is finalized, it should be approved by the library's administration and by its governing body. Lastly, policies should be easily located and readily available to staff and the public.

While many of the library's policies will deal with the service population as a whole, other policies or parts of a policy may be directed more specifically at children. Children's services staff should know the library's policies and must advocate to ensure that these policies do not impede or stifle services to children. Part of your job is to speak up for the children you serve. For example, the library's policy on who is entitled to get a library card is an across-the-board policy. Part of that policy may stipulate that a child must be able to write his or her name before being issued a library card. Does that policy conflict with the library's mission to connect children and books? Are there provisions that allow a child who has learning disabilities and can't write his or her own name to get a card? The specific policies covered in this chapter, while certainly not the only ones that will affect children, are ones where the children's librarian must take care to advocate for young patrons. Library administrators and boards may try to overly restrict children's use of the library or implement more stringent rules for conduct. For example, one branch manager wanted to implement a policy that only allowed children to enter the library without an adult if the library had a signed note with parental contact information on file.

Few children will be concerned about the library's policy on fees for special services, but they are heavily impacted by the policies on intellectual freedom and how the library deals with unattended children. Other policies, such as those on partnerships, religious programming and decorations, and proctoring of exams, will influence and impact the services and programs the children's librarian can offer. Read all of the library policies, ask questions about anything that is not clear, and be prepared to provide input into revising current policies or developing new policies to better serve children. Be sure that you communicate your desire to be involved in the development of policies that affect children's programs and services; don't assume that the library director, board, or governing authority will automatically include you in this function. Pay special attention to the policies, including several that are examined more closely in the next section, that have particular relevance to children's services.

Intellectual Freedom Policy

Two basic tenets of library science are free and open access to information and the freedom to read, or view, what you want without government interference. This is based on the First Amendment of the United States Constitution, which guarantees the right of every American to read material without interference from others who may object to the content. Censorship, the act of deciding for others what they should or should not be able to read or view, is one of the most complex and impassioned issues faced by many public libraries.

Most public libraries have a policy that deals with intellectual freedom, and it is unlikely that there would be a separate policy directed specifically at children. However, the children's librarian may be called upon to explain, enforce, and defend this policy more than other librarians might. You should be familiar with the policy and be able to advocate for its application to all library users, regardless of age.

The issues related to intellectual freedom permeate almost every aspect of children's services and programs, from what is included or excluded in the collection, to Internet access and filtering of computers, and even the speakers or presenters who appear at library programs. Parents, caregivers, and members of community organizations are concerned about the welfare of children and want to protect children from real or perceived dangers, including physical, intellectual, and emotional dangers. It is critical that a policy be in place before a challenge to materials in the collection arises or a community member complains about a holiday program the library is holding. Review the policy regularly and know the procedures to follow when a complaint is filed.

In a diverse society, individuals will frequently have different ideas about what is appropriate for children and what is objectionable. Librarians cannot presume to know what others may or may not find to be offensive or inappropriate and cannot serve in loco parentis—in place of the parents—"either by limiting access to materials or services solely on the basis of the user's age or by attempting to enforce parentally dictated controls" (Conable, 2014). Parents have the right to restrict what their own child reads, views, or participates in but cannot make those decisions for another child. It is nearsighted and naive to think that there are any values, interests, or ideas that are universally accepted or that a topic will not be of interest to someone in the community. Therefore, library collections, and by extension programs, may include—indeed probably will include—something that is objectionable to someone in the community.

Librarians may feel pressured to either label media to warn of potentially objectionable content or to restrict children from checking out that media. (Conversely, movies that come with the Motion Picture Association of America ratings on the packaging should not have those ratings removed even though they "label" the content. Eliminating the ratings is considered to be expurgation, or "cleansing," and is another form of censorship.) Attempts may be made to restrict exhibits or programs that include viewpoints or values that are different from those held by some segment of the community. Censorship attempts can come from any direction and are not limited solely to people with conservative views or who adhere to a specific religion. The library's policy on intellectual freedom should clarify the reasons for any limitations on access.

Although libraries support open access to information and intellectual freedom, the Children's Internet Protection Act (CIPA)—federal legislation—requires the use of filtering software on computers that will be used by children if the library receives federal funds for technology. If the library decides to install filters on computers in order to obtain federal funds, the reasons should be outlined, and many libraries post a CIPA

SAMPLE CIPA STATEMENT

The library operates by the Internet filtering protocols required by the Children's Internet Protection Act (CIPA), which mandates that any public library using federal funding must filter Internet access for children. The intent of CIPA is to filter information that is considered "harmful to minors." Any person under the age of 17 years must have filtered access to the Internet.

statement such as the example on page 158. The policy should also allow for exceptions to the filtering when requested by adults.

Even with filters, there may be complaints about material viewed by children. The main goal of filtering software is to block access by children to pornographic or obscene material. While filtering systems vary, most do not block material that may be violent, discuss sexuality, or show disturbing images. Because of the complexities of this policy, some libraries will have a separate policy on Internet filtering that would be referenced in the general policy.

Policies on Accessibility of the Collection

While most libraries have a collection development policy that outlines how materials will be selected and added to the collection, some libraries also have a policy that deals with access to the various parts of the collection. This policy may also tie in with policies on intellectual freedom by reaffirming the rights of young people to have as full access to information as possible.

The American Library Association provides interpretations to the Library Bill of Rights that clarify the basic statements in that document. These include interpretations regarding free and open access to the library by minors, along with access to nonprint materials. Other interpretations deal with minors and Internet activity and expurgation of library materials, such as altering or obliterating parts of a book or magazine out of concern that the material may be inappropriate for young people.

According to the interpretation "Access to Library Resources and Services for Minors: An Interpretation of the Library Bill of Rights," "Library policies and procedures that effectively deny minors equal and equitable access to all library resources and services available to other users violate the Library Bill of Rights" (ALA, 2014). Attempts to restrict access may stem from concern about the content in adult fiction, leading to circulation policies that restrict children to checking out materials solely from the children's collection. The restrictions may also stem from economic concerns, such as not allowing children to check out expensive DVDs or discouraging children from requesting items through interlibrary loan.

Open access to young people should extend to all elements of the library's services, materials, and programs even if the library staff think that few children would be interested in the topic. Access should also be available in a fair and inclusive manner. For example, librarians may want to set policies that offer more time for computer use to adults, assuming that adults will be using the computers for more worthy purposes. Some libraries set restrictions that target young people by setting guidelines that label research or adult searching as more legitimate uses of the technology resources than children who want to play computer games. Of course, the library can set policies that regulate the amount of computer time for certain uses, such as limiting game playing to 30 minutes, but the limits should apply to all patrons and not reduce, impede, or restrict access by minors.

Unattended Children/Child Safety Policies

We all are, or should be, concerned about the safety of children, and library staff need policies that help them to identify the appropriate expectations, responsibilities, and actions required to ensure that children are safe in the library. Most libraries have a policy to deal with children who are in the library unaccompanied by a parent or other responsible adult. Additionally, the topic may be addressed in various other policies, such as those related to appropriate library behavior. All policies, but especially those dealing with behavior, that are vague or unevenly enforced may not be legally enforceable.

A general policy on patron behavior may address appropriate conduct in the library but staff should take care not to include language that compels a higher expectation of compliance from children than from adults. Policies on patron behavior are put in place to provide a safe and comfortable environment for *all* library users. It is unfair to expect children to be silent, for example, while permitting adults to hold conversations in the public areas or to talk on cell phones. Focus on the actions, not the age. Loud conversations are inappropriate whether held by children or senior citizens.

In developing a policy on unattended children, the library must be sure to define what is meant by "unattended." In larger libraries, parents may be expected to keep their children with them at all times, while in smaller facilities it may be fine for a child to be in the children's area while a parent is browsing in the nearby adult area. Often this is covered by the outline of expectations on behavior so that a nine-year-old child who is quietly studying or reading a book would be able to stay alone while a parent uses the computers.

Preschool children should never be left in any area of the library unsupervised by a responsible adult. In some jurisdictions, laws may establish the minimum age for a child to be anywhere without a parent or guardian and, indeed, leaving a young child alone, even for a few minutes in a public library where staff are on hand, may be construed as child neglect or abandonment under certain circumstances.

Policies on unattended children in the public library generally address "latchkey" children, a term that has come to mean children between the ages of about 6 and 12 who take care of themselves after school or during holidays until their parents or guardians return home. Many of these children come to the public library because it is perceived by parents to be a safe place for them to stay or as an alternative to being home alone. Public libraries should not be expected to offer entertainment for a child for hours on end, and even the best-behaved children can become bored, hungry, or too energetic.

The library policy may include a statement about older children acting as supervision for younger siblings and provide an age for that sibling to take responsibility. The policy would outline ramifications if a teen sibling is not attentive to a younger child in his or her care. Keep in mind that often older siblings don't want to be in the position of babysitting and will be distracted by their own activities, friends, and interests.

Public library staff must take care not to put themselves in the role of child care provider. Even in smaller communities it is impossible to know every child and who they may or may not go with when they leave the library. As with selection of reading or other materials, the library staff cannot act in place of the parent. Doing so, even with the best intentions, may expose staff and the library to liability when they accept responsibility for children who come to the library without a parent. Although library staff has no legal duty to help a child who has been left at closing, any library staff who do help have a responsibility to see the situation through to its conclusion. If, for example, the librarian waits with a child for a short period of time after closing but then decides to go ahead and leave, she may be held responsible for any problems that occur after her departure. "By taking on the responsibility of waiting with unattended children, the library has assumed a duty of due care" (Minow and Lipinsky, 2003: 270). Policies help staff provide a welcoming environment without accepting child care responsibilities and help parents understand the parameters of library use by minor children.

Children may need to be reminded about the library's closing time and offered the opportunity to call a parent some time before the library closes. The policy may indicate how staff will handle situations when a child remains in the library at closing time and no parent has arrived. In no case should a library staff member provide transportation for a child who has been left alone at the library, regardless of age. The library policy should address the steps to take in attempting to locate the parents, culminating with a call to the police if the parent cannot be located. Remember, it is not the child's fault that the parent left her at the library without supervision.

Additional safety issues that may be addressed include truancy or being in the library during school hours, providing food during programs when parents or caregivers are not in attendance, posting of children's names in public places (such as nametags for storytime or summer reading participation), photographing children at public programs, and adult use of children's bathrooms. It is probably not possible to anticipate every danger and write a policy or policies to cover every possibility, and the library may want to combine them into one policy.

Additionally, the library should have an emergency preparedness plan in place that covers how to handle natural disasters and other emergencies. This policy should include how the staff will deal with children if the library must unexpectedly close or if conditions require that patron's shelter in place for a period of time. We all hope that we never face situations where children and others are in danger, but we need to be prepared.

The sample policy provided below is not intended to be a model for every library. You must determine the parameters for your own library, based on local mores, issues, and laws. More specific guidance on developing policies can be found in *The Public Library Policy Writer: A Guidebook with Model Policies on CD-ROM* (Larson and Totten, 2008).

POLICY ON UNATTENDED MINORS IN THE LIBRARY

Introduction

The safety and well-being of patrons is a primary concern for the Bluebonnet Public Library. Parents may think of the library as a safe place to leave children; however, it is a public place and the library cannot provide child care services. Library staff cannot be responsible for children who are in the library. Secondary concerns are related to the impact of the behavior of unattended children, who may be bored or resentful, on the ability of other patrons to use the library and the amount of time staff must devote to addressing inappropriate behavior. This policy establishes guidelines for children who are visiting the library without adult supervision.

Definitions

Unattended child: A person 15 years of age or younger who is in the library without a guardian or parent.

Vulnerable child: A person 15 years of age or younger who, for whatever reason, cannot ensure his own safety and well-being and who might be endangered if asked to leave the library. Children under the age of six are always considered to be vulnerable.

Policy

Parents or a legal guardian are responsible for the safety and well-being of their child. They are also responsible for the actions and behavior of their child. Children under the age of six should never be left alone in the library. Children from the age of six to eight may be in the children's area alone, but a parent or guardian must remain in the library building. Children older than eight may use the library unattended if they are following library behavior rules.

Unattended children who become disruptive or who damage library property will be asked to leave. If a parent or guardian is not in the library, the child will be permitted to call a responsible adult and inform that adult that she or he needs to be picked up or will be leaving the building alone.

Library staff may notify the appropriate authorities if they have a reason to suspect that there is significant evidence of abuse or neglect or if a child is considered vulnerable and would be subjected to potential danger upon leaving the building.

If a child has not been picked up at closing and cannot leave alone, two staff members will remain with the child while the police are called to locate parents. Under no circumstances will staff transport a child.

Procedures

1. If a child under six is found alone in the library, staff will attempt to locate the parent. If the child knows where the parent is, try to locate that person. If the child can give you a phone number, attempt to contact the parents. If no parent or guardian can be located, staff will contact the police.
2. If a child over six is misbehaving or being disruptive, remind the child about library rules. If the disruption continues and the child is under eight, locate the parent in the library. If the parent cannot be located, staff should contact the police.
3. Children over eight who are disruptive or misbehaving may be given a warning to behave. If the disruption continues, allow the child to call a parent for pickup or ask the child to leave if she or he can walk home safely. If the child cannot safely leave, staff should contact the police.
4. Continued disruptive behavior or misuse of library materials and services should be reported to the director. A child who is continually disruptive may be banned from the library for a period of time.
5. Complete an incident report for all situations where a child is asked to leave the library or parents are called.

Confidentiality

Librarians consider what people read or view to be private, and in fact most states have laws that protect the privacy of patron records except under specific circumstances. There are also federal laws related to records that are or are not subject to open records laws and federal regulations related to privacy. State and federal laws, including the USA Patriot Act, outline the circumstances under which law enforcement agencies can subpoena records, and the library policy should outline procedures to follow if the librarian is required to reveal records. While the children's librarian is not usually responsible for developing the library's policy on confidentiality, it is important to be familiar with the provisions and how the policies and laws impact children.

When working with children, the issues related to privacy and confidentiality can become a little sticky. Parents or guardians usually have to sign a child's library card application accepting responsibility for lost materials and late fees. Older children and teens may be able to obtain a library card without a parent's signature. In that case, parents usually would not be entitled to access their child's records without the child's permission. The library, as mentioned in the section on access to materials by minors, wants children to be able to select and borrow materials from the collection. Parameters of confidentiality of patron records should be disclosed during the library card registration process.

Ethically, and often legally, the librarian cannot and should not discuss what a patron reads or disclose what a patron has checked out. The policy should protect the rights of young patrons while also delineating the ways parents can access records. Often the parent is a cosigner on the account and has access to the circulation records by virtue of having the account number and password. Parents may also ask their children to reveal their library records, and since that information is available from the minor, librarians should not breach confidentiality by disclosing the information.

Confidentiality also applies, in most cases, to use of services and attendance at programs. It may seem counterintuitive, but confidentiality includes not releasing the names of students who participate in, or complete, library programs without parental permission. Instead of sending the names of students who finished the summer reading program, the library can encourage the children to show their certificates to the school when they return in the fall. Alternatively, the library can request permission, in writing, from the child's parent or legal guardian to release the information to the school.

Remember also that the library's website is most likely subject to the Children's Online Privacy Protection Act. This federal legislation, administered by the Federal Trade Commission, requires websites that collect personally identifiable information from children ages 12 and under to obtain consent from their parents or guardians. For this reason, many commercial sites don't allow children under 13 to register for the site. (Keep this in mind when planning programs that encourage children to use Facebook, play online games, or share photographs. You will need parental permission or find another way to complete the program.)

Protection should be in place to guard privacy when using other online resources, such as databases and the Internet, by keeping browsing history to a minimum, and clearing stored information regularly. To the extent that it is technically possible to do so, data records should be deleted when they are no longer needed.

The issues in these, and other, library policies can be complex and overlapping. To the extent possible, policies should support intellectual freedom, access to information, and confidentiality for minors while also doing what is possible to ensure the safety of children.

Evaluating Children's Services

It is good practice to systematically evaluate the programs and services that the library provides. Funders want to know if library services have done what was intended. They also want to know if the services and programs are cost-effective. It is easier to plan for the future when what has worked in the past is known and when thought has been given to fixing or improving those things that didn't work.

There are various methods for evaluation, and in some cases the funder, or the library's administration, will require that specific evaluation measures and tools be used. State libraries or state library associations may also have standards that can be used to benchmark services and programs. In a nutshell, evaluation deals with numbers or anecdotes, or both, to demonstrate the library's successes and shortcomings. In most cases, the children's librarian will collect some of the data but will report these statistics to someone else who compiles the monthly and annual reports.

A lot of evaluation is focused on outputs: counting things, comparing numbers, and calculating growth or increases. Success is measured by comparing the number of children who attend a program against the number of children anticipated. Did attendance at the programs result in an increase in circulation or library card registrations? Library annual reports collect required information, often to be reported to a state agency, and statistics are a measure of growth in services.

While statistics are important, they only tell part of the story. The youth librarian should know, or be able to quickly find out, how many items circulate in a year, how many children attended various programs, how many books and other items are added to the collection each year, and how many children visit the library annually. For budgeting, it is helpful to know how circulation and use of youth materials compares with the circulation of adult materials. Grant applications will request data on library use, attendance at programs, or whatever facet of library services and programs will be funded by the grant. These numbers also serve to support the stories that communicate the outcomes of library services.

Some federal funders, including the Institute of Museum and Library Services, as well as some nonprofit foundations, require, or at least strongly encourage, that grantees use outcomes-based evaluation (OBE) techniques. Evaluating outcomes provides a measure of the impact of library services on the users. OBE answers questions like "So what? What difference did the program make?" and "What changes really occurred?"

The OBE process begins when the program or service is being designed, or redesigned, and helps library staff articulate and establish clear benefits (outcomes) they anticipate will result from the program. Outcomes look at the expectation of results while the program is being planned and focus on the users—the children and their families—rather than on the library. To do that, staff identify ways to measure those benefits (indicators) while clarifying the individuals or groups for which the program's benefits are intended (target audience). Activities are carried out to reach that audience and achieve the desired results. Outputs are still collected and can help track progress toward the intended outcomes, but they don't tell the whole story.

The benefit of OBE comes when the library can show that, for example, 48% of parents reported that they read to their child regularly after attending eight weeks of storytime. This figure can be compared with statistics collected during the first week of the program and show that this is an increase of 12%. That evaluation tells much more than simply knowing that 14 children and their parents attended storytime every week. The program resulted in more parents reading more often to their children. An excellent resource that clearly explains OBE is provided by the Institute of Museum and Library Services (http://www.imls.gov/applicants/outcome_based_evaluations.aspx).

Other evaluation methodologies include surveys, focus groups, and benchmarking or comparisons. Checking sign-up statistics for summer reading programs allows you to know whether your marketing plan has been successful. After the first week of summer reading, have as many children registered as by the same time the previous year? Collections can be benchmarked against lists of best books to ensure that the library is purchasing some percentage of the highest quality books released each year. Quick survey forms can be distributed at storytimes asking parents whether they check out books following the program. Teachers can be surveyed to find out if they are referring students to the library's homework help center. Focus groups provide an opportunity for those who use a service to give feedback on its quality and effectiveness.

Of course, the most important aspect of evaluating services and programs is what you do with the information gained. Use it to start the next planning cycle for summer reading programs or to establish budget guidelines for the next fiscal year's collection spending. Figure out what didn't work and do research to find ways to improve your services. Evaluation is not only an exercise in accountability; it is a tool for planning, budgeting, and management of your services.

Marketing Children's Services

It's easy to assume that libraries don't need to do any marketing. After all, the programs and services are free! However, parents don't always realize that the public library offers a great selection of programs and services. Parts of the collection may go unused or underused unless the areas are brought to the attention of library users. Even if plenty of people are using the library, marketing keeps the services and programs in the public eye—something that can be critical during budget times. Some people need to be reminded that the library is here; others, including new immigrant families, may not know that the library exists and is available for them. While many children from middle-class families will flock to the library, underserved and disadvantaged families in the community may need more encouragement to benefit from what the public library has to offer.

There are many definitions of marketing, but in essence it is a process that allows a business or organization to analyze itself and compare it with competition. You are positioning the library's products and services and promoting them through various means. Product, price, place, and promotion are Philip Kotler's four Ps of marketing, to which a fifth, purpose, was added in 2013 (Anand, 2013). Often libraries limit their marketing to promotion or publicity, overlooking the other aspects. For example, we often say that public library services are free, but that is not technically correct. Return on investment and "bang for the buck" are marketing considerations. The taxpayer is paying the price for library services. Unlike many businesses, the library's place is generally set in stone; it's not easy to move the library to a better location. Some libraries do lease space in shopping malls or strip centers; however, even then the library does not move to another location quickly or easily. Even when you "take the show on the road" by presenting programs off-site you are marketing the library as *a place* to come for specific services and you are promoting the place of the children's department within the library.

Developing a marketing plan is a good idea to ensure that all aspects of marketing are considered, and it is imperative that the children's librarian be involved in plans for marketing children's services. Marketing includes public relations, promotion, advertising, and customer service. Larger libraries may have a staff member or department that is responsible for the overall marketing of the library and, usually, for publicizing children's programs and services. In smaller and medium-sized libraries, frontline staff may be required to promote their programs and market the services of their department. Even when other staff handle marketing, the children's librarian will want to provide input and offer suggestions for targeting promotions and will market library services through outreach programs, through public speaking, and during interactions with patrons in the library.

Promotion includes advertising, direct marketing, publications (flyers, brochures), signage, word of mouth, media, and more. It's letting the public know about the library and what the library is doing. It also includes image, slogans, and branding. Many libraries develop a brand that quickly identifies the library. Some prefer to use the American Library Association's @ Your Library brand, part of the ongoing Campaign for America's Libraries, to increase public awareness of the value of libraries and librarians (http://www.ala.org/advocacy/advleg/publicawareness/campaign@yourlibrary/).

Few public libraries have funds to buy advertising space in newspapers or magazines, but the media will generally run notices of library programs. If the library has marketing staff or a public information office, the children's librarian usually will provide the program particulars to them and the marketing staff will write and submit press releases to the newspaper, websites, and other media outlets.

If writing press releases is part of the children's librarian's duties, then it's important to know how to write a short, precise one, and there are many resources available to help with this process. Even in our digital age, press releases follow a rather standard format but must also include enough information to attract interest and sound newsworthy. Your press release should include the most important information first. The media will most likely cut out all but the essential details so make sure those are obvious and easy to find. A sample press release is provided on page 167. Follow these tips as you write your own:

- Use simple sentences, straightforward language, and short paragraphs.
- Put the most important information first and include additional information further into the press release to be used if space permits.
- Double-check spelling and grammar, the date and time of the event, the address, and the phone number. Ask someone to proofread your press release.
- Limit the release to one page or less.
- Attach a program flyer, if available, to your press release.
- Include contact information so the media will know how to reach the program director for more information or to cover your program in more detail.

Most community newspapers prefer press releases sent by e-mail, but they should still follow the standard format unless you are told otherwise. There are also smaller, free newspapers like *The Greensheet* or parenting news magazines that welcome public notices and reach a lot of people.

Targeted Marketing

While generalized marketing is important, it's also important to spread the word about specific programs. There's nothing more disheartening than having planned a program that no one knows about, and therefore participation is low or nonexistent. It is impossible to guarantee that the public will show up for anything; there are conflicts, transportation challenges, bad weather, and any number of other factors beyond the library's control. However, people can't come if they don't know what the library is offering.

With targeted marketing, consideration must be given to how to best reach the intended audience. To reach Spanish-speaking families, the message must go out through Spanish-language radio stations and newspapers, for example. Look for ways to reach the target audience by looking for places that already reach that audience. A bedtime storytime program, for example, might be promoted through local preschools and child care centers so that parents who are working during the day can bring their children in the evening. Advertising for the summer reading program will reach the target audience through outreach at schools. Keep in mind that when working with children, especially young children, that while they are the target audience, the message also needs to go to the parents and caregivers who serve as the gatekeepers of a child's time and transportation. By focusing on the patrons, or customers, who might be encouraged to use the library's services and programs, it is possible to effectively match the appropriate information, the method of getting the word out, and the venue for marketing materials.

Methods for Marketing

There are a number of methods for marketing library services. Some happen in-house, while others are more effective out in the community. Some publicity and marketing requires more effort and resources, either financial or staff, than others. In addition to press releases to the media, flyers, social media, brochures, displays and bulletin boards, and word of mouth are generally most available.

Flyers are an excellent and inexpensive way to promote library services. The information is in writing and a flyer gives the patron, or potential patron, something to hang on to and be reminded about the details. They can be distributed in-house or taken out into the community. Of course, within the library, the publicity is reaching people who are already library visitors. To be effective, flyers must first include the pertinent information about the program or event: what is happening, where, when, and for whom. Don't assume that everyone in town knows where the library is located. To avoid misunderstandings, include the year with the date; flyers have a habit of turning up even after several years. Include contact information, such as the library phone number and website. Double-check the details and have someone else proof the flyer. It's very easy to accidentally include the wrong phone number, for example.

Even if the flyers are not designed by a graphic artist, they should be neat and attractive. Clip art and copyright-free images are readily available either free or at a small cost. Publishing software like Microsoft Office includes art files, and organizations like the American Library Association sell files that can be tailored for use on flyers, banners, and websites. The Association for Library Services for Children is one organization that provides publicity kits for special programs like El día de los niños/El día de los libros, a national celebration of bilingual literacy covered in chapter 7. The publicity kits often include art, such as the logo pictured in figure 8.1, and other materials that can be used promoting your events and activities.

The library's website is a very effective means of promoting children's services. Patrons may already be visiting the site to search the online catalog or use a database and will see an advertisement for a guest speaker or a special event. Work with the staff member who maintains the website to ensure that youth programs are adequately covered. Some

Figure 8.1. Día Logo. *Used with permission from the American Library Association*

Tween Scene Ages 8-12
Tuesdays, 4:30–5:00 pm

September 30
Straw Houses

Pflugerville Public Library (512) 990-6375

Figure 8.2. Web Ad Straw Houses. *Courtesy of Pflugerville Public Library, Texas*

website software allows for rotating images to appear, such as the images for a family program and a tween program shown in figure 8.2 and figure 8.3, which rotate with about six or seven other images every few seconds. Often these images are taken from flyers or other promotional pieces that were created for distribution, reinforcing the program's marketing. The website may also include a calendar area that should be kept current to advertise storytimes and after-school programs. Some libraries provide copies of flyers and brochures in pdf format on their website, allowing patrons and teachers to print them as needed.

Displays and bulletin boards, such as the one in figure 8.4, offer attractive in-house marketing but should be kept clean and up-to-date. A summer-themed bulletin board

Figure 8.3. Web Ad Cody Fisher Magic Show. *Courtesy of Pflugerville Public Library, Texas*

Figure 8.4. Summer Reading Program Bulletin Board. *Waterford Public Library, Connecticut*

can advertise summer programs while also promoting the collection. A program on rocketry can be promoted through a display of books on astronomy and outer space. A lot of artistic talent is not necessary to create eye-catching displays and bulletin boards but it does take some creativity. Hand-lettered signs almost always look tacky, so use a computer to create them. Software packages often have templates to help with layout of the information. Library vendors like Demco sell table top easels and risers to hold flyers and add interest to displays. Teacher stores, as well as library vendors, sell precut shapes and thematic borders for bulletin boards. For book displays promoting the collection, Brodart and other companies offer some interesting display units and shelf display products. Nothing is as pitiful looking as an outdated bulletin board or a display with nothing to display so be sure to keep these promotional tools current.

An increasingly effective means of promotion for library programs is social media. Although these methods primarily reach parents and caregivers, don't overlook the library's Facebook or Twitter account. In addition to reaching regular library users, social media is a good way to reach new audiences.

There are many other ways to promote, market, and advertise library programs and services. Keep in mind that consistency, timeliness, and repetition are important in marketing. People need to hear, see, or read the message several times before it sinks in. Also, for every person who attends a program or responds to the advertising, many others received the message and know that the library offered a program or service even though they did not attend it. Word of mouth is very effective, and endorsements, both implied and explicit, carry a lot of weight. Be sure that teachers, child care workers, and staff at other agencies that work with children know about the programs and have publicity pieces so that they can help spread the word.

⟲ Funding and Fund-Raising

Few libraries have enough money to provide all of the services and programs they would like. Although the children's librarian's role in funding the library may be limited, it is important to know where the money comes from, how it can be spent, and whether there are ways to get more. Even when funding is reasonably adequate, you may need to apply for grants to start new programs or services to show that they will be successful before local funding is provided.

Budgets

Money is at the root of most activities in the library. Whether money is buying staff, materials, program presenters, or equipment, the budget sets the parameters for what can be accomplished. In most public libraries the budget is a public document; even if the children's librarian has little responsibility for budget development, it is important to know the budget and understand the budget process.

The budget process is generally scheduled to begin several months before the end of the library's fiscal year. The children's librarian may be asked to provide input on costs and needs both for ongoing services and for the development of new programs. If the collection is sorely out of date, for example, the children's librarian will need to calculate the price of books and other materials to establish an amount of money needed to replace weeded materials. If the library wants to begin a family literacy program, the cost for staff, supplies, and materials will be needed. In larger libraries the head of children's services may be required to calculate the costs for staff, benefits, supplies, materials, travel, training, and other expenses.

Part of the budget process may include providing statistics and justification to support continued and increased funding. Justification statements may include the need for the service as well as information about demand and actual usage. If storytime programs are regularly attended by 30 or 40 children and parents, and there is a waiting list to register to attend, that may be used as an indication of the need for an additional program. It justifies the request for an additional part-time children's librarian. Statistics on the turnover of the children's picture book collection—circulation figures divided by the number of items in the collection—may be an indication that increased funding is needed to replace worn-out materials and to expand the size of the collection. Circulation figures will generally be collected thorough the library's integrated circulation system but the children's librarian will want to review them regularly to look at trends and dips in materials usage. Other relevant statistics that may be collected and reported regularly include program attendance, library visits (door count), in-house use of materials, reference and reader's advisory questions answered, web hits, and class visits. Many of these statistics are collected by the children's staff and are useful in providing justification for budget requests.

Grants

Publicly funded budgets often provide only funds for traditional or basic library services. The children's librarian may be expected to apply for grants or assist in the development of grant applications being written by other staff members. Although grants can be instrumental in starting new programs, they cannot be relied on for continuation of programs and are always subject to the funds being available and the grant funders potentially shifting priorities. Some libraries choose to avoid grants as a source of income because they adhere to the philosophy that only local funds, with a reasonable expectation for ongoing support, should be expended. On the other hand, grants can provide the start-up funding to test a new program or service.

It is important to look for grants that match the library's mission and priorities. Generally it is better to seek out funders for programs that the library is already trying to institute or expand. Some grant writers look at available grants and then try to develop programs or services to match the grant guidelines. Usually, this results in less successful programs because they were not developed out of a recognized need and a well-thought-out plan to meet that need.

When looking for grants, be sure to consider the amount of time that will be invested in researching and writing the grant application relative to the amount of money that might result if the grant is approved. It is also important to look at the cost to actually administer the grant if it is received. What strings are attached? Some grants require that the grantee match grant funds with local funds, either from the library budget or from other donors. Grantors may also want to know about in-kind funding—resources that are allocated to the program or project such as craft supplies, donated refreshments, or even the value of volunteer time. Grant applications also often ask if and how the program will continue once the grant funds end.

What reports are needed? Can the library's fiscal system easily track expenditures and can other systems capture data that is needed for required reports? For example, a grant to add parenting books to the children's collection may require that the library track circulation of the individual books purchased with grant funds. How difficult will that be to do? It's also important to be sure that applying for, and receiving, grant funds does not result in commensurate cuts in funds from other sources in the library's budget. Some grant funders also require that the library's administration promise not to cut funds if the grant is received.

Some grants are worth pursuing even though they won't result in a lot of money for the time invested. These grants show the library and organizational administration that another organization supports the library and its efforts and may serve as a catalyst for receiving other funds. They also show that the library is actively seeking other means of funding programs and working to get a "fair share" of available grant monies.

When looking for grant sources, be sure to carefully read the guidelines. Some foundations and granting sources limit their geographical range. Others may limit the size or type of library to which they will award funds. The Tocker Foundation, for example, only gives to small public libraries in Texas. It would be a waste of time for a library that is not in Texas to apply.

Be sure to check that the library is an eligible recipient of the funds. Some foundations will only give to organizations that hold IRS 501(c)(3) status. Even though, by definition, a public library is nonprofit, cities and county libraries are rarely established under this tax code designator. The registered applicant for the grant may need to be the Friends of the Library or the library foundation, if there is one. Several databases and directories are available to help in locating grant funding sources and larger libraries may have some of these resources in the reference collection. The Foundation Center, publisher of *The Foundation Directory*, provides a listing of cooperating collections, 250 free funding information centers around the country that provide a core collection of materials for grant seekers. A limited amount of information may be found for free on the Internet, and some state library agencies compile lists of potential grants for public libraries. Inexperienced grant writers would do well to read books like *Winning Grants: A How-to-Do-It Manual for Librarians with Multimedia Tutorials and Grant Development Tools* by Pamela H. MacKellar and Stephanie K. Gerding. Gerding and MacKeller also host a blog, *Library Grants*, to help librarians keep up with grants and deadlines.

Carefully check deadline dates and allow enough time to gather needed information and letters of support and to have someone else read a draft of the application and then proof the final document. A few typographical errors may be overlooked but numerous errors, especially errors in mathematical calculations and grammatical errors may reduce the library's chance for success. A poorly written application is often taken as a sign that the library will not be able to properly administer the grant.

It's good practice to also review all of the required items and any specific instructions for applying one last time before submitting the application. Some funders have very specific instructions about the number of copies, the order of documents, number of pages permitted, and more. It's heartbreaking to send off an application only to discover it will be disqualified because not enough copies were sent or unallowable attachments were included.

Be careful also to know the procedures required for grants by the library administration and the library's governmental body. Some cities require that grants be approved by city council. Some governmental agencies require signatures approving promises for matching funds, funds that the local library will put up along with the grant funds, or for future funding of programs that are begun with grant funds. It can take time to get these signatures and approvals, so know ahead of time what will be required. Finally, be prepared to carry out the grant and to administer the funds if the grant is awarded, and always follow up with reports and publicity to the funder.

Community Fund-raising

Grant writing is a type of fund-raising effort that is targeted toward foundations and governmental philanthropic organizations. Community fund-raising differs from grants in that the requester is going directly to companies and individuals in the community for money or in-kind donations to support programs. A common program that relies on community fund-raising is the summer reading club. Librarians who want to be able to offer snacks at a program might ask the local grocery store to supply cookies or ask a fast food chain to supply drinks. Prizes and small incentives might be solicited from a local big box store or a bookstore, or coupons might be donated for fast food restaurants or for entry to local amusement parks.

If in-kind items can't be obtained, the librarian may need to seek out small monetary donations. The Friends of the Library, local clubs that work with children, and specialty organizations like the Rotary may be open to providing small gifts, usually under $1,000, so that fun bookmarks or small items can be purchased in support of programs. Larger grocery stores may be able to donate gift cards that allow the library staff to buy wrapped snacks for after-school programs or homework centers.

Know what the library has to offer in return for the donation. Usually the library offers recognition and indirect advertising through listing on various library documents and promotional materials. It is also important to send a thank-you letter after the program. Community businesses want to be part of the community, but they also need recognition for their efforts. A certificate of appreciation, photographs of children enjoying a library program, and thank-you posters signed by the participants will often be displayed in the business (and further promote the library). When possible, it is also a good idea to verbally thank the donors at the beginning of a program. It's possible someone from the company will be in the audience, but it's also possible a competitor will be spurred to give the next time.

The items and funds provided by these donors can amount to a nice sum of money and enhance the library's programs, but getting them also takes time. Start early by making a list of potential donors. Look at the members of the local chamber of commerce and businesses that are utilized by the community. Seek out those businesses that have an interest in serving children and families.

Throughout the year, keep an eye out for possibilities and ask volunteers and the Friends for help in soliciting. Usually it is good to send a letter to the appropriate person and to then follow up with a phone call. Know what the library needs so that the request is specific. It is easier for a company to give a negative answer to a broad question like "Does your company have anything to contribute to the summer reading program?" than it is to say no to a request for six dozen cupcakes for the end-of-summer party.

Keep track of who is asked so that no single business is bombarded with requests, and always check with library administration to be sure no one else is making a request to the same business. Often businesses will limit their gifts to a specific organization to one or two a year, and it would be counterproductive to ask right after another department has asked. Additionally, be sure to report the value of in-kind and small monetary donations to library administration to document the funds received.

Professional Development

Learning never stops. Children's librarians are expected to be experts on many topics and therefore must continue to seek out and share new information. In addition to assisting in the performance of a current job, professional development and continuing education can help prepare youth librarians for advancement both in the field of youth services and also moving up in library management or moving out to positions in related fields.

Learning can happen in formal classes, many of them now available online, through universities and colleges. Courses that were not taken as part of an undergraduate or graduate program can fill in educational gaps. Many librarians find that courses on child development, reading and language development, and early childhood education may enhance their ability to provide effective programs and services in the public library.

In *Our Library* by Eve Bunting (figure 8.5), the community takes ownership of their library after Miss Goose tells the children that the building is closing because it is old. The kids pitch in to help with repairs and raise the money needed to operate the library. Books help the animals figure out how to fix up the building and hold bake sales to raise funds.

Figure 8.5. *Our Library. Cover for OUR LIBRARY by Eve Bunting. Jacket illustrations copyright © 2008 by Maggie Smith. Reprinted by permission of Houghton Mifflin Harcourt Publishing Company. All rights reserved.*

Continuing education courses help librarians develop, enhance, or refresh skills. Workshops and training sessions are offered by state or regional library agencies and by the state and national professional organizations, such as the American Library Association (ALA). In addition to annual conferences, where it is possible to hear well-known speakers and learn about the latest research, some associations offer webinars and other online learning opportunities throughout the year. Out-of-state librarians are often welcome to participate in continuing education programs offered by other state library associations and organizations. Vendors and publishers also offer continuing education webinars. These are generally free and last about an hour. They often introduce new books and products while providing information about a topic. A recent webinar, the Very Ready Reading Program, offered by Demco, for example, featured librarian Sue McCleaf Nespeca and Dr. Pam Schiller, early childhood consultant, discussing the importance of parental involvement in the development of critical early literacy skills (Demco, 2014). *Booklist* and *School Library Journal* frequently work with publishers to offer webcasts that introduce new books and other media or share ideas for books and resources that will appeal to reluctant readers, tweens, or other groups of library users. Frequently, these webinars are archived for later viewing by those who could not attend the live event.

The Association for Library Services to Children (ALSC), a division of ALA, offers online courses and webinars throughout the year on topics ranging from graphic novels to programming for tweens. These are available to members and nonmembers. A sampling of recent courses includes Storytelling with Puppets; Science, Technology, Engineering, and Math Programs Made Easy; or Best Practice for Apps in Storytime. Webinars are generally 60–90 minutes, while courses may encompass several sessions.

Conference attendance provides an opportunity to network with colleagues, meet the authors of some of the books children are reading, examine new books and other library materials available from publishers and vendors, attend programs and lectures on innovative services and new technology, and tour libraries in the host city. Conference attendance is expensive, and many libraries do not budget funds to support attendance. Being a conference speaker or serving on a committee may be a requirement for institutional support of travel to conferences. Both also provide great opportunities for learning. Being a conference presenter requires that the speaker organize the information and consider how best to present the material for an audience that includes both newcomers to the field and old hands. Speakers often need to pull in material from other libraries to show how programming is done by different people in different settings. Committee membership may enhance skills such as critiquing books on award committees, but also helps librarians gain experience with public speaking, management, and teamwork. Involvement in the professional associations may also lead to opportunities to write for professional journals like *Book Links* and *School Library Journal*.

Listservs and online discussion forums offer opportunities to ask colleagues for help with problems, to share ideas, and gain input about issues related to library work. Some lists generate a great deal of traffic, and reading every posting can take a great deal of time. Be judicious in selecting lists to monitor. Some focus on in-depth discussion of a narrow topic. For example, Child_lit (https://email.rutgers.edu/mailman/listinfo/child_lit) is a forum for examining the "theory and criticism of literature for children and young adults" (Child_lit, 2014), and dozens of postings may ensue as members discuss and debate points about a specific topic or book. Others, such as PUBYAC, a listserv for public library youth librarians, provide opportunities for members to ask questions about practical aspects of public library work with youth. Many postings on PUBYAC ask for help with programming or in identifying a book that a patron has described. Professional associations also provide discussion lists as forums where subscribers can communicate about ideas, issues, and activities that deal with a mutual interest or concern. ALSC-L is one of the lists offered through the Association for Library Services to Children. ALSC also supports targeted lists for discussion of preschool services, storytelling, legislation that affects children, and more.

It can be expensive to participate in continuing education opportunities, and even free opportunities cost staff time, but to remain up-to-date and involved in the profession, as well as to keep personal skills and enthusiasm fresh, it is critical that children's librarians add to their value to the field by continuously learning and sharing experiences.

Key Points

Although many of us become children's librarians because we love working with young people and their programs, we are also managers and administrators of library services. Children's librarians deal more frequently and more directly with issues related to intellectual freedom and censorship. Library policies may disproportionately affect children and youth services. These issues, along with responsibility for marketing and promoting youth programs and finding funds to implement new services, may fall to the youth librarian. Ultimately, these management skills make you a better children's librarian, able to offer top-notch services that greatly impact the lives of children.

- Policies should be written and enforced fairly with little or no regard for the age of the patron.
- Library staff cannot and should not serve in loco parentis—in place of parents—when serving children.
- Marketing and promoting youth services is a team effort but requires ongoing actions by the youth librarian to be successful.
- It is important to evaluate children's services and programs to ensure that they are effective, provide a good return on investment, and meet current needs of children and families.
- Knowing where funding comes from and how to get more allows programs to continue and be created.
- Continuing education and professional development should be ongoing, allowing you to continue learning and providing information and skills to improve programs and services.

References

ALA (American Library Association). 2014. "Access to Library Resources and Services for Minors: An Interpretation of the Library Bill of Rights." August 30, 2014. http://www.ala.org/advocacy/intfreedom/librarybill/interpretations/access-library-resources-for-minors.

ALSC (Association for Library Services to Children). 2014. "Competencies for Librarians Serving Children in Public Libraries." Accessed August 16, 2014. http://www.ala.org/ala/mgrps/divs/alsc/edcareeers/alsccorecomps/index.cfm.

Anand, Nupur. 2013. "Kotler Adds a 5th P to His Set of Four—Purpose." DNA, March 18, 2013. http://www.dnaindia.com/money/report-kotler-adds-a-5th-p-to-his-set-of-four-purpose-1812393.

Child_lit. 2014. https://email.rutgers.edu/mailman/listinfo/child_lit. Accessed August 18, 2014.

Conable, Gordon M. 2014. "Public Libraries and Intellectual Freedom." American Library Association. Accessed August 18, 2014. http://www.ala.org/advocacy/intfreedom/iftoolkits/ifmanual/fifthedition/publiclibraries.

Demco. 2014. The Very Ready Reading Program. http://www.demco.com/goto?webinar_6. Accessed August 18, 2014.

Resources Mentioned in This Chapter

ALA (American Library Association). 2014. "Campaign for America's Libraries." http://www.ala.org/advocacy/advleg/publicawareness/campaign@yourlibrary/.

ALA (American Library Association). 2014. "The USA PATRIOT Act." http://www.ala.org/advocacy/advleg/federallegislation/theusapatriotact.

ALA Electronic Discussion Lists: ALSC-L. http://lists.ala.org/wws/info/alsc-l.

ALSC (Association for Library Services to Children). 2014. "Día! Diversity in Action." http://dia.ala.org/.

Brodart. http://www.brodart.com/.

Bunting, Eve. 2008. Our Library. New York: Clarion Books.

Child_lit. https://email.rutgers.edu/mailman/listinfo/child_lit.

Demco. http://demco.com/.

Faighes, Judith Regina. 2014. The Foundation Directory. New York: Foundation Center.

Federal Trade Commission. "Children's Online Privacy Protection Rule ("COPPA")." http://www.ftc.gov/enforcement/rules/rulemaking-regulatory-reform-proceedings/childrens-online-privacy-protection-rule.

Foundation Center. 2014. "Funding Information Centers." http://foundationcenter.org/fin/.

Institute of Museum and Library Services. 2014. "Grant Applicants: Outcome Based Evaluation." http://www.imls.gov/applicants/outcome_based_evaluations.aspx.

Larson, Jeanette, and Herman L. Totten. 2008. The Public Library Policy Writer: A Guidebook with Model Policies on CD-ROM. Chicago: Neal-Schuman Publishers.

Library Grants. http://librarygrants.blogspot.com/.

MacKellar, Pamela H., and Stephanie K. Gerding. 2011. Winning Grants: A How-to-Do-It Manual for Librarians with Multimedia Tutorials and Grant Development Tools. Chicago: Neal-Schuman Publishers.

PUBYAC. http://www.pubyac.org/.

Tocker Foundation. http://tocker.org/.

Additional Readings and Resources

Dresang, Eliza T., Melissa Gross, and Leslie Edmonds Holt. 2006. Dynamic Youth Services through Outcome-Based Planning and Evaluation. Chicago: American Library Association.

Fasick, Adele M., and Leslie Edmonds Holt. 2013. Managing Children's Services in Libraries. Santa Barbara, CA: Libraries Unlimited.

Hernon, Peter, Robert E. Dugan, and Joseph R. Matthews. 2014. Getting Started with Evaluation. Chicago: American Library Association.

Institute of Museum and Library Services. 2014. "Grant Applicants: Outcome Based Evaluation." http://www.imls.gov/applicants/outcome_based_evaluations.aspx.

Koontz, Christie, and Lorri M. Mon. 2014. *Marketing and Social Media: A Guide for Libraries, Archives, and Museums.* Lanham, MD: Rowman & Littlefield.

Minow, Mary, and Tomas A. Lipinsky. 2003. *The Library's Legal Answer Book.* Chicago: American Library Association.

Nelson, Sandra. 2001. *The New Planning for Results: A Streamlined Approach.* Chicago: American Library Association.

Ohio Library Council. "Marketing the Library." http://www.olc.org/marketing/index.html.

Porter-Reynolds, Daisy. 2014. *Streamlined Library Programming: How to Improve Services and Cut Costs.* Santa Barbara, CA: Libraries Unlimited.

Turner, Anne M. 2004. *It Comes with the Territory: Handling Problem Situations in Libraries.* Jefferson, NC: McFarland.

Competencies for Librarians Serving Children in Public Libraries

THE ASSOCIATION FOR LIBRARY SERVICE TO CHILDREN (ALSC), a division of the American Library Association (ALA), recommends the following Core Competencies to all children's librarians and other library staff whose primary duties include delivering library service to and advocating library service for children from birth to age 14. The policy of this organization is that a master's degree in Library and Information Science from an ALA-accredited graduate school is the appropriate professional degree for the librarian serving children in the public library, but ALSC expects the same standards applied to paraprofessional staff. Through specialized coursework in undergraduate and graduate study, on-the-job training, and/or continuing education opportunities, librarians serving children should achieve and maintain the following skills, orientations, and understandings to ensure children receive the highest quality of library service as defined in the ALA Library Bill of Rights, and the ALA and Association of American Publishers (AAP) joint Freedom to Read Statement.

I. Knowledge of Client Group

1. Understands theories of infant, child, and adolescent learning and development and their implications for library service.
2. Recognizes the effects of societal developments on the needs of children.
3. Assesses the diverse needs, preferences, and resources of the community on a regular and systematic basis.
4. Identifies patrons with special needs as a basis for designing and implementing services following the Americans with Disabilities Act (ADA) and state and local regulations where appropriate.
5. Demonstrates an understanding of and respect for diversity in cultural and ethnic values.
6. Understands and responds to the needs of parents, caregivers, and other adults who use the resources of the children's department.

7. Cultivates an environment which provides for enjoyable and convenient access to and use of library resources.
8. Maintains regular communication with other agencies, institutions, and organizations serving children in the community.

◎ II. Administrative and Management Skills

1. Participates in all aspects of the library's planning process to represent and support service to children.
2. Sets long- and short-range goals, objectives, strategic plans, and priorities.
3. Analyzes the costs of library services to children in order to develop, justify, administer, manage, and evaluate a budget.
4. Conducts job interviews, trains, and evaluates staff who work with children, parents, caregivers, and other adults using children's services.
5. Writes job descriptions and encourages continuing education for staff who work with children.
6. Demonstrates critical thinking, problem solving, decision making, and mediation skills and techniques.
7. Delegates responsibility appropriately and supervises staff constructively.
8. Documents and evaluates services and needs assessments through various research methods.
9. Identifies outside sources of funding and writes effective grant applications.
10. Follows federal, state, and local legislation in the development and enactment of library policies and procedures.

◎ III. Communication Skills

1. Defines and communicates the role and scope of public library service to children for administrators, other library staff, and members of the larger community.
2. Listens and interacts actively when speaking individually with children, families, other patrons, and staff, paying genuine attention to what is being communicated, and confirming understanding.
3. Writes proficiently and adjusts content and style to accommodate diverse functions and audiences.
4. Communicates effectively when addressing or presenting to large or small groups of children and/or adults.
5. Conducts productive formal and informal reference and readers' advisory interviews.
6. Successfully communicates library policies and procedures to patrons of all ages.

◎ IV. Knowledge of Materials

1. Demonstrates a knowledge and appreciation of children's literature, periodicals, audiovisual materials, Websites and other electronic media, and other materials that contribute to a diverse, current, and relevant children's collection.

2. Provides a wide and diverse variety of electronic resources, audiovisual materials, print materials, and other resource materials to best serve the needs of children and their caregivers.
3. Keeps abreast of new materials and those for retrospective purchase by consulting a wide variety of reviewing sources and publishers' catalogs, including those of small presses, by attending professional meetings, and by reading, viewing, and listening.
4. Keeps up-to-date on adult electronic and print reference sources which may serve the needs of children and their caregivers.
5. Develops a comprehensive collection development policy consistent with the mission and policies of the parent library and the ALA Library Bill of Rights.
6. Considers the selection and discarding of materials according to collection development, selection, and weeding policies.
7. Maintains a diverse collection, recognizing children's need to see people like and unlike themselves in the materials they access.
8. Understands and applies criteria for evaluating the content and artistic merit of children's materials in all genres and formats.
9. Addresses materials against community challenges.
10. Demonstrates a knowledge of cataloging, classification, indexing procedures, and practices to support access to children's materials.

⑥ V. User and Reference Services

1. Instructs children in the use of library tools and resources, empowering them to choose materials and services on their own.
2. Conducts reference/readers' advisory interviews to assist children and their parents/caregivers with the identification and selection of materials and services, according to their interests and abilities.
3. Respects the patron's right to browse regardless of age, and provides nonjudgmental answers to their questions.
4. Assists and instructs children in information gathering and research skills.
5. Understands and applies search strategies to give children the widest possible range of sources.
6. Compiles and maintains information about community resources.
7. Works with library technical services on cataloging, classification, and indexing to ensure easy access to materials for children.
8. Encourages use of materials and services through bibliographies, booktalks, displays, electronic documents, and other special tools.

⑥ VI. Programming Skills

1. Designs, promotes, presents, and evaluates a variety of programs for children of all ages, based on their developmental needs and interests and the goals of the library.
2. Identifies and utilizes skilled resource people to present programs and information.
3. Provides library outreach programs which meet community needs and library goals and objectives.

4. Establishes programs and services for parents, individuals and agencies providing childcare, and other professionals in the community who work with children.
5. Promotes library programs and services to underserved children and families.

VII. Advocacy, Public Relations, and Networking Skills

1. Utilizes effective public relations techniques and media to promote an awareness of and support for meeting children's library and information needs through all media.
2. Considers the needs, opinions, and requests of children in the development and evaluation of library services.
3. Ensures that children have full access to library materials, resources, and services as prescribed by the Library Bill of Rights.
4. Collaborates with other agencies serving children, including other libraries, schools, and other community agencies.
5. Lobbies on behalf of children for the highest quality library service, through library governance and the political process.

VIII. Professionalism and Professional Development

1. Acknowledges the legacy of children's librarianship, its place in the context of librarianship as a whole, and past contributions to the profession.
2. Stays informed of current trends, emerging technologies, issues, and research in librarianship, child development, education, and allied fields.
3. Practices self-evaluation.
4. Knows and practices the American Library Association's Code of Ethics.
5. Preserves patron confidentiality.
6. Mentors library school students, paraprofessionals, and new librarians.
7. Participates in local, state, and national professional organizations to strengthen skills, interact with fellow professionals, promote professional association scholarships, and contribute to the library profession.
8. Pursues professional development and continuing education opportunities throughout her/his career.

IX. Technology

1. Possesses up-to-date computer and technology skills necessary for effective communications and presentations.
2. Acquires familiarity with emerging technological trends and tools.
3. Applies technological skills to provide reference services and programs for children and families.
4. Supports access to Internet and electronic resources for children.

Created by the ALSC Education Committee, 1989. Revised by the ALSC Education Committee: 1999, 2009; approved by the ALSC Board of Directors at the 2009 American Library Association Annual Conference.

Reproduced with permission from the Association for Library Service to Children, a division of the American Library Association. Copyright 2009.

Awards and Best Lists

AWARDS FOR CHILDREN'S BOOKS and media range from highly literary to popularity. Most commonly awards are given to a single book or material proclaimed as the best in the grouping, with a handful of additional books recognized as honor titles. Best lists are often released annually and look at the range of titles released during the review period. Both awards and best lists offer librarians the opportunity to benchmark their collection against the materials experts and reviewers deem to be worthy of recognition. Some awards focus on a specific subject or theme, such as the Jane Addams Children's Book Award, which recognizes books that promote peace and justice, or groups of writers and illustrators, such as the Coretta Scott King Award for books by African Americans. While it is not a good idea to automatically purchase every item that is honored, it is worth considering them if they are not already in the collection.

It is not possible to compile a comprehensive list of awards for children's books and media. Most states now have a state award for children's books. There are also general awards, such as the National Book Awards, that include one or two categories for youth books. A few awards recognize translations or books published in other countries, but most of the awards included here are for materials from U.S. publishers. It's a good start for most children's librarians.

Awards

The Jane Addams Children's Book Award (http://www.janeaddamspeace.org/) recognizes outstanding children's books that promote peace and justice.

The American Indian Youth Literature Awards (http://ailanet.org/activities/american-indian-youth-literature-award/) are presented every other year for the best literature by and about American Indians.

The Américas Book Award for Children's and Young Adult Literature (http://www4.uwm.edu/clacs/aa/index.cfm) recognizes the best U.S. works in English or Spanish that authentically portray Latin America, the Caribbean, or Latinos in the United States.

The Hans Christian Andersen Award (http://www.ibby.org/index.php?id=273) is presented every other year by the International Board on Books for Young People (IBBY) to an author and an illustrator for the lasting contributions of their complete works to children's literature. Each country member of IBBY submits a nomination, and although the winners may be from any of these nominations, the author and illustrators are all highly regarded.

The Arab American Book Award (http://www.arabamericanmuseum.org/bookaward) encourages the publication of books that recognize and preserve the knowledge and culture of the Arab American community by recognizing a winner and honor book for children.

The Asian/Pacific American Award for Literature (http://www.apalaweb.org/awards/literature-awards/) recognizes the literary and artistic merit of books about Asian/Pacific Americans and their heritage.

The Batchelder Award (http://www.ala.org/alsc/awardsgrants/bookmedia/batchelderaward) recognizes an outstanding book first published in another country in a language other than English and subsequently translated into English and published in the United States.

The Pura Belpré Award (http://www.ala.org/alsc/awardsgrants/bookmedia/belpremedal) is awarded to a Latino/Latina writer and illustrator for books that celebrate the Latino culture.

The Irma Black Award for Excellence in Children's Literature (http://bankstreet.edu/center-childrens-literature/irma-black-award/) is presented by the Bankstreet College of Education for a book in which the text and illustrations are inseparable. Third and fourth grade students select the winner from a list of finalists.

The Amelia Bloomer Project (http://ameliabloomer.wordpress.com/) recognizes excellent literature for children that reflects significant feminist content.

The Boston Globe-Horn Book Awards (http://www.hbook.com/boston-globe-horn-book-awards/#_) are presented by *Horn Book* magazine and the *Boston Globe* newspaper for children's and young adult books in three categories: picture book, fiction and poetry, and nonfiction.

The Caldecott Medal (http://www.ala.org/alsc/awardsgrants/bookmedia/caldecottmedal/caldecottmedal) is presented to the illustrator of the most distinguished picture book published in the United States during the previous year.

The Carnegie Medal (http://www.ala.org/alsc/awardsgrants/bookmedia/carnegiemedal) honors the best films and videos produced for children during the previous year.

The Children's Choice Book Awards (http://www.cbcbooks.org/ccba/) are given by the Children's Book Council for books that children will enjoy. The list of finalists is compiled based on votes by children across the United States, who also vote for the winner.

The Geisel Award (http://www.ala.org/alsc/awardsgrants/bookmedia/geiselaward) is presented to the author and illustrator of the most distinguished book for beginning readers published in the previous year.

The Coretta Scott King Awards (http://www.ala.org/emiert/cskbookawards) are presented each year to outstanding African American authors and illustrators whose works show an appreciation of human values and African American culture. The John Steptoe New Talent Award is notable for its recognition of new writers and illustrators.

The National Book Awards (http://www.nationalbook.org/) are presented by the National Book Foundation to U.S. citizens. One category considers Young People's Literature and the long list reflects some of the best literary writing from the previous year.

The Odyssey Award (http://www.ala.org/alsc/awardsgrants/bookmedia/odysseyaward) recognizes excellence in the production of audiobooks for children and young adults.

The Orbis Pictus Award (http://www.ncte.org/awards/orbispictus) is presented by the National Council of Teachers of English for outstanding nonfiction works. Although only one book wins, honor books and other recommended books are also notable for their literary quality and accuracy.

The Newbery Medal (http://www.ala.org/alsc/awardsgrants/bookmedia/newberymedal/newberymedal) is presented to the author of the most distinguished contribution to American literature for children published in the previous year.

Texas State University awards the Tomás Rivera Mexican American Children's Book Award (http://www.education.txstate.edu/c-p/Tomas-Rivera-Book-Award-Project-Link.html) to books that depict the Mexican American experience.

The Schneider Family Book Award (http://www.ala.org/awardsgrants/schneider-family-book-award) recognizes the author or illustrator of a book that embodies "the disability experience" for a child.

The Sibert Medal (http://www.ala.org/alsc/awardsgrants/bookmedia/sibertmedal) recognizes the most distinguished informational book published in the previous year.

The Skipping Stones Awards (http://www.skippingstones.org/) recognize books that promote an understanding of the world's cultures and respect for differing viewpoints.

The Stonewall Book Award (http://www.ala.org/glbtrt/award/honored) recognizes GLBT (gay, lesbian, bisexual, transgender) books, including a category for books for young people.

The Sydney Taylor Book Awards (http://jewishlibraries.org/content.php?page=Sydney_Taylor_Book_Award) are presented by the Association of Jewish Libraries to books that authentically represent the Jewish experience.

The Carter G. Woodson Book Awards (http://www.socialstudies.org/awards/woodson) are presented by the National Council for the Social Studies for distinguished books in the social sciences that sensitively and accurately depict ethnicity in the United States.

The author of the best picture book text published in the United States during the previous year receives the Charlotte Zolotow Award from the Cooperative Children's Book Center (http://ccbc.education.wisc.edu/books/zolotow.asp).

⌖ Notable and Best Lists

Booklist honors its editors' choices (http://booklistonline.com/Booklist-Editors-Choice/pid=6588764) in categories that include youth books and media, as well as reference materials.

The staff of *The Bulletin of the Center for Children's Books* annually compiles its Blue Ribbons list (http://bccb.lis.illinois.edu/BlueRibbons/blue13.html) of their choices for the best books published in the previous year.

Notable Children's Books (http://www.ala.org/alsc/awardsgrants/notalists/ncb) is compiled by a committee of the American Library Association to recognize outstanding books published the previous year.

Notable Children's Recordings (http://www.ala.org/alsc/awardsgrants/notalists/ncr) are selected by a committee of the American Library Association from sound recordings, including audiobooks and music, released in the previous year.

The Notable Children's Video (http://www.ala.org/alsc/awardsgrants/notalists/ncv), awarded by a committee of the American Library Association, recognizes the best film productions for children released in the previous year.

The National Science Teachers Association (http://www.nsta.org/publications/ostb/) publishes a list of Outstanding Science Trade Books for Students K–12 each year.

The *New York Times* (http://www.nytimes.com/) releases its list of Notable Children's Books each year, dividing their recommendations into three categories: young adult, middle grade, and picture books.

School Library Journal (http://www.slj.com/) annually releases lists of their editor's choices for best books in a variety of categories, including picture books, fiction, nonfiction, and Latino-themed books.

The Teachers' Choices Reading List (http://www.reading.org/Resources/Booklists/TeachersChoices.aspx) is compiled by the International Reading Association. Books placed on the list are new books that encourage children to read and contribute to learning across the curriculum.

Index

About the Author

Jeanette Larson (MLS, University of Southern California, 1979) is the author of *El día de los niños/El día de los libros: Building a Culture of Literacy in Your Community through Día* (2011), *CREW: A Weeding Manual for Modern Libraries* (2008), *The Public Library Policy Writer* (2008), and *Bringing Mysteries Alive for Children and Young Adults* (2004) as well as numerous manuals for the Texas Reading Club. She is also the author of *Hummingbirds: Facts and Folklore from the Americas* (2011). After more than 35 years working in and with public libraries, she now teaches for Texas Woman's University and is an independent consultant and trainer. She has spoken and written extensively about children's library services. In 2002 the Texas Library Association honored her work with children with the Siddie Joe Johnson Award and named her Librarian of the Year in 1998.